THE RELUCTANT REBEL

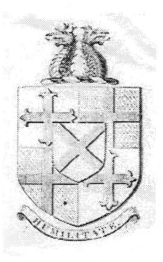

The
Reluctant Rebel

Memoirs of an English Farmer in Wales

E.P. Carlisle

First published 2006 by Real Lives, an imprint of
Wye Valley Publishing Company Ltd, Hereford

A CIP catalogue record for this book is available from
the British Library.

ISBN: 0-9550050-2-7 / 978-0-9550050-2-2

Typeset & Cover Design by Tim Watkins, Hereford

I would like to express my great gratitude to Alan Pool for typing my illegible draft, my wife Rosemary for her many re-collections and unfailing support, Jason Ashworth for his father's Indian Army photographs and to Peter Burden and Tim Watkins of Real Lives for their admirable editing and design respectively. Without their help these memoirs would never have got published.

Foreword

I don't suppose my life has been so very different from thousands of other men – ex-soldiers, wartime officers – who, having left the army, chose to take to the land, perhaps in the belief that the skills they had acquired in warfare might fit them well for a career in farming and land management in post-war Britain.

But somehow, throughout my life I seem to have attracted more controversy than most. Quite why, I don't know, although it has, for me, nearly always been on a matter of principle. I've always been prepared to stick my head above the parapet when I felt circumstances demanded it, and, from time to time, it's been blown off – metaphorically speaking, of course.

The first chapter, Forebears, is really for those interested in the genealogy and history of the Carlisle family, and for easier reference, I have included diagrammatic family trees.

Further chapters contain a broadly chronological account of my life, juxtaposed with events in the wider world. Public events inevitably impinge to some extent on our private lives and I have unashamedly included my own observations on those which I felt affected me.

I hope this account of a long, occasionally adventurous and sporadically litigious career, with all its peaks and troughs, triumphs and debacles will strike a chord for some, provide information and entertainment for others and a small dash of life-enhancing controversy for all.

EPC, Cusop, 2005

Chapter One

Forebears

"CARLISLE" is a Celtic word meaning 'Camp of the Legion', in this case situated at the Western end of Hadrian's Wall. *The History of the Ancient Family of Carlisle*, published in 1822 commences with Sir Hildred de Carlisle, a Norman knight, who was granted estates by Duke William of Normandy after his conquest of England in 1066, and who, in 1092, built a large castle from which to dominate the neighbourhood. The crest of two dragons heads reversed above the coat of arms seems somewhat incompatible with the mild motto of HUMILITATE inscribed beneath it.

Known pedigrees of the Carlisles begin with a Sir William de Carlisle of Torthorwald – a forbidding ruined keep which stands today on a small hillock five miles north of Dumfries. His son was created Lord Carlyle of Torthorwald in 1474. The barony survived for only a century, being extinguished after death of the 4th Lord Carlyle in 1573.

The next notable Carlisle was a naval captain, who settled on a plantation in Antigua in the 16th Century and married the daughter of the governor. There is still today a Carlisle Bay near to the capital of Antigua. Perhaps more notably, Thomas Carlyle, the celebrated philosopher and author was born in 1750 to a collateral branch of the family living at Ecclesfechan. Another distantly connected Carlisle founded the Church Army in the 19th century.

From five generations of Adam Carlyles, farmers at Bridekirk all bailies of Annan near Dumfries, John Carlyle moved to Sedbergh in West Yorkshire, where he married Elizabeth Lewis and his son William, born in 1719, married first Eleanor Herd of Howgill, a small manor house five miles north of Sedbergh. Their son William was born in 1762, attended Sedbergh school and afterwards went to Magdalen College, Oxford where he obtained an MA before spending his life as vicar of Ipstones near Leek, Staffordshire.
William's sons, John and Frederick, then aged 22 and 18, led a party

of ten men, described as the parish poor, on the 1820 settlement scheme to the Cape Colony of South Africa. The scheme was promoted by the British Government to reduce unemployment and unrest in Britain after the Napoleonic wars, and to settle an agrarian community on the disputed Eastern frontier of the Colony, whose presence would discourage Xhosa tribesmen from crossing the frontier. An additional purpose was to increase the English speaking population of the recently acquired colony, still predominantly Dutch in its language and customs.

In all, some thousand families sailed in sixty ships, but the Carlisle party, sailing in the SS Chapman, was among the smallest. They landed at Simonstown and moved inland to what was called the Albany Settlement around the present town of Grahamstown, where they were granted 1,268 acres, two miles to the south, which they named Belmont after their home in England. This was later increased to 5,000 acres and John was appointed Sheriff of Albany. Six years later his brother Frederick succeeded him as Sheriff while John kept the farm.

The settlers survived an extremely precarious few years before getting established. Both John and Frederick married daughters of two Philipps, who had led another party of settlers. These were relations of the Philipps family of Picton, in Pembrokeshire, from whom descended Lords Milford Kilsant & St Davids.

When I visited Belmont in 1990 I found the house to be a ruin, the property subsumed in a larger farm but Frederick's house, now called Carlisle House, is among the finest in Grahamstown. Numerous descendants have since lived in South Africa and what was Rhodesia, farming, engaged in legal and other professions and, in one case, politics. The nearest claim to aristocracy in South Africa is descent from one of the 1820 British settlers.

William Carlisle of Sedbergh married secondly Margaret Croxton, daughter of a substantial farmer at Cautley, two miles East of Sedbergh. They had one son, John who was educated at Sedbergh school and went on to Magdalen College, Oxford where he obtained an MA before becoming vicar at Chipping, in the Forest of Bowland in Lancashire from 1786-1807. Here he married Elizabeth Parkinson of Blindhurst. They had three sons and two daughters. The eldest,

William was born in 1795 and married to Betty Alston. By 1822, he was a wine and spirits merchant in Lancaster, trading with Spain and Portugal. Until that time Lancaster had been the principal port of NW England, but the River Lune was silting up and the city was being superseded by Liverpool. The second brother Richard was now living as a merchant in Rio de Janeiro, then capital of Brazil, and the third, John, was a merchant, in Buenos Aires. BA was still part of the Spanish Empire but shortly to become capital of Argentina as Spanish rule was overthrown by revolutionary movements all over South America in the 1830s. Those were the great days of the square riggers and it must have been a voyage of about six weeks from England. Communications were sporadic, and there is no record of either brother ever marrying or coming home.

William had three sons and four daughters. Thomas, born in 1813, John and Richard, two and four years younger, between them in about 1837 formed the company of Carlisle Ltd, export merchants in Liverpool. They traded in cotton goods from the fast expanding Lancashire mills to Buenos Aires and Calcutta, where John and Richard opened merchant houses.

From the beginning of the 19th century for a hundred years the mighty Lancashire cotton manufacturing industry clothed the world. The Carlisle brothers must have prospered mightily, for by 1855 Thomas was living at Dawpool, a very large house near Birkenhead which became a hospital during the First World War.

By 1870 John must have retired early as he built a large Italianate villa designed by a famous London architect at Bowden, Cheshire, called High Lawn. He had married Ellen Nield from Bowden and they had a large family of six boys and six girls. From all those six boys there are today no Carlisle descendants, and though two daughters remained spinsters for life the other four have left only two heirs. The youngest, Leonard must have married money as he first lived at Ulverston Hall, near Barrow in Furness. He must also have spent some years in the family firm, as he was a guarantor until he died in 1952, leaving £100,000, a substantial sum at the time. He had by then lived many years at Upper Brook House, Marchington, near Uttoxeter and spent his life hunting with the Meynell Hounds. One of his brothers and his son went to Harrow School.

Richard, born in 1817, appears to have had a wife and five children in India, although little is known of them, but in 1864 he married secondly Rose Moseley and retired to live at Llanvapley Court (near Abergavenny), which included an hundred acre farm. He died in 1893 and is buried in a large vault just inside the lych-gate along with a son, Archer, who died in 1866 aged 2 years. His wife removed to Menton on the French Rivera where she died in 1898.

Their daughter married a White-Spunner, from a family of the Protestant Ascendancy in Ireland, whose grandson, Barney commanded The Life Guards in 1998 and was subsequently a Brigadier oC 16 Air Assault Brigade in Bosnia with the United Nations peacekeeping force 2002.

Thomas married Ellen Dodson Potter, of Bootle, in 1841 and had eight sons and one daughter. The eldest, William died in infancy as happened to so many children in those days. The daughter Frances married 1867 George Pilkington, heir to the famous glass manufacturers of St Helens, near Southport. Their son Hector built the grandest house in Alderley Edge and their daughter Mabel married Lord Kensington of St. Brides Castle near Haverfordwest. Pilkingtons is now the leading glass manufacturer in Europe.

Charles, born in 1844, my grandfather, was educated at Liverpool Grammar School and became managing director of the family firm. In 1881 he married Mary Royds, daughter of Canon Francis Coulman Royds, vicar for life of Coddington, Cheshire, and had seven sons and one daughter.

Arthur became a schoolmaster at Haileybury and left no heirs.

Thomas managed the firm's merchant house in Calcutta and married Margaret Hinde in 1881 He retired in 1898 and bought a farm on the Brendon Hills in Somerset, and later retired to Caxton House, Old Cleeve. Their eldest son, Hartley, became a Lt Colonel, Royal Horse Artillery, won a DSO and MC in the Great War and died in 1968. His son, Michael was a lieutenant in the Royal Navy during in the last war.

Thomas's second and third sons, Edgar and Ronald both went out to the Argentine where Edgar was shot dead on a ranch in 1934, leaving no issue.

Ronald returned to join the army in the Great War,

becoming a Captain in the Welsh Horse and gaining an MC and a Mention in Despatches at Gallipolili 1915 Palestine 1916. He married Jessie Stuart, a house-mistress at Cheltenham Ladies' College and died at the young age of 43 in 1933. A memorial plaque to him can be seen in Old Cleeve church, Minehead.

He left one son, Archie, born in 1918, who was Captain, Royal Fusiliers in the Second World War after which he was with Barclays Bank in Nigeria. He never married and died about 1980.

With increasing prosperity, Thomas sent his last four boys to public schools, which had steadily expanded to accommodate a growing Victorian middle class.

Samuel (Sam) and Frederick (Fred) were twins born in 1849. They were both educated at Harrow School, the first of twenty three Carlisles, mostly in the leading house, Elmfield, over three generations, the first two of which were all very good games players, several of whom won scholarships.

Edmund Septimus, born in 1851, looked quite unlike any of his brothers. He was small and dark, whereas all his brothers were tall and fairish, though adultery by his mother seems unlikely. He spent only two years at Harrow and was said to have got a housemaid into trouble. He emigrated to America, shortly followed by his twin brother Harold, who had been head boy at Harrow. Both Edmund and Harold married and acquired farms in Kansas, a section of 500 acres of state land being given to emigrants.

The American Civil War, 1861-1865, which devastated the country and brought about the abolition of slavery, had brought about the shooting of all the buffalo which had roamed the great plains of the mid-west, for their meat and hides, no doubt to clothe and feed gold miners and railway workers. The Civil War was followed by the Indian Wars, which resulted in all the Red Indians, as they were then miscalled, now Native Americans, being confined in reservations, in Kansas the Cheyenne tribe. There was therefore a great sea of grass in unoccupied and unclaimed land. The idea, started by a French aristocrat near Denver, of cattle ranching on a big scale developed, and in 1880 about forty British companies were formed, many of them headed by English or Scots peers. This was due in part to the fact that capital, other than for building railways, was available only in Europe.

My grandfather Charles, then managing director of Carlisles Ltd, formed one of these companies with a few friends and relations as shareholders, along with his two brothers already farming in Kansas, at Mount Hope and at Salt Creek, near Arkansas. They gave the company the grandiose title of *The Kansas & New Mexico Land and Cattle Company* and Edmund and Harold moved five hundred miles west to set up the company offices at Durango, at the lower end of the Rocky Mountains in Colorado, and occupy land in New Mexico, south of the San Juan river, near Bloomfield, and in southern Utah around Monticello and the Blue Mountains sixty miles north.

The land was completely uninhabited and free for the taking, and in a very short time the company had amassed thirty thousand head of cattle which roamed over an area as large as two English counties, being driven up into the mountains in summer and down to the rivers in winter. To some extent, the success of such a large operation depended, presumably, on the cowboys employed being more aggressive than those on neighbouring ranches. The brother of Butch Cassidy, the celebrated outlaw, was one of the Carlisles'.

It is likely that the cattle came out of New Mexico or had gone wild during the Civil War. Similarly, the collapse of the Spanish Empire in Mexico had resulted in large numbers of horses turning feral, before being caught and domesticated by the Red Indians.

For a while the company prospered greatly, and Harold soon built what was described as the finest house in the Mid West, at Monticello. Unfortunately, all the other ranches also increased their numbers of cattle, until eventually the beef price collapsed, making it too expensive to rail freight from Dodge City to Chicago, the major cattle market for the developing industrial areas below the Great Lakes.

Instead, the ranchers had to drive their steers six hundred miles north, and across the Rocky Mountains to this market. Many Western films have been built around the cattle drovers and the skulduggery that occurred. These problems were exacerbated by the attitude of the cowboys who considered it their job to herd the cattle would not undertake the menial tasks of ploughing and reaping, hence the practice of grazing the cattle in the mountains in summer and down by the rivers in winter. In 1887/8, the winter was very hard and the land was covered in snow for several months. Without any cultivated winter fodder, half the cattle were wiped out, which added greatly the ranchers' financial problems.

By that time, all the companies had borrowed money from American banks who wasted no time in taking action against Limey absentee landlords and foreclosed on their overdrafts. To compound these difficulties, immigrants were flooding into the States from Europe and moving ever westwards where these homesteaders, as they were called, were granted a section of 500 acres or a half section of 250 acres. They brought sheep, which grazed where cattle could not survive, introduced the newly invented barbed wire and settled along the rivers. This resulted in bitter cattle wars between homesteaders and cattle barons as they were called, with incidents of flocks of sheep being driven over cliffs by cowboys and the inevitable shoot-outs that followed.

Having no good title to the land, by 1890 all the companies had gone bankrupt, except the mighty King Ranch in Texas, which still exists to this day. If they'd had title to their land the descendants of the early ranchers would have been multi-millionaires today.

Edmund, who had married Mary Heame returned to his farm at Mount Hope where he had three boys, Frederick, Alfred and Guy and two daughters Mabel and Constance. He died in 1894 at the young age of 43 and is buried at Mount Hope. His wife and one son continued in the farm till about 1950 when it was sold.
A grandson became a commander in the U.S. Navy.

Harold, who had married Henrietta Stevens, continued to live at Monticello until about 1920, when he sold the farm to Mormons, who were moving south from Salt Lake City. Today Monticello is an entirely Mormon small town, no more than an English village, but the history of Monticello records the Carlisle herd of cattle, branded with a broken cross, taking three days to drive through.

After selling Monitcello, Harold retired to St Louis, Mississippi, where he died in 1928.

Sam and Fred, born in 1849, went out to the firm's office in Calcutta where they joined the Calcutta Light Horse, a territorial regiment, and photos remain of them resplendent in uniform playing polo at

Talygunge Club in the early 1870s.

The Calcutta office was closed in the early 1980s as the Indian Government started to import textile machinery to manufacture their own cotton goods, making the import of English textiles uneconomical.

The twins became involved with operations in Argentina and married two sisters, Jessie and Flora Methven respectively, daughters of the owner of a sugar factory at Concepcion near Tucuman in Argentina, at the foot of the Andes and alternated between managing the office in Buenos Aires, living at a substantial house at San Jose de Flores, and the head office at 52 Princes Street, Manchester, when they lived at Toft Hall near Knutsford, Cheshire. In about 1890 the head office had moved to Manchester, which had become the centre of the cotton trade after the opening of the Manchester Ship Canal.

Sam had two sons, the younger Malcolm, born in 1884, was for two years in both the cricket and football XIs at Harrow. He went on to Sandhurst and afterwards joined the Northumberland Fusiliers in India. Later, while attached to the Durham light Infantry for a course, he died tragically as a result of an accident while playing polo. He was just 22.

The elder son, Kenneth, born in 1882, was also a very good games player at Harrow. He later captained the Oxford University Cricket Club and played golf on plus 4 handicap. He took over the office of Carlisles Ltd in Buenos Aires and was Argentine amateur golf champion in 1908. However, he would appear to have paid more attention to golf than to business as the firm nearly went bankrupt in 1911 and the office was moved to Montevideo in Uruguay, where his nephew Frank took on as manager.

At the beginning of the century the firm had been offered the dealership of General Motors for all of South America but had turned it down. Inevitably, the people who did take it soon became millionaires.

Kenneth then joined the bankers, D'Erlangers until the Great War when he came home and was commissioned into the Royal Artillery, lieutenant, twice wounded in 1917 and 1918. He had married in 1907 Minnie Donner the daughter of a very rich German family that had moved to England. After the war he joined *Liebigs*

Extract of Meat Company, then run by Charles Gunther who had married a sister of Minnie's. The firm had been formed by Count Liebig, the first man to discover how to can beef. He owned ranches in Argentina and a meat canning factory at Fray Bentos in Uruguay on the border. They also made OXO cubes. Kenneth became chairman of the London office in 1930, until he retired in 1936, living at Oakley Hall near Basingstoke. He and Minnie had three sons.

The first, also named Kenneth, born in 1908, was always known as Peter. He was very good at games, being in the Harrow cricket XI for three years and football XI for two, and as well as an Oxford scholar. He joined Liebigs, married Elisabeth McLaren, sister of Lord Aberconway, of Bodnant near Conway and signed on with the Rifle Brigade at the outbreak of WWII, serving in North Africa and Greece and leaving with the rank of major in 1945 to return to Liebigs, of which he became chairman in 1956. Later he became deputy chairman of Brooke Bond Liebigs and held that position until 1973. Peter and Elizabeth lived at Wyken Hall, Stanton, near Bury St, Edmunds and in 1941 had a son, also Kenneth, who, like his father, joined Liebigs after Harrow.

In 1979, Kenneth, who had been elected MP for Lincoln, became Minister of State, Department of Transport and was knighted on his retirement 1997. He married Carla Heffner from Mississippi, USA, who was a journalist on *Country Life* magazine. They now run a vineyard at Wyken Hall and have one son Sam.

Christabel, born in 1939, became a racing motorist of mini production cars but stopped racing after a serious crash. She wrote travel books and married Sir James Andrew Watson, 5th Baronet.

A daughter, Katherine, born in 1941, married V Newall 1969 and another daughter, Barbara, born in 1951 is unmarried.

Kenneth and Minnie's son, Ian, born in 1912, was an academic, artist and lay preacher near Bury St. Edmunds, and Bruce, born in 1914, had a colourful career at Magdalen College, Oxford, becoming master of the drag hounds, a steeplechase rider and chairman of the Bullingdon Club. Bruce worked at the stock exchange until the outbreak of war, when he joined the 9th Lancers, participating in the conquest of Madagascar, later being wounded as captain in northern Italy. After the war he went out to the Argentine and after some years in insurance joined Liebigs, becoming their manager in Buenos Aires. He married Anne Murphy, an Irish Argentinean Catholic. They lived in BA but also owned a small estancia at Vichacheras and had children – Sam, Caroline, Marina and Nicholas. The boys both went to Harrow and all married Argentinians. At the time of the Falklands war Nico, joined the Argentinian army but did not take part in the disastrous invasion. He subsequently became a banker.

Fred, twin of Sam, born in 1849, was in the Harrow football team for two years and afterwards played cricket for Lancashire before joining the family firm and going to India. Having taken over, with his brother, responsibilities in Argentina and England, he and his wife, Flora (Methven) had three daughters and one son Montague, who was born in 1889 at Toft Hall.

Montie, who was two years in the Harrow cricket eleven and at Pembroke College, Cambridge, became a scratch golfer and captained the university Golf Team. During the Great War, he served in the Highland Light Infantry and later the Northumberland Fusiliers, being wounded at Gallipoli. Every officer in his regiment was either killed or wounded. He was wounded again in France in 1916 and then became staff captain having gained an MC and a mention in despatches. He continued in the army until 1921, when he joined Lloyds and later set up his own firm of *F M Carlisle & Co*, Insurance brokers. During the second war he served again as staff captain, Southern Command. He had married in 1914 Katherine "Kitty" Apcar, the daughter of a rich Armenian merchant and they lived in Onslow Gardens, London and later at a beautiful country house, Pyt House, Ashampstead.

Kitty was a very talented woman and prolific needlewoman. She assembled a remarkable collection of miniature furnished rooms which she embellished with her needlepoint work and later donated to the National Trust, who exhibited it at Greys Court, Henley, where much was lost as the result of a burglary. The remaining rooms are now displayed at Nunnington Hall, North Yorkshire.

Montie and Kitty had three boys and a girl. Anthony, born in 1917, married Stella Groves and worked all his life at the Bank of England, except during the war when he served as Lieutenant RAMC and later, RA in India and Burma. Their adopted daughter, Janet has been literary correspondent for *The Times* and adopted son, David lives in America.

Brian, born in 1919, joined the navy on the outbreak of war and served throughout in various ships of the Home Fleet, Mediterranean Fleet and escorting the supply convoys to Russia. He was awarded the DSC and promoted 1st Lieutenant. In 1953, he married Hazel Binnie, whose father worked for Ferranti, the electronics firm and was tragically lost at sea when he had gone to check some equipment on a ship which was sunk by a U boat.

Brian and Hazel had three girls Juliet, Sarah and Celia and a boy John. After the war, he joined the Sudan Colonial Service, becoming a district commissioner until Sudan achieved independence. He then joined Shell Oil, where he rose to a high position before leaving to set up his own oil company, Saxon Oil, which he later successfully sold.

Brian was awarded the CBE in 1973 as a result of his negotiations between Shell and OPEC. Living at Hartley Wintney, he and Hazel have devoted much time to charitable work, particularly on behalf of the Sudanese church. Brian died in 2005.

Christopher, his brother, born in 1924, joined the Coldstream Guards in 1944 and was taken prisoner by the Germans in Italy in 1944 with the rank of captain. After the war he became a director of the firm started by his father *F. M. Carlisle & Co* Insurance Brokers at Lloyds. He married Carol Hutt and they had three children, Isabel, Lucy and Nicholas, who went to Harrow like his father.

Diana, born in l932, married Alexander "Sandy" Gray, Major, Grenadier Guards, who became a land agent with Savills on retirement. They had children, Catherine, Penelope and Alexander, known as Alex, and live at Souldern House, near Bicester.

My grandfather, Charles Stewart Carlisle, born in 1844 the eldest son of Thomas, had followed his father as managing director of the family firm, Carlisles Ltd, after it had moved to Manchester. He had married Mary (née Royds) in 1881 and lived at The Grange, North Rode, near Macclesfield until about 1910, when the firm nearly went bankrupt in the Argentine and they moved to a much smaller house in Alderley Edge.

There were many large houses built on the Edge by the cotton manufactory owners, it being on a railway line and only fifteen miles from Manchester. Up until then, merchants had always considered themselves socially superior to the much richer factory owners. Alderley and nearby Prestbury have to this day almost the highest property prices in the country, now attracting pop stars and overpaid footballers. Charles died in 1914, Mary in 1944. Both are buried in the cemetery near Alderley.

Charles had long been a Justice of the Peace, and in 1884 he took time of and went round the world, visiting the firm's office in Calcutta and the company's cattle ranches in Colorado, USA, that were managed by his brothers Edmund and Harold. His wife, something of a grand dame, was chairman of the committee that built the Alderley Edge cottage hospital.

The religious and philanthropic Royds family were descended from James Royds (1758-1842), a woollen manufacturer, who epitomised the motto beneath his family coat of arms, 'Semper Paratus', meaning 'Always Ready'. James built a large house, Mount Falinge, now a school, whose surrounding acres have become the municipal park. He married Mary, daughter of Charles Smith of Summer Castle, Rochdale, and in 1811 bought the advowson – or gift of the living – of Brereton church near Congleton, Cheshire, which had glebe lands worth £82 per year and tithes from 4,000 acres, worth the very large sum of £1,010.

He also bought the livings of Haughton, near Stafford and Heysham in Lancashire. These were very good investments as large rectories came with them and a job for life for the incumbent vicar. In these he put his younger sons, Edward, Charles and Frank. Each was held in the family for over 100 years.

His eldest son Clement, born in 1785, founded a bank, *Clement Royds & Co*, and followed his father at Mount Falinge. He was appointed High Sheriff in 1850. His son, Albert Hudson Royds succeeded him at Falinge and as owner of the bank. He, too, was appointed High Sheriff and later, Deputy Lieutenant. He was also a very prominent Freemason, being Deputy Grand Master for East Lancashire, and later, Grand Master of Worcestershire. In those days, the order of Freemasons was a respected organisation, acceptable to the Church of England. Nowadays it is much distrusted and often corrupt.

In 1870, Albert built the large and ornate church at Falinge, which incorporates many Masonic symbols. It would appear that this expensive exercise nearly ruined him, as his son Clement, also Grand Master for East Lancashire, had to sell Mount Falinge, and also sold the family bank to Williams Deacons & Co, although he did join them, becoming chairman.

James's son, Edward was born in 1790, educated at Christ College, Cambridge and became vicar of Brereton in 1819. He married Mary Molyneux, whose father, Thomas, was a merchant in the firm of Molyneux and Taylor and lived at Newsham House, where Queen Victoria once stayed. Newsham was eventually sold to Liverpool Corporation and became the Judges' lodgings.

In 1822, Edward became Rector of the C12th St Giles Church, Haughton, Staffordshire. He was followed by his brother Charles, in 1831, who extensively renovated the chancel in 1838. His son Gilbert followed him as rector in 1879, and undertook even more extensive alterations, practically rebuilding the church except for the tower in 1887, and putting in fine East and West windows in memory of his parents and grandparents.

He was eventually succeeded by his son, Thomas, who retired in 1947. There is a memorial to Thomas's son, Clement, born in 1923, who became a flight-lieutenant with the RAF and was killed in action in 1945. The patronage of the church is still today in the Royds family after 186 years.

St Peter's church, Heysham, near Lancaster was first consecrated AD 967. It is a very small church standing on low cliffs, right above the sea and adjoining the site of an earlier ruined chapel dating from the late C6th. John Royds became rector in 1858 and set about extensive renovation in 1864, adding a north aisle. He was succeeded by his brother, Charles from 1865-1900. His son Charles was rector from 1908 to 1943, followed by his son, John, from 1943-1956.

The fine East window was dedicated to the memory of the Royds family, who hold the patronage to this day.

Charles's second son, Everard Royds, who had been ordained but resigned on divorcing his wife, lived at Glasbury-on-Wye in Breconshire. He went into business as a corrosion engineer, painting ships, and for many years was the devoted leader of a Boy Scout troop, to whom he was always known as George. In 1950 he started the Riding for the Disabled charity, which went on to have branches all over the country. He married Felicity Wedgewood of the porcelain family and had three boys, John, Richard and Tom. Everard died in 1998 and is buried at Glasbury.

A direct descendant of James Royds of Falinge joined the Navy and commanded Captain Scott's ship, Discovery on his first expedition to Antarctica, 1901-1904, where Cape Royds, which later became Shackleton's base, is named after him. He was subsequently promoted Rear Admiral, CMG and died in 1926 when Deputy Commissioner of the Metropolitan Police. His brother, Percy was also a Rear Admiral, RN.

Edward, who died in 1845, and Mary had ten children. Edward, their eldest son, born in 1820, was educated at Rugby and Brasenose College Oxford, and followed Thomas as vicar of Brereton until his death 50 years later in 1895. He married Anne, daughter of Thomas Littledale of Highfield House, West Derby and had eight children of whom the eldest, Edward, educated at Eton and Trinity Hall, Cambridge, was killed whilst climbing in the Alps aged 23.

Their second son Alfred, educated at Winchester and Trinity Hall married Eleanor, daughter of John Dixon of Astle Hall, Chelford and followed his father as vicar of Brereton till 1919 when he retired — the last Royds after 108 years. Neither Edward or any of his six sisters left any children.

Edward senior's second son, Clement, born in 1822, was drowned in the Mersey aged 20. Henry, twin of Clement, and Thomas, born in 1824, became merchants in the firm of *Molyneux & Taylor* in Liverpool, whilst their fifth son, Francis Coulman, born in 1825, married Cornelia, daughter of Canon Blomfield of Hollington Hall, Cheshire, and became vicar for life of Coddington near Chester. Francis, who was to become a Canon, was my great grandfather. Charles and Edmund, born, respectively in 1827 and 1830, went out to Australia in 1851 where they ran a sheep station for 40 years at Juandah, Queensland. They never married.

Francis and Cornelia Royds, my great grandparents, had ten

children.

Alice, born in 1853, married the Rev John Howell, vicar of Penmaenmawr; Frances, born in 1854 and Ellen, born in 1855 never married; Frank, born in 1856, joined the Navy and was killed at the battle of El Teb in Egypt in 1884 while commanding a gun troop of the Naval Brigade. He was buried at Sea and is remembered by commemorative tablets at Coddington church, Rossall School and in the Anglican church in Alexandria.

Edith, born in 1858, married Archibald Skipwith in 1880. Their son Frank became a major in the Royal Scots Fusiliers. He married the Hon Bridget Byng and was killed in France in 1915. Their daughter, Nora married Lord George Seymour, son of the sixth Marquess of Hertford, and had sons Paul – Squadron Leader RAF, killed in 1942, George, a Lt. Col., Royal Scots Fusiliers MC, who died in 1953 and Frank, Lieutenant RN, killed in action 1944.

Edmund, born in 1860, became a solicitor, forming the firm of *Royds Rawsthorne and Co.* at 46, Bedford Square, London, WC. He lived at Stubton Hall Newark and married Rachel Fane of Fulbeck, the next parish, whose forebear had raised Fane's Horse at the time of the Indian Mutiny, later 19th Lancers, Indian Army. Edmund was Conservative MP for Sleaford from 1910 to 1923 and served during the Great War as a Major in the Lincolnshire Yeomanry and Lt. Col. Commandant in the Lincolnshire Volunteer Force. He was awarded the OBE in 1919 and was a Deputy Lieutenant and High Sheriff of Lincolnshire in 1931. He was knighted in 1939.

Edmund and Rachel had two children, Anthony, the eldest, who was born mongol, and Jasper, who became a Sub Lieutenant in the Royal Navy and was tragically killed in a motorbike accident in 1917, leaving no heirs.

Mary, born in 1863, married my grandfather Charles Carlisle.

Evelyn, also born in 1863, married Hugh Aldersey of Aldersey Hall, who owned a 2,000 acre estate in the parish of Coddington near Chester. The family had also owned Spurstow Hall, which is recorded in the Domesday Book. They had three sons.

Mark, Lieutenant, Cheshire Regiment and Hugh, Captain, Cheshire Yeomanry, were both killed in France in 1915. A memorial to them stands by the roadside in Aldersey Green.

Their brother, Ralph, Captain, Cheshire Regiment, was a horticulturist who lived all his life at The Crook, Aldersey. The Hall was occupied by the army during the war and left in such a bad state, it was demolished.

Their last child, Agatha, born in 1865, married James Steuart RA, a Scots artist. They had one daughter Sylvia, a charming spinster lady and accomplished water-colourist, who was a Red Cross worker during the war, but otherwise lived a leisured life in London until her death in 1970.

Her elder sister, Norah Royds, daughter of Francis and Cornelia, was born in 1859 and married George Gribble of 17 Hans Place, London, a wealthy businessman and owner of a dock warehouse company. In 1890, they bought a derelict Queen Anne house, Henlow Grange, six miles from Hitchen, Hertfordshire, in a park of one hundred an twenty acres, with surrounding farms of another fourteen hundred acres. They restored the house of twenty-four bedrooms and employed a housekeeper, three kitchen staff, four menservants, three housemaids, a lady's maid, three nursery maids, three grooms, nine gardeners and two keepers. George also owned a yacht on which he employed a crew and in which the family annually cruised the French coast. Today, Henlow Grange is a well known Health Farm.

In about 1909, George and Norah moved to Biddesden (now owned by Lady Moyne of the Guinness family) and from there moved to Kingston Russell House, which George had purchased and renovated in 1913. This was another extensive property situated in Longbredy near Dorchester.

Norah died in 1923 and George in 1927 leaving £500,000, the equivalent of about £25 million today.

They had six children.

Phyllis, the eldest, born in 1882, married Wolverley Fordham of Fordham, Essex, the owner of a brewery. They had no issue.

Norah Le Grand, born in 1886, married Eustace Hill, a banker, and had a son. Anthony, who formed the firm of *Hill Samuel Ltd,* a leading London bank.

Leslie Grace, born in 1883, married Hugh Seebohm, a member of a prominent Quaker family, who owned the *Hitchen*

Bank, which was taken over by Barclays, who also had strong Quaker traditions. Their second son, Frederick, born in 1909, joined Barclays and served in the Royal Artillery during the Second World War. He achieved the rank of Lt Col., was mentioned in despatches and became chairman of *Barclays Bank DCo*, the overseas business, in 1964. He was knighted in 1965 and given a peerage in 1972, as Lord Seebohm, having been chairman of the Joseph Rowntree Memorial Trust for fifteen years and prominent in other social work. He was High Sheriff of Hertfordshire 1970. His eldest daughter is Victoria Glendinning, the author.

Vivien Massie, born in 1888, married Douglas Doyle-Jones and had a daughter, Cressida.

Philip Le Grand, born in 1891, was educated privately due to ill health. He served during the Great War in the Hampshire Regiment and held the rank of Major in the Royal Flying Corps. In the 1920s he founded the *Rhodesian Tobacco Company*, representing that industry in London, and during the Second World War served as war correspondent for the *News Chronicle*. He published a book entitled *Diary of a Staff Officer*, describing his experiences in France with the BEF before Dunkirk.

Philip Gribble, also known as Bogie, was married four times, first, in 1915 to Morwenna McNeil, daughter of Robert McNeil, MP for Canterbury, who died in 1924 without issue, and secondly to Joyce Lyall by whom he had two daughters and a son, David, who, after Eton and Cambridge became a master, later head, of the progressive co-educational school Dartington Hall in Devon. Philip's third wife was Anthea and his fourth Jean MacFarlane by whom he had a son, Aylmer Philip, born 1st October 1948. After the Second World War, Philip lived at Tackoldneston Hall in Norfolk, where he bred horses, with how much success is not known. He wrote an autobiography entitled *Off the Cuff*.

Julian Royds Gribble, George and Norah's second son, born in 1897, was educated at Eton, where he was an all-rounder, and the Royal Military College, Sandhurst, where he was given a commission on 13th May 1915 and joined the Royal Warwickshires. He then spent a year on the Isle of Wight, was transferred to France on 21st May 1916, promoted to Captain on 23rd March 1917 and earned the VC for holding his position against overwhelming odds when attacked by the enemy at Hermies Ridge, Beaumetz on 23rd March

1918.

During that encounter he was stunned by a shot in the head, ending up in the hospital for British prisoners at Hameln, Hanover, from whence he was moved to the Citadel, a prison in Mainz for officers of allied countries. There he quickly recovered from his ordeal and was scheduled to return home with fellow officers to this country on 24th November 1918. But it was not to be. Sadly, Julian contracted Spanish flu, which was sweeping the world at that time, killing more people, it was reported, than were killed in the war itself, and he succumbed to it in Mainz hospital at 00.30 hours of the 25th November.

A replica of his VC (the original was destroyed by fire in Bogie's house) can be seen at The Royal Regiment of Fusiliers Museum in Warwick, who in their publication, *Famous Sons of the Regiment*, describe the events that led up to the following citation:

> *On 21st March 1918, the 10th Bn was near Velu with orders to hold on in face of heavy German attacks. On the 23rd, the Germans broke through on a wide front, but Captain Gribble and his Company would not yield. His orders were to hold on to the last, and he sent a runner to say that he would stay until ordered to retire. This resolution he inspired his men to accomplish. When last seen he was still fighting, surrounded by the enemy. By his courage and determination the Germans were unable to obtain complete mastery of Hermies Ridge for some hours, and the rest of the Brigade was able to be withdrawn. He was wounded and taken prisoner.*

Julian is remembered in this country by a stained glass window of Saint Julian, designed by his sister Vivien and installed by Norah at St. Martin's church, Preston, Hampshire. Only a few yards from this window one can see two solitary overgrown graves, one of Julian's sister, Leslie, who died in 1913 and the other, next to it, of Norah herself, truly reflecting the awful pain of the loss her two children.

Norah, was a very beautiful, accomplished and highly intelligent woman, well known for her evening soirées to which she often invited artists from the London stage to perform at Kinston Russell. A portrait of her by the American artist, John Singer

Sargent in 1888 is now in the hands of the Art Museum of Western Virginia.

My grandparents, Mary (née Royds) and Charles Carlisle who had been married in 1881, had seven children.

George Blomfield, born in 1883, was educated at Radley College and Oxford, where he won several scholarship prizes. He went into the church in Africa and was chaplain to the forces in East Africa from 1910 to 1918, being mentioned in despatches. Later he was appointed vicar of Boksburg near Johannesburg. He married Joan Burden, thereafter returning to England where he became, first, vicar of Holmes Chapel in Cheshire in about 1930, then vicar of Luton, and later, vicar of Shenley in Hertfordshire and a canon of St. Albans.

George and Joan had 3 girls:

Penelope, who became a missionary teacher in Uganda.

Judith, who married a doctor, Michael Montagnon, practising in Caerleon, and had four girls, Mary, Ruth, Jane, Sarah.

Elizabeth, who was a horticulturist and married David Booth. They had two girls, Nancy and Helen and retired to live at Moylegrove near Cardigan.

Thomas Roger Massie (Roger), born in 1884, went to Woolwich and was commissioned into the Royal Artillery. He commanded a battery during the disastrous Mesopotamian campaign and was taken prisoner with the whole force by the Turks after the 143 day siege of Kut-el-Amara in 1915. He was awarded the DSO and mentioned in despatches.

The British and Indian troops were very badly treated by the Turks, being marched hundreds of miles back to Turkey, many dying on the march. Officers were reasonably treated and transported by rail, but of 8,000 British and Indian soldiers taken prisoner, only 2,000 survived.

After the war, while serving in India, Roger married Maud Cowan, his commanding officer's wife, who had nursed him through a serious illness. She had two daughters who became missionary teachers in India and a son, William who became a farmer in Cardiganshire. Roger retired as Major in 1936 to live in Worthing and died in 1962. He and Maud had no children.

Evelyn Rose, born in 1885, married Ralph Barbour who

owned a firm making heavy electrical switchgear. They lived at Shenley, Hertfordshire and had a girl Lynette, who never married but devoted her life to good works, and three boys, Hugh, David and Philip educated at Stowe.

Hugh, a scholar, was converted to Communism by a master at Stowe and was taken on a visit to Russia in 1936. I don't know if he was disillusioned by what he saw there, as were Malcolm Muggeridge and other intellectual "commies", but the poor man died of a brain tumour shortly afterwards.

David served as an officer in the Royal Engineers during the war and afterwards was a manager in the nationalised coal board. After retirement he owned a fishing tackle business.

Philip started as a conscientious objector, which required considerable courage but later joined the Army Medical Corps. After the war he edited *Which* magazine.

In 1960, their father bought a large farm in Shropshire, which he let to a tenant but gave to his sons, and also two farms in Pembrokeshire which he gave to Lynette, but let to me.

Frank, born in 1886, joined the family firm and went out to manage the office in Montevideo, Uruguay, where it had recently moved from Buenos Aires. He married Renee Bankier and spent his whole life in Uruguay except for 18 months in 1928/9 when he brought his family home and exchanged jobs with my father, who took his family out there.

Frank and Renee had four children, two boys Gerard and Ronald (known as Billy), and two daughters, Yvonne and Adelaide (Betty).

Gerard went to Radley and joined the firm in Manchester in 1938. He served during the war as Captain, RASC in Africa and Italy, and then returned to Uruguay where he took over the running of the company office until his death in 1961. He married Genevieve Clavel but had no children.

Billy went to Radley, then to Loughborough University and became an engineer, a reserved occupation during the war. He married Margaret, daughter of Canon Youens living at Rotherham and had two daughters, Nicola & Christine. He also died young.

Yvonne was a very beautiful girl who came over to join the FANYs for the war. They descended from the First Aid Nursing Yeomanry of the First War and were mostly composed of upper class girls in confidential intelligence jobs or drivers for generals in the army. They were later subsumed into the more proletarian ATS – Auxiliary Territorial Service.

Yvonne married Jack Ladenburg, a stockbroker, and had three sons Michael, Simon and Richard. She died like her mother and two brothers of cancer in her late forties.

Betty, born in 1923, spent her life in Montevideo, marrying late in life Edouardo de Caballero, a psychiatrist. They had no children.

Charles Valentine (Val), born in 1887, was at Radley and Oxford, gaining several scholarship prizes. He became a solicitor, joining *Royds Rawsthorne & Co.* the firm started by his uncle, Sir Edmund Royds. On the outbreak of war he joined the Artists Rifles OTS and was commissioned into the 16th Lancers and wounded as Lieutenant in 1917. He married Mariquita Webbe, a colourful singer and high diver, and they had three daughters – Fiona, born in 1925, Donella and Gillian, who married David Spencer-Jones – and an adopted son, Hildred.

Val, also my godfather, acted as solicitor for the family firm. He was divorced from Mariquita in about 1935 and died in 1958.

Geoffrey, born in 1899, was also at Radley, winning several prizes. He joined the Cheshire Yeomanry as 2nd Lieutenant shortly before the end of the war and though he did get to France, survived unwounded. A classics scholar at Corpus Christie Cambridge, he went out to the South African church where he was curate at Pretoria from 1926 to 1932 and vicar of Barberton from 1932 to 1938, returning home to be appointed vicar of Buxton from 1938 to 1953 and Master of St. Cross, Winchester, built as a monastic hospital, from 1953 to 1970. He retired to live in Canterbury, where his son Julian was diocesan secretary, and stayed there until he died in 1985.

He had married Ethel Mentjies, an Anglo-Boer, in Pretoria in 1929. They had a son, Julian, in 1930 and a daughter Anne in 1934.

Anne married the Rev. Philip Norwood and they had one son, Michael.

Julian married Jill Fearnly Whittingstall and had three sons – Timothy, Matthew and Simon – and a daughter Helen. Julian was in the colonial service in Tanzania for a few years after the war as a district officer until self-government in about 1960. That was the time of the disastrous groundnut scheme of the colonial development corporation promoted by Clement Atlee's Labour Government, which had won the 1946 election with a huge majority. This victory had been largely due to the votes of servicemen who had been indoctrinated in socialist propaganda by the army educational service, and their relations who thought Labour was more likely to demobilise and "get the boys home" quicker than a Conservative Government, lead by the ageing Winston Churchill. It was this Labour Government that gave us the National Health Service and was responsible for the disastrous nationalisation of the coal and steel industries, and the railways.

Philip Edmund, my father, was born 1889 and also went to Radley, where he rowed in the school eight but was the only one of the four brothers not to appear on the scholarship prize boards or to go on to University. On leaving school he lived at home in Alderley Edge and joined the family firm in Manchester, taking over as managing director after my grandfather died in 1910.

With the outbreak of the war in 1914, he handed over management of the Manchester office to his uncle Sam and joined the Cheshire Yeomanry, now dismounted as infantry. He was wounded in France in 1917 and transferred to a hospital at Dawpool, a large house near Birkenhead that had been owned by his grandfather, Thomas, in the middle of the 19th century, when the firm's offices had been in Liverpool. His father and all his uncles had been brought up there.

He was nursed at Dawpool by my mother Mary (Molly) Gamon, a Red Cross Nurse throughout the war, and married her in 1919.

The name Gamon probably originates from a follower of William, Duke of Normandy, who conquered England in 1066. But the first ancestor to be identified is Richard, who was born in 1630 at Dunham Hill, and farmed at Picton. His son, Thomas, was baptised at Thornton-le-Moors in 1671 and married Mary Garrett of Plumstall. He died in Plumstall where he was buried.

In 1730, their son Richard, described as a yeoman of Willaston, moved to Thornton. He had eight children, of whom three sons are described as being of Ince, but his son Charles, born in 1750 acquired the 1,000-acre Thornton-le-Moors estate. His son, also Charles, born in 1783, and William, 1789, are both described as being of Thornton Green, the mansion house. They were corn merchants, owners of the Dee corn mills, and also town councillors of Chester. Richard was buried at Thornton as are all his descendants to this day.

A rhyme about a miller on the river Dee runs as follows, although I don't know if one of them was the miller about whom it was written.

> *There was a jolly miller once lived on the River Dee.*
> *He worked and sang from morn till night, no lark more blythe than he*
> *And this the burden of his song was ever wont to be:*
> *I care for nobody , no not I, if nobody cares for me.*

When feeling depressed by farming difficulties I would often sing this ditty to cheer myself up and emulate the example of my forebears.

Charles left no heirs but William had nine children. Among them were, William, born in 1832, who married Catherine Grindley of Hoole and continued living at The Green and in ownership of the Dee corm mills; John, born in 1838, who became a solicitor in Chester and married Mary Vernon of Towcester, with whom he had five sons, all apparently clever, as Geoffrey was a scholar at Winchester, BA Christ College Oxford; Hugh went to Harrow and obtained a BA at Exeter College, Oxford; Humphrey, Vernon and William all went to Marlborough College.

Hugh became a barrister, and Geoffrey and Humphrey were solicitors — they started the firm of *Gamon & Co.* solicitors of Chester.

William and Catherine had nine children born at The Green. Charles, the eldest, my grandfather, born in 1858, married Mary Stott, whose family owned a shipping line trading between Liverpool and the Baltic and whose brother was MP for Derby. Charles was a broker on the Liverpool cotton exchange, and Lt. Colonel, VD (Victorian Decoration), in command of the territorial battalion of The Cheshire Regiment, 18981 1900.

Charles and Mary lived at Parkgate on the Dee until 1920 when Charles retired and they moved back to The Green, which had been unoccupied for some years. Today, it is a nursing home. Then, of course, The Green had no electricity; I found oil lamps and candles most attractive when staying there as a child. A well in the cellars provided water, which was somehow piped up to a bathroom. Their daughter Mary, my mother, born in 1890, never went to school, education for girls being then considered unimportant.

Their eldest son Charles, born in 1889, was educated at Sedbergh in West Yorkshire and during the Great War served in the Cheshire Regiment in the army commanded by General Allenby that drove the Turks out of Palestine and Syria – an operation aided by irregular forces of King Feisal, led by the dashing Colonel Lawrence of Arabia, which had driven the Turks out of Saudi Arabia. Lieut Charles Gamon, was mentioned in despatches.

The regiment was later transferred to France where Charles, then a Captain, was severely gassed in 1917. He was left chronically disabled with bronchitis and spent the rest of his life living with his mother at The Green, chicken farming. He never married and died of pneumonia in 1940.

The estate of 1,000 acres was comprised of four tenanted farms and thirteen cottages in Thornton-le-Mooors village. I sometimes stayed there as a child during the harvest and would lead the horses out, riding back on top of the corn sheaves on the wagons. All Cheshire farms used beautiful great Shire horses then. It was only during and after the war that tractors, mostly Fordsons, took over their tasks. Casual labourers from Ireland travelled from farm to farm for hay-making and harvest. They slept in the barns and were given huge plates of potatoes and gravy for their meals.

Tragically, as Charles had left some debts when he died, his cousins, solicitors in Chester, regrettably advised his mother to sell the estate both to provide an annuity for her and to pay off an aunt in Australia, who had a share in the estate. It would have realised about £20 per acre or £20,000, which is to be compared with a value of £3,000 per acre today, i.e. £3million. Charles' mother, Mary continued to live at The Green till her death in 1950.

Mary's younger son John (Jack), another of my godfathers, was born in 1900. He went to Dartmouth Naval College and was already at sea as a midshipmen, aged 16, during the Great War. Later, he served on the battle cruiser, *Renown* when it took the Prince of Wales and Lord Louis Mountbatten to Australia and around the world.

He retired in 1936 with the rank of Lieut. Commander and took holy orders. Having been appointed curate at Northwich, Cheshire in 1938, he married Beatrice (Bea) Campbell, a distant cousin of my father's who had been a social worker in Manchester.

When WWII broke out, Jack was recalled to the Navy and became naval chaplain at Grimsby, where he and Bea had two daughters, Ruth and Mary.

Ruth married Christy Griffith, headmaster of Hurworth House, a prep school in Darlington. He retired early and they went to live near Denbigh, where Ruth became a County Commissioner of the Girl Guides and later Chief Guide in Wales and a Deputy Lieutenant. They had two daughters, Eleanor and Caroline.

Mary became house-mistress of the prep school for Repton School, married Michael Grinter, a naval officer by whom she had a son Jonathan, in 1967 and a daughter Naomi in 1970. However they were divorced when he deserted her. In retirement she lived at Patterdale with the headmaster.

On the invasion of France in 1944, Jack was appointed senior naval padre in Normandy. After the war he became vicar of Chelford, Cheshire, where he and Bea had three more children, all boys:

Andrew became a senior manager in the National Health Service married Jean Bramley, with whom he had daughters Jean, Sarah & Jane. He subsequently married Barbara Claridge with whom he had a son, John.

James (Jim), after a few years as a prep school master and 10 years in agriculture, married Patricia Gilder and started a business in Hay-on-Wye, hiring out canoes and mountain bikes. They had no children.

William (Bill), my godson, became a producer of documentary films and married Rowena Perez. They had two daughters, Farni and Hannah. Bill was tragically killed in a road accident aged 30 years.

After Chelford, Jack became vicar of Tattenhall, Cheshire, followed by Norbury and Snelston, near Ashbourne. He retired and died at Tilston in 1986, aged 86. He was buried at Thornton le Moors, as was his wife, Bea when she died in 1989.

Mary (Molly) Gamon, born in 1890, having met him while

nursing him at Dawpool, married my father, Philip Edmund Carlisle in 1919. For what must have seemed a very glamorous honeymoon at the time, they sailed to South America on a three-month honeymoon/business trip, visiting Uruguay, Argentina and Chile, to which the firm exported textiles.

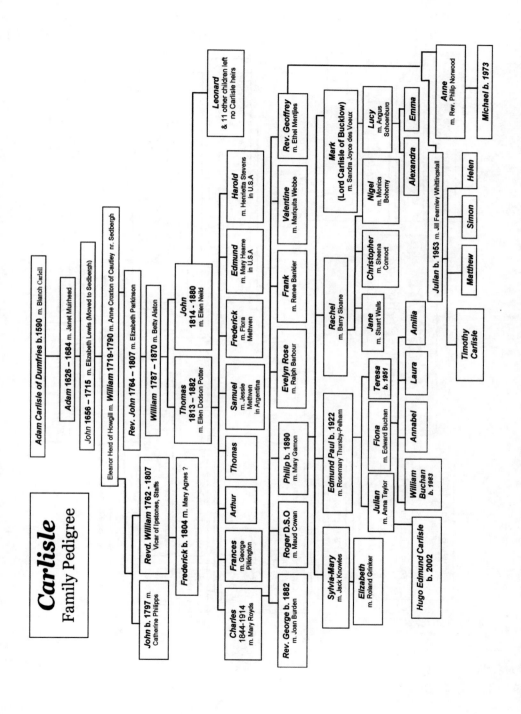

Carlisle
Family Pedigree

Adam Carlisle of Dumfries b.1590 m. Blanch Carlell

Adam 1626 – 1684 m. Janet Muirhead

John 1656 – 1715 m. Elizabeth Lewis (Moved to Sedbergh)

Eleanor Herd of Howgill m. William 1719-1790 m. Anne Croxton of Cautley nr. Sedbergh

Rev. John 1764 – 1807 m. Elizabeth Parkinson

William 1787 – 1870 m. Betty Alston

Revd. William 1762 - 1807
Vicar of Ipstones, Staffs

John b. 1797 m. Catherine Philipps

Frederick b. 1804 m. Mary Agnes ?

Thomas 1813 – 1882 m. Ellen Dodson Potter

John 1814 - 1880 m. Ellen Neild

Leonard
& 11 other children left
no Carlisle heirs

Harold m. Henrietta Stevens in U.S.A

Edmund m. Mary Hearne in U.S.A

Frederick m. Flora Methven

Samuel m. Jessie Methven in Argentina

Arthur

Thomas

Frances m. George Pilkington

Charles 1844-1914 m. Mary Royds

Rev. Geoffrey m. Ethel Mentjies

Valentine m. Mariquita Webbe

Frank m. Renee Bankier

Evelyn Rose m. Ralph Barbour

Philip b. 1890 m. Mary Gamon

Roger D.S.O m. Maud Cowan

Rev. George b. 1882 m. Joan Burden

Mark
(Lord Carlisle of Bucklow)
m. Sandra Joyce des Voeux

Rachel m. Barry Sloane

Edmund Paul b. 1922 m. Rosemary Thursby-Pelham

Sylvia-Mary m. Jack Knowles

Nigel m. Monica Bohomy

Christopher m. Sheena Connoct

Jane m. Stuart Walls

Fiona m. Edward Buchan

Julian m. Anna Taylor

Elizabeth m. Roland Grinter

Lucy m. Angus Schoenburg

Alexandra

Emma

Amilia

Laura

Annabel

Teresa b. 1951

William Buchan b. 1983

Hugo Edmund Carlisle b. 2002

Anne m. Rev. Philip Norwood

Michael b. 1973

Julian b. 1953 m. Jill Fearnley Whittingstall

Timothy Carlisle

Matthew

Simon

Helen

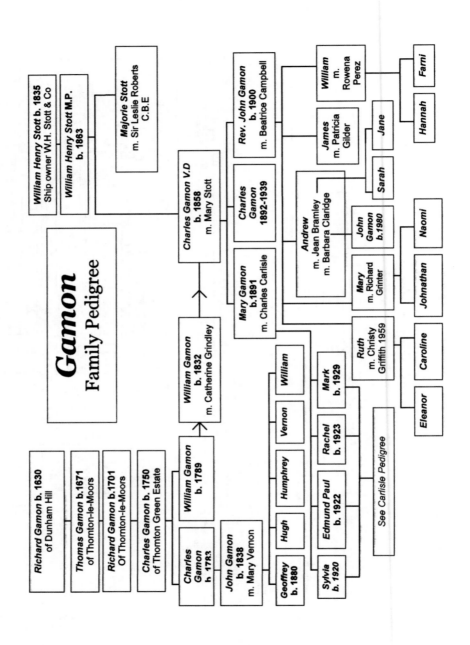

Gamon
Family Pedigree

Chapter Two

When my parents returned to England from their honeymoon, they bought a house called South Bank in Alderley Edge, where they lived for the rest of their lives. This house, now demolished, was only a five minute walk to the railway station from where my father travelled to his office in Manchester, 5½ days a week until after the war when the office ceased to open on Saturdays. South Bank was only a mile from his mother's house and as my father was a very devoted son, he went round to see her with books from Moodies' library several times a week. She died in 1945 aged 78. This prevented them from living in the country which was a loss to my mother, who always wanted to keep horses.

For many years my father was on the local council and, for part of that time, chairman and Justices of the Peace. During the war he was chief air raid warden for the village and my mother worked part time at the local hospital as a Red Cross nurse. He was 6'1½", handsome and reserved. My mother, at 5' 10", was a beautiful if unsophisticated woman. As was the manner of the upper classes at the time, there was little overt display of affection between them and never any conflict. They were, nevertheless, both devoted to each other and wonderful parents to me, being both firm and tolerant.

Although my father's salary never exceeded £1,500 year, we always had a cook general and a nursemaid when we were young. He managed to put four children through public schools – fees were then £200 a year - and we never wanted for anything. We always had three weeks holiday at the sea in summer and often a week at Easter. In winter my parents played golf and bridge, and in summer tennis at the excellent Alderley Edge Cricket & Tennis Club, which had the best cricket team in the county.

On Sunday mornings we went to church where the vicars regularly harangued us on the sins of fornication. These days state schools encourage it with sex education, and the Church is silent. After lunch there were bible stories and a long walk, finishing with tea at our grandmother's house.

My elder sister Sylvia was born at Alderley in 1920, followed in 1922 by me, Edmund Paul, Rachel in 1923, and Mark in 1929, when we were living in Montevideo.

One of my earliest memories is of the nursery at South Bank, where a nursemaid locked me in a cupboard for being disruptive; she was sacked next day. And I can sill recall being vaccinated against smallpox by our doctor, who in those days came to the house to do it. Vaccination for children then was rather like the present TB test on cattle, but much more vicious. Boys were scratched with vaccine on the upper arm, girls on the upper leg, which caused two scabs about the size of a 10p piece. It was painful and irritating and left one scarred for life.

I also vividly remember my fear of going in the sea, and being terrified if my father, driving our Morris soft top car, had to stop on a hill to engage first gear, which seemed to involve much elaborate double-declutching; I was sure we would roll back down the hill. Once, I remember, a front wheel dropped off our car and went bowling down the road ahead. I remember once being scared out of my wits by a policeman telling me to "Go along with your mother" on a Manchester street when I was tugging on her hand in the opposite direction. I was also fearful of going upstairs in the dark and, as we had no bedside lamps, always made a running jump into bed, in case there was someone underneath it. Another memory is of sneaking down to the kitchen, which was out of bounds, to steal butter.

In short, I suppose, I was a nervous, highly strung and slightly rebellious child and I can still feel the pain of being slapped on the back of the hand by my mother, who wore rings, for any indiscretion. And talking of pain, there was the dentist's drill; that was agony – there were no injections in those days:

In 1928, my father took our family to Montevideo, the capital of Uruguay – a stable country, often described as the Switzerland of South America. My father had arranged to exchange houses and offices with my uncle Frank, who managed the South American end of the family merchant business, and brought his family over to live in our house for 18 months. In Uruguay, I can only remember the fig tree in the garden and the huge jellyfish which littered the beach at

Punta-del Este, where we went for holidays. At that time there were just a few bungalows behind sand dunes, contrasting with the town's present day status as a major resort and marina for Round the World yacht racers, and the holiday choice of Argentineans from the other side of the River Plate. We also took with us to Montevideo our much-loved governess, Miss Carleon (Carlo), who taught my sister and me, so that we wouldn't fall behind when we got back to England.

We sailed both ways on the Blue Star liner, *Deseado*, although all I remember of the journey home with our new born younger brother, Mark, a great storm that hit us in the Bay of Biscay, washing away the gangplank and sending chairs and tables sliding across the saloon. It was their worst experience for twenty years, the sailors told me.

Back home in Cheshire, Carlo taught us for another year until, aged eight, I went to a prep school, The Ryleys, which involved a one mile walk to avoid the taunts of the boys attending the village school near-by. My parents caused me much distress by refusing to allow my hair to be cut short, which they considered common, and I developed a nervous habit of blinking whenever I spoke to anyone. After a year I was allowed to cycle to school – the cause of some concern to my mother, even though there was little traffic on the roads in the early 1930s.

My mother, unusually at that time for women, had learned to drive, in her case in our newly acquired Talbot touring car. She occasionally drove me, but motoring in those days could be very cold, which necessitated wrapping oneself up in rugs and invariably caused sickness on a long journey. Fifty miles per hour was going it some.

At ten, I was sent away to Moorland House at Heswall in the Wirral. It was owned by Mr Dobie and Mr Daniels, both bachelors, around seventy, of strange demeanour. There was a good deal of bullying there and I was not very happy, although I never told my parents. In summer we played cricket and cultivated individual gardens; in winter we usually played rugger in the afternoons. The school had its own chapel and on Sundays I frequently found myself fainting during the long services, which were followed in the afternoons by tedious crocodile walks around the district.

One master had the habit of stroking our legs beneath our shorts when we stood by his desk to have our work corrected. He would presumably be prosecuted today but it caused us only amusement and mild embarrassment.

Another bachelor master, a glamorous ex-RFC pilot with a metal plate in his head – the result of a war wound – wanted to take me skiing during my last winter holiday but, to my mystification, my parents forbade it. However, the education must have been adequate as I passed my common entrance into Radley, although there was never any talk of a scholarship.

I remember in 1931 seeing the Graf Zeppelin fly over, and hearing the news of the huge Hindenburg airship, which, after making ten transatlantic crossings in regular commercial service in 1936, was destroyed by fire in 1937, landing at Lakehurst, New Jersey. Thirty six of its ninety two passengers and crew were killed, a terrible disaster, which, coupled with the burning out of our R101 in France, was to signal the demise of airships for good.

Another disaster was the sinking of the submarine *Thetis* whilst undergoing trials in the Mersey. For three days it lay with its bow stuck in the mud and stern projecting from the water. I wondered then why a cable could not have been put under it and a hole cut in the stern. Only three men had got out of the escape hatch which presumably then malfunctioned. When eventually refloated and renamed *Thunderbolt*, she survived the war.

In those days, winters were harder. I remember building snowmen, tobogganing and skating most Christmas holidays. In summer I collected birds' eggs – considered a good hobby in those days – but took only one egg per nest. I had my own garden, growing lettuce, radishes and onions. I kept rabbits and, later, hens, climbed trees and went for long cycle rides on empty roads.

In September we always had three weeks holiday at the sea, staying at a number of different places – Sandsend in Yorkshire, Silecroft in Cumberland, Morthoe in Devon, Rhosneigr in Anglesey and Criccieth in North Wales. We stayed in boarding houses and went on picnics every afternoon.

In those days Lancashire factory workers were given a

week's holiday at Blackpool, but farm workers were only allowed bank holidays off. The beaches were empty as August was more popular with the middle classes, but more expensive. We went shrimping, prawning, canoeing and bathing. A skinny child, I would shiver for an hour after coming out of the water, despite going for a run. In the evenings at home we played family games like old maid, rummy, hearts and whist and, when sick in bed, bezique, piquet and draughts.

When young, our parents read to us from the books of Beatrice Potter about talkative bunnies and squirrels, followed by the fables of Hans Christian Andersen and Grimms' Fairy Tales. Winnie the Pooh, Eyeore and Kanga were great favourites, although A A Milne blighted the life of his son, as Christopher Robin. Fortunately the debased American Mickey Mouse had not yet appeared. The girls were then enraptured by the adventures of *Swallows & Amazons,* by Arthur Ransome, who, it was recently disclosed, had been a British secret agent in Russia at the time of the revolution in 1916. Having communist sympathies and being married to Lenin's secretary, he had very bravely tried to arrange negotiations for our Foreign Office. Boys were reading the stories of G A Henty, about plucky Empire soldiering, and Sapper's tales of *Bulldog Drummond* – surely an ancestor of James Bond? John Buchan's hero, Richard Hannay inspired us, as did the stories of Percy Westerman, describing brave British seamen in "Q" ships defeating dastardly German U-boats in the Great War. Children's stories have, sadly, gone downhill ever since.

Before WWII, football was already the national game of the working classes. Most of the players were professional, although the leading player, Stanley Matthews probably earned little more than any workman. There were no international games then, and the practice of buying and selling players had yet to emerge. It's worth noting that the modern horror of football hooliganism had not yet appeared either.

Rugby, the more upper class game, was all amateur, apart from the Welsh and Lancashire Leagues, and matches were regularly played between England, Scotland, Wales and France.

Cricket was played in all private schools and in every village. County teams were mostly professional, but always captained by an amateur. Five Test matches were played each year, but only against

Australia, either here or there. Batsmen wore only pads, gloves and a box. Bumper bowling by the fast bowlers, Larwood and Voce, expressly to intimidate the batsmen became known as "bodyline" and was considered unsporting by the Australians and nearly put an end to test cricket. Nowadays fast bowlers regularly aim at the body and batsmen have to wear helmets, visors and body padding.

I occasionally listened to cricket broadcasts on the radio we acquired in 1936, but it needed earphones so was little used. Otherwise we read books and did jigsaw puzzles. At Easter we often went to Aberdovey for a week, where we walked and I played golf with my father.

In 1935, the popular and progressive but unstable Prince of Wales, who had had affairs with several married women, notably Ladies Cunard, Warwick and Furness, became besotted with the American Mrs Wallis Warfield Simpson. His behaviour, like that of his grandfather, was considered to be acceptable in those days and was not reported in the then deferential British national newspapers. The foreign press, on the other hand, printed photos of Edward and Mrs. Simpson while yachting in the Mediterranean.

In 1936, King George V died and Edward was proclaimed king but was told by Prime Minister Baldwin that Mrs Simpson could never be queen. He decided therefore, to general relief, to abdicate in favour of his shy brother, Albert, who succeeded to the throne on December 11th 1936.

Albert was crowned as George VI on 12th May 1937 at a spectacular coronation, highlighted by parades and village parties across the country. Mrs Simpson was distinctly unpopular, a feeling echoed in the strains of a ditty attributed to the boys of Eton College, which ran as follows:

Hark, the herald angels sing,
Mrs Simpson's pinched our King

On the evening that Edward's abdication was formally announced, he departed with Mrs Simpson to stay with friends in Austria and married her in France on 3rd June 1937. Soon after the abdication of Edward, King George VI conferred on him and his wife the titles of Duke and Duchess of Windsor. She was not, however, accorded the privileges of a royal duchess in this country, and they elected to live abroad.

When war started, Edward was made Governor of the Bahamas – "to get him out of the way", probably because, foolishly, he and the duchess had visited Hitler and been accused of pro-Nazi sympathies. After the war they lived chiefly in the United States and France, and remained exiles from this country for the rest of their lives.

At Radley in the winter of 1936 my tutor (Housemaster of a Social) was Clem Morgan, who had just been appointed Sub-Warden and given the most modern house. Since its formation in 1847, Radley had always been a strongly Church of England school, accepting no Jews, Catholics or foreigners, with an ordained Warden (Head master) until 1950. Attendance at Chapel every evening and twice on Sundays was compulsory.

The school comprises a series of fine building set out in beautiful spacious grounds situated above the Thames, halfway between Oxford and Abingdon. It caters for the sons of the professional & business classes – 'aristos' go to Eton, the rich to Harrow.

Like all public schools, it was really run by twelve prefects who had the power to beat boys quite savagely for serious offences or for getting five 'checks' awarded by house prefects for more trivial offences. I was beaten once by my Tutor for cutting the school concert on the last night of term. I omitted to put on thick pants and, to the distress of mother, had visible wheals for the next three weeks. No one wanted to be beaten twice. It's my view that if birching were practised today, 90% of crime would be stopped.

Apart from lessons and top games there was little contact with masters. We had to play rugger every day in winter, unless it was raining, when we were required to take part in long country runs or expect to take a beating if we cut them.

In my first summer, not being selected for Junior Colts cricket game, I elected to go rowing, a sport in which half the boys participated and at which the school then excelled, winning the Ladies Plate in 1938, when it was open to all University Colleges at Henley Regatta. Since 1939, schools have competed for the Princess Elizabeth cup.

Only four boys of the eight that rowed in the event in 1938

survived the war. The whole school travelled to Henley by special train and we all took punts on the river. I was more keen on sculling, at which I had some success in what was a less brutish occupation than rowing in an eight. I also played chess for the school in one or two matches. I played fives every Sunday and squash when possible. In the case of squash, I played for the school team. There was a racquets court but few played as it was very expensive on balls. Nevertheless we did produce national champions from time to time.

On the whole I was pretty happy at Radley and worked hard until I took School Certificate with 5 credits (Matric) at sixteen, but thereafter lost interest in working for the Higher Certificate at eighteen for entrance to Oxford or Cambridge, which my father was not offering, and there were no grants then. In any case, the war had started and I was impatient to leave school and join the army.

During the summer of 1940, senior boys formed a platoon in the Home Guard and patrolled the Thames at night in the school launch, keeping watch for German parachutists, who never came, although I did spot a few couples up to no good on the banks and heard nightingales singing the night through.

Being deprived of the company of girls, it was inevitable that affections developed between boys. During my first summer term I was asked by a senior boy in my social to meet a prefect and leading rugby player and rower in another social, Jim Arkell.

Scholars cut no ice but good games players were much admired. After some persuasion – no doubt slightly flattered – I agreed and we went for an evening walk, finishing up innocently sitting in the dark in the Memorial Arch. Someone must have spotted us, for, next day, my Tutor called me into his study and questioned me about it.

I was surprised at his interest but, at the same time, embarrassed when he asked if I knew about sex. Unable to see what an innocent friendship had to do with it, of course I said I did, although afterwards, I rather regretted not hearing what he had to say. During the whole of my time at Radley I never knew of any homosexual act being committed, although public schools have always been accused of this happening.

On leaving school, Jim went to Sandhurst and joined the Indian Army and rose to the rank of major in the 6th Gurkha Rifles.

He won an MC and bar but was tragically killed in Sumatra after the end of the war when his regiment, among the troops sent there to supervise the surrender of the Japanese, was involved in putting down an insurrection by 'freedom fighters' resisting the return of the Dutch colonial regime.

In my final year at Radley, like many others, I was enamoured of a blue eyed boy David Dill, a relation of the Field Marshall. David joined the 60th Rifles and later transferred to the SAS, seeking adventure while the great majority of the British Army sat in Britain, inactive from June 1940 to June 1944. He was in a group rashly dropped by parachute behind enemy lines during the German offensive in the Ardennes in December 1944. They were all taken prisoner by the Germans and shot illegally by the brutal SS on the orders of Hitler against any infiltration operations. He was awarded the Croix de Guerre and mentioned in despatches. A total of two hundred and seventy five Old Radleians were killed during the war – many, as is often the case, as a result of an accident. That was almost exactly the same number lost during the Great War.

During all the holidays of my teen years I spent much of the time with my close friends Oliver and Christopher Hamilton-Dixon cycling and playing golf at the Wilmslow Golf Links which was three miles away. In summer we played tennis and practised cricket at the nets of the excellent Alderley cricket club. Oliver joined the Fleet Air Arm and was tragically shot down in the Mediterranean in 1942.

We boys had no contact with girls, except our sisters. In fact I was scared of girls and most unwillingly attended the one or two dances held for children around Christmas dressed in my father's dinner jacket. One was given cards on which to book partners – no smooching with one girl then!

However, I was deeply in unrequited love with the Norwegian skating and film star, Sonja Henie, whose photo I carried close to my heart — pin-up pictures were not displayed at school and pictures of scantily clad females only became a feature of the licentious soldiery during the war. Pirelli calendars of discreetly naked women appeared in every garage soon after.

There are now over five hundred boys at Radley; in my time there were about four hundred. Parents would visit in summer and winter terms but we weren't allowed to stay out at night. We had cold baths each morning and hot baths after games. Meals in a fine dining hall were served by waiters and we slept in individual cubicles within the dormitories and worked in studies for two boys, after the first year in social hall. We wore gowns which became increasingly tattered and green with age. We were allowed bicycles which enabled trips down to the River Thames where we would sometimes swim in the filthy water (until a swimming pool was built in 1940). With a Tutor's permission, we could cycle to Abingdon or Oxford. In the school theatre, we saw brilliant Dons' plays and boys' productions. We hunted with the beagle pack (started in 1938) and took part in a weekly drill parade of the OTC – Officers' Training Corps. In my first year, I remember vividly being required to break into a run on hearing the shout of 'Fag!', to perform minor jobs for a prefect.

Overall, I'm sure that I was given a good education but was never pushed as hard as I could have been. Nowadays, though Radley rides high scholastically and at games.

Few Old Radleians have made a great mark in life, except, perhaps, for the comedian Peter Cook, Clive Stafford Smith, who has devoted his life to defending prisoners on Death Row in the United States, cricketers Ted Dexter and recently, Andrew Strauss, four generals, one air marshal (now Lord Craig of Radley), Lord Scarman QC and my late brother Mark, the only politician among them, who became a life peer, albeit without having achieved distinction at Radley. Mark's nursemaid told me long after that as a child, he was the most untalkative she had ever known. But he certainly took to talking at University and became chairman of the Young Conservatives in the North West.

The twenties and thirties were dominated by the depression and industrial unemployment, fear of communism from Russia, disarmament and fear of another war with Germany, left devastated with rampant appalling inflation and unemployment by the Treaty of Versailles.

In Russia, Stalin's purges were responsible for the deaths of most of the senior army officers and sent millions of intellectuals and so-called dissidents to prison in the appalling Siberian gulags.

Forced collectivisation of farms in the Ukraine caused famine and the deaths of millions.

In Germany, the National Socialist German Workers' (Nazi) party was led by Hitler who was appointed Chancellor of the Reich in 1933 and brilliantly transformed the country. He had been imprisoned in 1924 for eight months after a failed 'putsch' and, whilst there, wrote his autobiography Mein Kampf. This clearly described his intention of driving out the Jews, whom he blamed for undermining Germany during the war, of obtaining more land 'liebensraum' in the east for their burgeoning population, and of fighting Russian communism. He expressed admiration for the British Empire and wanted power only in Europe.

Mein Kampf was published in Britain in 1938. Regrettably, our own politicians appear to have been too stupid, or too complacent to read it.

Hitler immediately repudiated the Treaty of Versailles and set about rearmament on a huge scale. He introduced conscription, which provided full employment, and ensured that all children were dragooned into the Hitler Youth Movement, a sort of militant Boy and Girl Scouts. Within the Youth Movement the young people were systematically and brilliantly indoctrinated with the idea that the Jews were a despicable people responsible for Germany losing the Great War, and that they themselves belonged to a superior Aryan race which, led by their great Fuhrer, Hitler, were destined to avenge the iniquitous Treaty of Versailles and build a greater Germany at the expense of the despised Slavic nations to the east. Incredibly these beliefs sustained them through six years of war, to the very end.

In 1934, after a fire destroyed the Reichstag parliament building, Hitler blamed the Jews and his storm troopers turned on them on Kristallnacht, burning their synagogues and smashing their shops. Thereafter, all Jews were compelled to wear a yellow star of David on their arm and many tried desperately to get out of the country. In the same year, in the 'Night of the Long Knives', the militant SS whom he had recruited attacked the rival SA Brownshirts, murdering their leader, the homosexual Rhom, and fifty three of his officers. The remaining thuggish rank and file were promptly incorporated into the SS, in which they would later be responsible for some of the vilest atrocities.

Meanwhile, in Russia, Joseph Stalin, who had seized power in 1923 after murdering Trotsky and the other leaders of the 1916 communist revolution, had turned on the independent farmers of the Ukraine, described as Kulaks. This purge resulted in an appalling three year famine, in which a staggering ten million people died. In 1937 he released the 'Great Terror' against so-called dissidents and most of the senior army officers, in which some two million were shot, or despatched to the Siberian Gulags. Despite this, left wing British intellectuals and trade union leaders continued to applaud the benefits of communism.

In 1936 Germany reoccupied the demilitarised Rhineland, and France failed to react. In Britain, the Labour party still insisted on disarmament, only Churchill and a few other Conservatives gave warnings. France, although frightened of Communists with a large party in their country, made a pact with Russia.

In 1938 Germany annexed the Sudetenland, part of Czechoslovakia, with a German population of 3,000,000 and Chamberlain flew to Munich, where he met Hitler and came back proclaiming, 'Peace in our Time'. Nevertheless, in spring 1939 Hitler invaded Czechoslovakia – and still France, Britain and Russia did nothing.

In the Spanish Civil war (1936-1939), in which republican communists fought monarchists and the church, Hitler and Mussolini saw an opportunity to cause difficulties for France and each decided to support Franco. This gave the Germans a chance to try out terror bombing, which they did to much effect, annihilating several small towns, including Guernica on April 26, 1937. Their participation in the war helped Franco to win and establish himself firmly as a dictator for the next 40 years. It was fortunate that Spain did not go to the aid of the Axis in the world war that followed.

In 1935 the Italians had invaded Abyssinia from their colony Eritrea, using poison gas and got away with it. Anthony Eden, unable to get agreement on sanctions against Italy, resigned as Foreign Secretary. In 1939 Mussolini invaded Albania.

To popular local acclaim, Hitler annexed Austria in March 1939 and on 24th August 1939 made a surprise pact with Russia undermining its alliance with France. America all the while, having left the League of Nations in 1921 and passed a neutrality law that prohibited material assistance to all parties in foreign conflicts, remained isolationist. France and Britain had guaranteed the state of Poland, so when Germany invaded in September, they both declared war, but again did nothing. The plucky Poles, although they fought bravely, could not withstand the German 'blitzkreig' of armoured divisions supported by dive bombers. They were defeated within a month and, as agreed with the Nazis, the Russians moved in to occupy the Eastern half of the country. The Russians also invaded the Baltic states and in the following year either shot, or deported to Siberia, 34,000 Latvians, 60,000 Estonians and 75,000 Lithuanians.

If we had gone to war in support of Czechoslovakia, which had two armoured divisions in the best army in Europe, the German generals, who loathed Hitler and desperately wanted to avoid war, would have overthrown him and made peace. Fear, however, of his secret police, the Gestapo, and his astonishing success hitherto, won their grudging support.

The French army sat tight behind their 'impregnable' Maginot line and the British Expeditionary Force of 200,000 men were sent to France to dig in on the Belgian border and the so-called 'Phoney War' began.

For seven months the only activity was at sea where U-boats, after allowing crews to take to their boats, sank ships with impunity until they were grouped together in convoys and a helpful Roosevelt sold us 50 old destroyers (in return for bases in the Caribbean) to protect them. Surface raiders continued to sink individual merchantmen until rounded up by the Navy and German aircraft dropped newly developed magnetic mines around the coast, which also sank many ships.

At the Battle of the River Plate, which began on 13th December 1939, the cruisers Exeter, Ajax and Achilles discovered and damaged the pocket battleship Graf Spee, which turned away and headed for the neutral port of Montevideo, where its aristocratic Captain Hans Langsdorf was to release, unharmed, two hundred men captured from merchant ships sunk by the Graf Spey during her most recent voyage. She remained there for three days until on the evening of 17th December, she sailed out of Montevideo to be scuttled three miles out by Langsdorf who had placed explosives in such a manner that the sinking would set them off after both he and the skeleton crew had got off.

Langsdorf, while in his room at the Naval Base in Buenos Aires where the ships officers were being held, committed suicide with a shot to the head. He was found on the morning of the 20th wrapped in the ensign of his ship. He was later buried in the Cemeterio del Norte in Buenos Aires - his final resting place. The destruction of the Graf Spey was a great boost to British morale, but why she didn't sail across to Buenos Aires I never understood, since Argentina was pretty favourable to the Nazis and, in fact, did not join the Allies until 1945.

All poor children had been evacuated from London to be compulsory billeted in country houses and cleaned up! Many children of the well-to-do were sent to friends in America until a liner was sunk by a U-boat without warning.

A submarine also penetrated the nets of our principal naval base at Scapa Flow and sank the battleship, Royal Oak, with the loss of 833 out of 1008 crew, and escaped undetected.

In November 1939, the Russians invaded Finland and in the ensuing winter war, to our delight and admiration, suffered huge casualties, but in the end the overwhelming numbers of Russians prevailed and Finland surrendered in March 1940. 125,000 Russians had died, and 48,000 Finns.

The French and Churchill had pressed without success for us to invade Norway through Narvik, to cut off the iron ore supply from Sweden on which the Germans were dependent, and to assist the Finns. They also wanted to start a second front in the Black Sea, to deny Germany oil from the Baku oil fields and in the hope of Rumania and Yugoslavia joining the war. However, no doubt bearing in mind the disaster of Gallipoli in the Great War, the plan was shelved.

Remembering the bloodbath of the Great War, both French and British were fearful of casualties and convinced that the blockade would compel Germany to sue for peace. The French generals were also convinced that if the Germans attacked they would be defeated by their superior numbers and much better tanks. The German generals shared this opinion but were overruled by Hitler.

On 9th April Germany invaded Denmark, which surrendered in two days. They then went on to invade Norway where they lost three cruisers and ten destroyers to Norwegian guns and British mines, but rapidly overcame resistance.

On 14th April, four French brigades of 12,000 men were landed at Trondheim and four British Brigades at Narvik. The French were pulled out on 11 May and the British on 8 June were defeated by inferior numbers of German troops though our navy sank several German warships.

The theory of fast moving armoured warfare had first been expounded in the '20s by Captain Liddel Hart and General Fuller, but the blimpish British generals had been too stupid to take it up, still even maintaining cavalry regiments, although they had performed so disastrously in the Great War. The efficient German generals, on the other hand, adopted the concept as 'Blitzkrieg'. The Germans also produced the Stuka as aerial artillery in support of their aggressive army. The plane dived accurately on its target emitting a terrifying scream from its siren. However, they were slow and easily shot down by fighter aircraft if caught. The British army, being built for defence, had no air support.

On 10th May the German army invaded Holland and Belgium, which had insisted on neutrality and, fearful of Germany, refused any co-operation. The British and 1st French army on the coast advanced into Belgium, but it was too late. Huge numbers of terrified refugees, regularly dive bombed, clogged the roads. The Dutch surrendered on 20th May and the Belgians on 30th.

Meanwhile the principal German attack of armoured divisions, brilliantly commanded by Generals Runstedt, Guderian and Rommel, had come through Luxembourg and the Ardennes forest round the north end of the Maginot line, bridging several rivers. Not even stopping to collect prisoners, they headed for Abbeville on the coast, which they reached on 28th May, overcoming French forces and cutting them off from the British army.

Hitler ordered a halt on the Belgian French border on 17th May but his generals disobeyed and pressed on. A counter-attack by a French armoured division commanded by General de Gaulle from the south and a British armoured division from the north to cut off their spearhead near Arras, caused heavy German losses and very nearly succeeded, but that was the last throw.

On 19th May, the commander of the BEF, General Gort, had warned the French that he was already considering evacuation and on 26th our troops started to leave from Dunkerque. The 51st Highland Division fought bravely in the only really major battle at Calais, until overrun, but astonishingly all German forces were halted on 28th May on Hitler's direct order when only 10 miles from Dunkerque.

The only possible conclusion is that he allowed the British army to get away because he hoped to be able to negotiate peace, thus leaving himself free to pursue his intended campaign against Russia without an enemy on his western front. There was in fact good reason to hope for this as many influential people in Britain were more frightened of Communism than of Nazism, but he reckoned without Churchill, who succeeded Chamberlain as Prime Minister and rallied the country with rousing speeches of defiance.

Fortunately, the seas were remarkably calm and despite some bombing by German aircraft, between the 26th May and 6th June, 220,000 British soldiers and 120,000 French were brought home from Dunkerque by the navy and a vast flotilla of ferries and small boats, but left all their tanks, guns, transport and equipment behind. In the British press it was hailed as a miraculous delivery – almost a heroic victory.

In reality, the campaign had been the biggest military disaster in our history, very different from the performance of the British regular army in the Great War. On 14th June the French Prime Minister Renaud resigned to be succeeded by General Petain, their most renowned commander of the Great War. He immediately sued for peace, rejecting all entreaties by the British and General de Gaulle to remove the French Government to their Algerian colony, there to continue hostilities from their empire. And, with the backing of Admiral Darlan, Petain refused to order the French fleet – second only to the British Navy – to sail from French harbours. The liner, *Lancastria*, evacuating British troops from St Nazaire, was sunk by German bombers with the loss of 3,000 men. This disaster was never reported at the time, although it was the worst in our naval history.

De Gaulle, who had been appointed Secretary of Defence, came to

London and immediately proclaimed the formation of the Free French. However, he was only able to recruit 2,500 soldiers from the 120,000 brought out of Dunkerque, to join him. The rest were all shipped back to France.

Mussolini had joined Hitler in the Axis pact and, when a German victory was assured, Italy invaded France to get a share of the pickings, demanding Corsica, Tunisia, even Nice and Savoy. By their armistice agreement, Germany occupied two thirds of France including all the Atlantic coast and the French Government moved to Vichy, keeping the rest free. In all, the French had lost 124,000 men and 200,000 wounded in the campaign, thus their defeat was not as ignominious as has been painted. Dutch, Belgian and British losses from some 600,000 troops had been comparatively light, but we had lost around 500 planes.

It was found long afterwards that eighty British prisoners of The Norfolk Regiment and The Royal Warwickshire Regiment had been massacred by the SS, who herded them into a barn at Esquelbecq into which they threw grenades before setting it on fire. The SS officer who ordered it survived, to become a senior officer but, disgracefully, was never put on trial when unmasked in 1985.

Hitler's peace overtures having failed, an invasion of Britain was expected. The Home Guard was formed, beach defences constructed and mined, as many large German barges were assembled in French ports. But our navy had command of the Channel.

To confuse German invaders or their agents, all signposts were removed from roads all over Britain. In fact, only two or three spies landed in the country throughout the war, yet, incredibly, the signposts were not replaced until 1944 and their absence created immense dislocation.

During August and September, large formations of German planes attacked our ships and aerodromes daily in what became known as the 'Battle of Britain'. Fortunately, while so many of our armaments were inferior, we did have a winner in our Spitfire and Hurricane fighters, and, moreover, we alone had radar, recently invented by Robert Watson-Watt, to guide them. Eventually the German losses became unsustainable and a few hundred brave fighter pilots, about a quarter of whom were Poles who had escaped their homeland, saved Britain. In the course of this mighty air battle, 3,000 brave pilots shot down 1,200 German aircraft and lost 800 of their own. Of 'The Few', 500 were killed.

Unable to gain command of the air, and with the British navy dominating the English Channel, Hitler called off the invasion and again tried peace overtures. Meanwhile, although General de Gaulle had been able to persuade French colonies in equatorial Africa to rally to his flag, those in north Africa – Morocco, Algeria and Tunisia – remained loyal to the Vichy government, which by then was regarded by Britain almost as an enemy. Accordingly the Royal Navy sailed to Oran, where a sizeable French fleet was anchored in the harbour and commanded them to join us. They refused, so we duly sank three battle ships with the loss 1,300 men.

This both infuriated de Gaulle and reinforced Vichy hostility, so, when an Anglo/Free French force later invaded Syria (a French mandated territory), serious fighting ensued and resulted in about 3,000 dead on each side.

After the defeat of the 33,000 French troops, only 7,000 could be persuaded to join the Free French. All the rest were shipped back to France.

In October, after we had rashly sent a few planes to bomb Berlin, the 'Blitz' on London began. It went on for several months, reducing much of Dockland and the East End to rubble and the death of about 6,000 people. But the spirit of Londoners was unbroken. The king and queen led by example, remaining in London while the people spent the nights in underground stations, on bunks or mattresses.

In return, we bombed German factories and railway yards but later, when it was realised that this was too inaccurate to be effective, the controversial 'Bomber' Harris took command of the RAF and deployed newly commissioned Lancaster heavy bombers, led by Pathfinders in low-flying Mosquitoes dropping flares, to destroy Germans cities – a strategy designed to terrorise and break the morale of the German people. Up until 1942, more British aircrew had been lost than German civilians killed.

Although later in the war, huge fleets of bombers were used – up to 1,000 at a time – and several German cities were flattened, most notably Cologne, Hamburg where 40,000 civilians died, and disgracefully, as the war was near its end, Dresden, killing 35,000, German morale held up.

In fact, as Germany's night fighters, aided by a large numbers of searchlights and ack-ack guns, gained mastery of the situation, heavy bombing raids proved to be highly expensive in planes –some 8,000 going down – and 55,000 crew were lost, including many from empire countries and Poland; as many as 10% of those died as a result of accidents during training.

A tour of duty was 30 flights and only one in four survived them, and very few a second tour. They were brave men, the stress of long flights must have been appalling. It is remarkable that of those who parachuted from planes shot down few were lynched and most finished up in prisoner of war camps. Officers were treated reasonably; other ranks could be made to work but there have been few reports of the conditions they experienced.

It was considered the duty of officers to try to escape but only a handful succeeded. In the most celebrated case, in which seventy broke out through a tunnel in 1944, the majority, on direct orders from Hitler, were shot on recapture by the SS.

Back at Radley, in the summer of 1940, I failed dismally the Higher School Certificate having had to study French and Spanish at my father's behest for his business with South America. I have never had much ability for languages and wish I had done science, which few boys did, though a large new science lab had recently been built. A very few, four or five, were headed for the Regular Army – all good at games but pretty thick. Wellington was then the army school.

I rode home for the holidays on my Hercules bicycle, a journey of 130 miles, without gears. I then spent a month working on a local farm with my friend Oliver and was proud to be told that we were worth a shilling an hour (5p today) during the harvest, setting up sheaves of corn in stooks behind the reaper and binder, pitch forking them on to carts drawn by a shire horse, and stacking them in the farmyard. Farm work was very companionable in those days, with much chat and tea in the fields.

In September my elder sister, Sylvia and I cycled 120 miles to Criccieth and returned home after three weeks, stopping the night in an hotel on the way. B&B was three shilling and sixpence, 17p today. Petrol was rationed so there were few trips in the car with picnics.

I was then sent back to waste another term at school and

after that persuaded to go into my father's firm for six months, an experience which convinced me that I did not want to spend my life in a Manchester office. After I left Radley I joined the Home Guard and would spend a night each week with my section, commanded by Sergeant Dennis Midwood, a delightful cotton manufacturer, who had been an officer during the Great War, watching for the German parachutists who never came.

Although when the Home Guard had first come into existence after Dunkirk. Some units had only pikes and shotguns, we did have rifles and it was fun – if not so hilarious as *Dad's Army* on television. In fact, I think the Home Guard must have been a great waste of time and resources as it never encountered the enemy and went on for much too long until it disbanded in 1944.

The 'blackout', which entailed covering house windows entirely with heavy curtains, was strictly enforced. Similarly, it became a legal requirement to cover car head lamps, except for a two-inch diameter hole in the middle. On the latter account, driving at night was generally avoided.

Petrol was rationed to about 8 gallons per month, or 150 miles, and clothes could only be bought with coupons, which was very difficult for families with growing children; the problem was generally solved by their elders who were obliged to 'make do and mend'.

Additionally, food was rationed to 8 oz of sugar, 2 oz butter and 2 oz of margarine, 3 oz of cheese, ½lb of meat, 2 eggs and 2 oz of chocolate or sweets.

Baked beans, tinned fruit and jams were on points, amounting to about one tin per week. Fish was never rationed but involved queuing to obtain. Offal was a favour from the butcher. Bread, potatoes and vegetables were always in free supply but bananas and oranges were never seen. Everything was bought loose, in brown or white paper bags, or simply wrapped in newspaper, as were meat and fish & chips. Vegetables were simply tipped from weighing scales into one's shopping bag and sugar was dispensed into blue paper cones.

Rationing was generally hardest on the elderly as factory workers were given lunch in a works canteen and office workers could get a reasonable meal for one shilling at a 'British Restaurant'. Nevertheless, it's worth noting that, overall, the health of the nation improved during the war.

Farmers and country dwellers did all right with rabbits, game and poultry and for some dairy products and mutton. Cigarettes were always available; Players cost 5p for 20 and Woodbines (small size) 2½p. There was no shortage of beer in the pubs at 3p a pint bitter and 2½p for mild, but spirits were difficult to get.

There was a considerable black market in petrol and food, allowing the unscrupulous with money to acquire whatever they wanted as usual. Everywhere were posters warning that 'Careless talk costs lives' as spy mania engulfed the country. Twenty seven thousand Germans were interned in camps on the Isle of Man, although many of them were Jews who had fled Nazi persecution and were keen to join the war effort; later many of them were allowed to do so.

The greatest source of entertainment were the cinemas, if you could get to them, and they were always full. At night, people listened to the news on the radio and occasionally to Nazi spokesperson, William Joyce, dubbed 'Lord Haw Haw', speaking from Berlin on the success of German arms and how we were certain to lose the war. He was hanged as a traitor after the war, though this was probably irregular as he was, in fact, an Irish citizen.

Conscription had started in 1939. Men were called up at the age of nineteen for the forces, except those in reserved occupations, such as farming. Women were conscripted for work in munitions or aircraft factories or in the land army to work on farms. Later in the war, some men – the 'Bevin Boys' – were made to work down the mines.

Cricket and football matches continued, albeit with older players, and there was some horseracing at the major courses and limited hunting. Private servants became a thing of the past, having been dispersed to join the war effort.

In December 1940, President Roosevelt introduced Lend-Lease, announcing that America would be the arsenal of democracy although they preferred to remain neutral. From that moment a great flood of armaments of all kinds crossed the Atlantic, but they had to be paid for, and for another year Britain stood alone against the might of Germany, described by Churchill as 'Our finest hour'.

In January 1941, the Germans flattened Coventry, destroying the cathedral. Over the following months, Liverpool, Southampton, Swansea and other towns were heavily bombed. Few of the raiders were shot down, though many missed their targets or ditched their bombs in open country.

After Italy had entered the war in June 1940 and attacked France, the British and Indian armies moved in on Italian Somaliland and Abyssinia from Kenya, and Eritrea from the Sudan, defeating the Italians after a short and brilliant campaign.

From their Libyan colony the Italians had also attacked Egypt, a British mandated territory and our principal base in the Middle East. They were soon defeated by General Wavell commanding the 8th Army, which comprised the British seventh armoured division, an Australian and a New Zealand division, and the 4th and 5th Indian Divisions, British artillery regiments and engineers.

Some 200,000 prisoners were taken and the British advanced as far as Benghazi, a significant boost to the country's morale after the depression that followed Dunkerque, and in March our Mediterranean fleet based at Alexandria defeated the Italians off Cape Matapan, sinking a battleship, three cruisers and two destroyers.

In November 1940, Italy managed to overcome Albania and went on to attack Greece, but the Greeks manfully held them all winter until the following April when Germany, now joined by Hungary, Romania and Bulgaria, invaded Yugoslavia and pressed on into Greece with the Italians.

We sent the Australian and New Zealand divisions from Libya to help the Greeks but within a month Greece was overrun and our forces were withdrawn to Crete, leaving all their heavy equipment behind.

In May the Germans launched an airborne attack on Crete with parachutists and glider-borne troops who secured the aerodrome at Maleme but suffered such heavy losses of men that they never again made an airborne attack.

Although there were also two Greek divisions on Crete, we had no air support against the German dive bombers and, indecisively led by the ageing New Zealand General Freyberg VC of the Great War, our troops were soon evacuating again, with the loss of three cruisers, six destroyers and 2,000 sailors. It was an ugly debacle; while 18,000 men were taken off, 1,700 were left behind dead, and 12,000 were taken prisoner.

Meanwhile, German forces under the brilliant General Rommel had landed in Africa and in May drove the weakened British 8th Army all the way back to the Egyptian border, apart from an Australian garrison which held out in Tobruk and remained under siege for eight months.

On the 10th May 1941, Hitler's deputy, Rudolph Hess flew himself in an Me110 plane to Scotland and landed on the estate of the Duke of Hamilton, whom he had met in Berlin before the war. Presumably he was trying to negotiate peace though whether with the knowledge of Hitler or on his own initiative was never established, or at least, not disclosed. He was locked up and declared insane, which seemed unlikely. He was to be kept in prison for the rest of his life by the Allies in Berlin after the war.

Soon after the Hess episode, the most powerful battleship in the world, the Bismarck, broke the British blockade and headed out into the Atlantic where, on 23rd May, she hit and sank with her first salvo the pride of the British Navy, the Hood, which went down with all but three of her crew out of a total complement of 1,421.

After a dramatic search, the Bismarck was found, her rudder damaged in an heroic attack by old Swordfish biplanes from the Ark Royal and destroyed by our battleships on 27th May 1941 with the loss of all hands.

A further British naval disaster occurred on the November 14th. The Ark Royal, our most modern aircraft carrier, which had downed over 100 Italian and German planes, was torpedoed and sunk by a submarine in the Mediterranean while accompanying a convoy to Malta. All the crew were saved.

Despite continual bombing, which devastated Valetta, and the loss of many ships in supply convoys, Malta held out, to inflict heavy losses by air attack on Axis convoys sailing to Africa until relieved by our assault on Italy in 1943. The island was awarded a new medal, the George Cross, equal to the Victoria Cross, for bravery by civilians in recognition of their heroism. Of 17 merchant ships in a heavily escorted convoy in June 1942, only two reached Malta.

By this stage in the war, the Blitz on London had reached new heights and the Houses of Parliament were heavily damaged, causing MPs to move to Church House, Westminster.

In a new initiative, Winston Churchill set up Special Operations Europe (SOE) with the expressed purpose of 'setting Europe alight', by dropping agents and arms to encourage sabotage of railways and factories by local resistance fighters, and to transmit intelligence by radio. These agents (technically spies) were not protected by the Geneva convention and many hundreds of brave men and women were picked up by the efficient German forces and shot after being brutally tortured to extract information on their resistance contacts, who often then suffered the same fate. It is doubtful if the immense effort involved in training and supplying these agents was worthwhile, or ethical; they certainly contravened international rules of warfare.

In June 1941, Germany attacked Russia using their Blitzkreig tactics with armoured formations supported by dive bombers. These were phenomenally successful and resulted in the capture of three million Russian soldiers, of whom two million died within a year, through starvation, overwork, brutality, and gassing. (The Germans had already gassed 70,000 mentally deficient and incurable people from their own population.) However, overrunning Yugoslavia and Greece had delayed the invasion of Russia – code-named 'Barbarossa' – by a month, which would prove to be fatal.

When the Germans reached Ukraine they were at first welcomed as liberators by the people who had suffered terrible years of starvation in the 1920s when Stalin liquidated the Kulaks (independent farmers) and forced collectivisation of the peasants into huge state farms. But subsequent brutality by the SS – Hitler's elite Storm Troopers – on Ukraine's substantial Jewish population, who they proceeded to round up, shoot and bury in mass graves, soon turned other Ukrainians against them and ensured their resistance to the German occupation.

By October the Germans were within sight of Moscow and

Leningrad (now St Petersburg once more) but the harsh Russian winter set in and they got no further. They did not have adequate winter clothing, their vehicles got bogged down and the Russians, reinforced by troops from the east, resisted with heroic and suicidal tenacity. Leningrad remained under siege for 18 months. Half a million civilians died of starvation and a million Russian and German troops were killed.

I had left Radley at Christmas in 1940 in a depressed state as my study companion and I had been reported for smoking down near college pond. It was my first cigarette, a Players full strength which made me feel green. I never found who sneaked on us but we were called before our Tutor and demoted from our positions as House Prefects, which I found a big blow to my self-esteem.

On the last night of term, boys leaving had a farewell talk from the Warden who with some embarrassment warned us against consorting with prostitutes. Afterwards he asked me if I would like a cadetship in the King's Royal Rifle Corps, otherwise known as the 60th Rifles, who were recruiting for officers from Eton and Radley, Having Cert A in the OTC entitled one to a commission after a short period in a recruit cadet squad, but I turned it down. However, I had agreed to go into my father's firm for a few months. He and my mother, remembering the first war, were probably trying to put off the evil day when I would get absorbed into this one, although it seemed that the whole British Army was sitting around doing nothing but training, and most were to continue so for another three and a half years.

Nevertheless, throughout 1941, losses at sea were appalling, averaging 400,000 tons each month. But fortunately, in March the British Navy captured the Enigma cipher machine and code books from a sinking German U-boat, and the code breakers at Bletchley Park, using what was in effect the first computer, were able to decipher virtually all German radio messages throughout the rest of the war.

My other close friend, Christopher Longridge, nephew of George Mallory, who may have been the first man to climb mount Everest in 1926, had joined the RAF and was lost in a ship torpedoed on his way to flying training in Canada.

Life was pretty drab, because with rationing there was little entertaining, though I do remember somehow being invited to a cinema and dinner with a blond girl called Rose, who lived in Wilmslow and to whom I lost my heart. We saw a soppy film called *Mrs Miniver*, starring Greer Carson as a plucky British housewife. The principal heart throb was Diana Durbin, an American teenager who sang divinely, all in black and white then. I could not ask Rose home as my parents did not know her parents. In those days Alderley did not speak to Wilmslow. They thought she might be 'common' or at least nouveau riche, and indeed her family were much richer than ours! In the next six years I never met another girl and often regretted I did not have Rose as a correspondent.

As for other sporting activities, I did play cricket for the Alderley second eleven a few times and got my golf handicap down to 16, but I have never played since.

Chapter Three

In June, when approaching my nineteenth birthday and the age of call-up, I went to a recruiting office in Manchester and volunteered as a Trooper in the Life Guards, being given the traditional king's shilling. In July, I was ordered to report to Combermere Barracks, the Regimental Depot in Windsor, where I found I was the only volunteer in a platoon of thirty national service conscripts. Training consisted of PT before breakfast, followed by drill parades on the square, weapons training that included bayonet practice, on some days long route marches in column, when we sang dirty songs, and church parades on Sundays before marching to Windsor after tedious inspection by the Corporal-Major Platoon Commander, 2 IC & C O.

In fact, the training as a whole was pretty unimaginative and more suited to the First World War. We had iron beds with blankets but no sheets and spent our evenings occupied with various chores, such as blancoing our belts and packs, polishing the brass buckles and boning our boots with spit and polish, which probably ruined them! All clothes had to be laid out each morning for kit inspection.

Although the language was appalling, there was no bad behaviour or bullying and despite being the only public school boy in the group, I quite enjoyed the experience. The Life Guards officers were then all aristocrats. There are none today! The Earl of Sefton was our OC and Lord Daresbury the Company Commander, whose family owned Greenalls Brewery. The Depot commander was Lord Dormer and our platoon commander was Lord John Manners, brother of the Duke of Rutland.

In those days, the warrant officers and senior NCOs really ran the show. The only time we saw officers was on parade, except for night exercises, when occasionally I would talk to one or other of them.

The depot also served the Royal Horse Guards, The Blues whose officers were more nouveau riche, even from families in trade! For the war the two regiments were combined as the Household Cavalry and the first Battalion had gone to Palestine on the outbreak of war, taking their horses, although they were mechanised soon afterwards, with armoured cars.

In the evenings one could walk into Windsor and drink in the pubs, beer at 2½p for a pint of mild and 3p for bitter. Pay, for which we had to parade, was 14 shillings (70p) a week.

There was an emergency treatment room beside the guard room at the gate where anyone who had been seduced by ladies of the town could call in for self-treatment, but I suspect they put bromide in the tea as I never heard of such activity! Condoms, then called French letters ('Capotes Anglaises' by the French), were not available and, incredibly, not sold by Boots until long after the war. I soon applied for a commission but not in the Life Guards, as I had no private income. There was little activity in England so, inspired by the tales of Rudyard Kipling, I applied to go into the Indian Army.

The interview before the commissions board of three officers in London was a formality, and soon, when on a course at Seaford being taught how to shoot down dive-bombers with rifles or Bren guns, I received orders to go on a week's embarkation leave and report to the Marylebone Hotel in London. There I joined about sixty others cadets, mostly from public schools, and after three days, was sent by train to the Clyde where we embarked on a P&O liner, the *Maloya*, of some 17,000 tons, which had nothing like enough life boats!

Our accommodation was near the water line and all portholes were secured. We were allocated a seat at a bench beside a long table for meals and at night hung a hammock above it, sandwiched between two others, head to toe. I slept with a pair of feet either side of my head, and my feet between two heads. We were each supplied with a lifejacket consisting of two kapok pads tied with string under the arms which had to be taken everywhere and served as a cushion when sitting on deck.

There were six thousand troops on board, including two women among the officers, who had the first class accommodation and lounges. We sailed in a convoy of thirteen ships, escorted by four destroyers, in a great sweep out into the Atlantic, out of range of German aircraft based in France, and reached Freetown in West Africa after three weeks. There we sweltered for three days over Christmas and a lunch of roast pork and potatoes as the ventilation

Ruins of Torthorwold Castle, Nr. Dumfries
Lord Carlisle 16th Century

St. Peter's Church, Heysham, Lancs
Four Royds Rectors 1858 – 1956

Capt. Charles Stott Gamon
Cheshire Regiment 1917

Mary Carlisle née Royds
1861 – 1945

Jack Stott Gamon
Age 19, 1920

Mary Carlisle née Gamon
Lt Com Rev. Jack Stott Gamon 1950

St Oswald's Church, Brereton
Four Royds Rectors 1819 - 1919

St Edmund's Church, Falinge, Rochdale
Built by Albert Hudson Royds 1870

Caynham Court Nr. Ludlow

High Lawn, Bowden, Cheshire
Built by John Carlisle – his home 1848 - 1880

would not work whilst the ship was stationary. Natives came alongside and with much filthy language offered trinkets and dived for coins

From Freetown we sailed faster unescorted under the brilliant Southern Cross to Durban. We cadets learnt Urdu. Housey-housey, now known as bingo, was our only amusement apart from singsongs on deck in the evenings. The weather was good and I enjoyed the voyage. The flying fish and the phosphorescence on the bow wave were always a fascination. We came within sight of a merchant ship which struck a mine off Cape Town and, I believe, sank; otherwise we were undisturbed

Meanwhile in the Mediterranean, on 25th November, a U-boat sank the battleships *Queen Elizabeth* and *Valiant* in Alexandria harbour, decimating our fleet there.

At Durban we were put ashore to spend three weeks in tents on Claremont racecourse while the ship went on to Singapore to deliver troops, just in time to be taken prisoner by the Japanese. As a result of disgraceful incompetence, some 130,000 men surrendered to a much smaller force of Japanese, who had come overland down the Malay peninsular as we withdrew before them on 15 February 1942, the greatest military disaster in out national history.

The Japanese had captured 25,000 British and Indian troops in Malaya. Most of the latter would be pressed into the Indian National Army but readily surrendered when put into action in Burma in 1945. The first Japanese atrocity in Singapore was the butchering of the patients and nurses found in the hospitals.

To add to our problems, without air support, the battleships *Prince of Wales* and *Repulse* had been sunk off Malaya with the loss of 800 men.

Japan had entered the war with the famous and devastating attack on the American fleet at Pearl Harbour in Hawaii on 9th December 1941, when 21 warships including eight battleships were sunk or heavily damaged and 164 planes were destroyed on the ground with the loss of 2,400 men. Fortunately two American aircraft carriers escaped as they were at sea and six months later were able to establish superiority over the Japanese by sinking three of their aircraft carriers at the battle of Midway.

However, the Japanese had also taken Hong Kong and overrun the American occupied Philippine Islands, committing appalling barbarities in both. At the same time Germany had foolishly declared war on America, which brought them into the European war.

Whilst in Durban, I had spent three nights with two friends on a ranch near Pretoria belonging to Ewan Campbell, whose brother Athol had been head boy of Radley in my first year and had been killed as a pilot in the South African air force in Libya. Ewan had a sugar plantation at Umhlanga Rocks just north of Durban, and showed me great hospitality. He took us swimming off an open beach in front of sand dunes to the south at Amanzimtoti, now a tourist centre encrusted with hotels.

Ewan's estate is now the property of a millionaire who owns game reserves in Zimbabwe and is a lot too friendly with the appalling President Mugabe. It is also unfortunate that his daughter is a girl friend of Prince Harry.

In February, we sailed in comfort in the *Isle de France*, the pride of the French liners, to Suez, where near panic reigned. In the previous November the British army, under the command of the great General Auchinleck, who had taken over from Wavell on the latter's appointment as Viceroy of India, had driven Rommel's army back to Benghazi and relieved Tobruk after a siege lasting 33 weeks. But our army, in their turn, had been driven back to the Egyptian frontier. Once again, a single garrison was left in Tobruk. On this occasion, however, it was soon overcome by Rommel who took 35,000 men prisoner, possibly because the commander was of a South African Division and most Boers were still pro-German. However, the 'Auk' was to hold the line at El Alamein.

After three days ashore in Suez, plagued by Egyptians selling 'feelthy' pictures, we boarded the *Ascanius*, a 10,000-ton refrigeration ship, where we slept in the hold over the screw without ventilation and there was not even room to sit on your lifejacket on the one deck. We had a very hot trip down the Red Sea to Aden, where the *Ascanius* took on coal, carried by navvies, and then continued to Bombay. There we entrained for a two day journey to Bangalore, then a small town bazaar and separate cantonment, as army lines were called. Today it is a city of several million people, devoted to computers, software and call centres for many British businesses.

At the OCTU (Officer Cadet Training Unit) on Agram Plain we lived in spacious tents, two to each with beds, desks and so on, and had meals in fine old colonial buildings. A bearer served four of us in our tents and at the mess. As practically always in India, we were called at 6.00AM with *chota hazri* of tea and banana. The first day we were dropped in the bush fifteen miles away and told to get home by compass.

My friend Mike Brew had come over from Venezuela to join the army. His father was in oil, so, against this background, Mike was a slightly romantic figure. He and I mildly distinguished ourselves by getting back first from the bush and then captaining tug-of-war teams.

After a few days I went down with jaundice, no doubt a legacy of conditions on the *Ascanius*, and spent ten days in hospital, where I fell for the QA nurse.

Bangalore is situated some 5,000 feet above sea level and never excessively hot, even in summer, and we spent most of the time on field training operations in the surrounding countryside, wearing shorts, khaki bush jackets and t*opees* (pith helmets). We also had individual lessons each day from a *Munshi* in Urdu, the language of the British Indian army and officialdom. All cantonments, including the present one, were extensively laid out so officers were provided with cycles to get about. On Sunday mornings a friend and I would ride to the 6.00AM meet of the Bangalore hounds, which hunted jackals.

I thought the training course unimaginative and felt it could have been done in half the time. Nevertheless at the end in September, officers from various regiments came to ask us to join them. Being 6'5", I considered I would look ridiculous as a Gurkha officer, and for the same reason would not fit easily into a tank, although my father had mentioned that Fane's Horse (the 19th Lancers), had been raised by a distant relation at the time of the Indian Mutiny.

I chose the Rajputana Rifles, which was at that time the most decorated regiment in the British or Indian armies, having two battalions in the 8th Army in North Africa.

Mike Brew got deflected to the Ajmer Regiment. With ten days joining leave, he and I went by local bus through the independent princely and spectacular state of Mysor and its jungle, to Ootacamund (Ooty), a hill station high in the Nilgiri mountains above Madras. We stayed there for a week before journeying by rail to Raj Rif Regimental HQ in Delhi.

In January 1942, the first American troops had landed in Britain bringing nylon stockings with which they seduced British girls! And in May, as the Russian countryside dried up after the winter, the Germans launched another massive offensive there.

Huge tank battles raged throughout the summer with a vast number of casualties until the Germans were stopped at Stalingrad on the River Volga in November when heading for the Russian oil fields. The battle raged for two months until, against Hitler's orders, the Germans surrendered. They had lost 300,000 men, killed or taken prisoner, many to die later in Russia's POW camps.

In June that year two brave Czechs, rashly dropped by parachute, assassinated the brutal German Gauleiter Heydrich. In revenge the Germans destroyed the village of Lidice, killing all the men in what was their worst atrocity in the West, until they did the same at Oradour in France in July 1944.

In Burma, British forces, ably commanded by General Alexander fought delaying actions against the advancing Japanese for 800 miles to India, losing 13,500 British, Indian and Burmese men, but still getting 4/5^{ths} out, though after great suffering.

In July, British convoy, PQ 17 carrying supplies to Russia in 33 ships was attacked and ordered to disperse. This disastrous move resulted in the loss of all but four ships, taking 2,400 planes and 400 tanks to the bottom. In all, 104 merchant ships and 20 warships were lost on these convoys. My cousin, Brian Carlisle sailed on many and was awarded a DSC.

In May, fearing that the Japanese might take Madagascar which was still under Vichy French control, British troops invaded and met quite strong opposition. My cousin Bruce, a squadron leader in the 9th Lancers was seriously wounded in the operation.

In May 1941, Iran had been invaded by the Indian Army, from the Persian Gulf, and the Russians from the north, with the objective of securing the oil wells and enabling arms and supplies to be sent overland to aid Russia. There was little resistance. Paiforce was to remain in occupation of Iran and Iraq for the rest of the war.

A year later, Rommel launched another offensive in Libya only to be halted again by Auchinleck at the Egyptian frontier. For no clear reason, the Auk was then appointed GOC, India and replaced as OC Middle East by the aristocratic Guards officer, General Alexander, while the cautious but efficient ascetic, General Bernard Montgomery was appointed commander of the 8th Army after Churchill's first choice, General Gott had been killed when his plane was shot down.

In August 1942, the disastrous Dieppe raid took place. It failed miserably and 2,500 soldiers, mostly Canadians, were taken prisoner by the Germans.

In North Africa, Montgomery was sent vast reinforcements of American Sherman tanks and British infantry which gave him a 2-1 superiority over the Germans, when he launched the battle of Alamein in October and drove them from Libya into Tunisia. Until then, it had been disaster all the way, but now the tide of war turned and only victories ensued.

After a few days at the Regimental Depot in October 1942, I was posted to the territorial Battalion at Loralei in Baluchistan, then a comparatively peaceful area of the North West Frontier. At the railhead in a town called Sibi in the Sind desert, I had to spend three nights at the 'Dak' bungalow to take the weekly local bus to Loralei. I was attached to the only Indian company commander, Major Hukm Singh, a substantial landowner from the Punjab, who had been through Sandhurst before the war.

Ever since the Mutiny all Indian regiments had had companies of different Hindu castes, Sikhs and Moslems. We had Rajputs, Jats and Ahirs, Hindus and Punjabi Mussalmans. There was a priest to look after the spiritual needs of the Hindus and a mullah for the Moslems. All were given two meals a day from separate cookhouses, but on active service abroad, Hindus would eat canned beef and Moslems pork Spam, while the Ramadan fast was disregarded

King George VI was emperor of India and the Oath of Allegiance taken by the troops was directly to him. The men were recruited from the so-called 'martial' races of northern India, except for the Madras Sappers and Miners from the south. There was great competition to join as, after 21 years the soldiers retired to be respected residents of their villages. For this reason there was no crime and they were always keen.

Since the Mutiny in 1857 half of India had been autocratically governed by a Viceroy, beneficently administered by a few thousand British of the Indian Civil Service and Police, and the Moslem and Hindu population were restrained from strife by the army. In fact, the country had the most efficient and least corrupt government of any country outside Europe. The other half was composed of independent states, each ruled by a Maharaja with his own forces but guided by a British resident.

For many years members of the Congress Party, led by the ascetic and charismatic Ghandi, portrayed as a religious fanatic in his loincloth and dhoti, and his Oxford educated son-in-law Jawahal Nehru, had agitated for self rule. After causing riots when Japan invaded Burma, a British colony, in early 1942 and drove our forces back to India, both Ghandi and Jawahal Nehru were put in prison for the duration of the war.

Fortunately the Sepoys, Jawans (young men), as they were now called, had no time for any Indian politicians and would happily put down any civil disturbance, as they were required to do occasionally later in the war.

The Indian army, which also garrisoned Hong Kong, Burma and Malaya, all colonies of the British Empire, was composed of twenty infantry or rifle regiments, ten cavalry regiments (then in the process of becoming mechanised with tanks or armoured cars) and ten Gurkha regiments. Many had more than one battalion, which, with depots and supporting arms, came to well over 100,000 men, which was more than the British army. In wartime it expanded to over two million, every man a volunteer, of whom 87,000 died in our service.

An Indian army Brigade was composed of two Indian battalions and one British, in which every regiment had Hindu and Mussalman companies recruited from different districts, all of farming stock and many related. An Indian infantry battalion had only twelve British officers whereas a British battalion had thirty two. In fact my battalion had only ten and often only seven or eight, with some away on courses or leave. Our platoons were commanded by Viceroy's Commissioned Officers (VCOs) of long service. They really ran the show like the senior NCOs in the British army.

The CO and 2 IC were regular soldiers, the company commanders and adjutant had been war service officers in British Regiments and had volunteered to transfer on the great expansion of the Indian Army in 1941. The Quartermaster had been a schoolmaster in Poona.

There were three other subalterns and me. The pay was better than the British army and there was more chance of promotion. Due to my height, 6'5½", I was inevitably called 'Lofty'. *Very* large men got called 'Tiny'.

Loralei was high in the mountains north of Quetta, the headquarters of the army in Baluchistan and seat of its staff college, which had been almost totally destroyed in an earthquake in about 1930. How it got its romantic-sounding name I never discovered but it had been long established, though just a tiny cantonment spaciously laid out for one battalion and built in brick.

In winter there was a little snow in these hills and the few Pathans living in the area were then peaceable and policed by the Zhob Militia of the North West Frontier Scouts. The Colonel even had his wife living with him in a substantial bungalow.

After about three months, I was sent off for a small arms course, which involved a hair-raising local bus journey down the mountain road to the railhead at Sibi before going on by train to Saugor in the middle of the Deccan Central Provinces of southern India. The course was being run in what had been the old cavalry school which had fine buildings, with bungalows and mess emblazoned with the stuffed heads of boars from pig-sticking days.

I'm sure I already knew all about small arms but the army were not imaginative and no doubt the Battalion had been allotted a place, so it had to be filled. One of the few things I remember was the cinema showing the voluptuous Betty Grable, later overshadowed by the even more glamorous Marilyn Monroe, but this was the last film I was to see for four years.

Meanwhile, in the wider world, on 7th November 1942, the Americans had landed 140,000 men in Morocco and Algeria against opposition from French troops, an operation which resulted in some 3,000 casualties on each side. The French troops involved were still loyal to Vichy and governed by Admiral Darlan.

Incredibly, America had recognised the Vichy Government of France since 1940, even keeping an ambassador there, and had refused to have anything to do with General de Gaulle or allow his Free French troops to participate. A substantial British force, the 1st Army, also landed. After a few days, Darlan was murdered by a Frenchman and they surrendered.

The Germans in full occupation of Vichy France had replaced the geriatric Petain with the traitorous Laval and the French naval fleet in Toulon scuttled itself in the harbour rather than sail to join the Allies.

The green American troops commanded by the inexperienced General Mark Clark proved most incompetent. When they met the German army on the Tunisian border they were only saved from disaster by the intervention of the British Guards' armoured division.

The 8th Army under Montgomery made slow progress from Libya and Free French forces came north from Chad. Eventually after much heavy fighting, the Germans, squeezed from both sides, surrendered at Tunis in May 1943, leaving 150,000 prisoners – German and Italian – in Allied hands.

During all the north African campaign, which lasted more than three years, there had been no atrocities. Prisoners had been well treated and among the British there was even a considerable amount of admiration for their enemies, particularly for General Rommel. They even adopted the German song, *Lily Marlene*, although Vera Lynn was without question the foremost heartthrob of the British throughout the war.

Our losses at sea had been immense, reaching a peak in 1942 of seven million tons, a figure that could have been far lower if Ireland, led by the traitorous De Valera, had permitted us to set up naval bases there.

In September 1942, a German U-boat sank the liner *Laconia* off Ascension Island carrying 1,500 Italian PoWs and 1,000 crew and guards. The U-boat commander sent out a message in English that he would not attack any vessel coming to their rescue, and took many survivors on board his own vessel. However, an American plane arrived and bombed the submarine, and a large number of men perished as a result.

At about the same time, an American submarine sank a Japanese ship carrying 1,800 British and Canadian PoWs from Hong Kong, of whom 840 drowned.

A total of 55,000 merchant seamen lost their lives during the war and did not receive even a campaign medal for it. But now, at last, the tide was turning and German U boats became the hunted. By the end of the war 500 German submarines had been sunk. Also the American marines, by far their best troops, were progressively recapturing islands in the Pacific, albeit with heavy losses due to suicidal Japanese resistance.

My journey from Saugur back to the Frontier took two days by rail. I always travelled first class in a two-berth compartment, sleeping on my valise, which went everywhere with one. Well-to-do Indians mostly travelled in similar second class accommodation. I never remember sharing a compartment with one.

In those days, there was little contact under the British Raj with educated Indians or even Anglo-Indians, who were excluded from British clubs. The rest of the population travelled third class, jammed on hard seats and often even standing on the outside running boards. For meals the trains stopped at stations where first and second class passengers would eat at the station restaurant, which almost always served chicken followed by caramel custard. Station masters, who were always Anglo-Indian, as they managed the railways and provided the drivers, would often ask permission of the first class travellers to restart the train.

To pass the time on the long, hot journey, I read *Fanny Hill* and *Lady Chatterley's Lover* to improve my education. Lady Chatterley was banned in Britain for another ten years but I found it much more useful than the ridiculous sex education classes taught in British state schools today.

On arriving at Mari Indus, near Peshawar, I prepared myself for the next stage of the journey to Bannu. It lasted for eight hours, with some passengers sitting on the roof of a really ancient train, the 'Heatstroke Express', which never exceeded 20 mph. Bannu was a cantonment on the edge of the plains and Brigade HQ for North Waziristan, the home of the Mahsuds, the most warlike tribe on the Frontier. There a traveller might have waited several days in the comfortable 'dak' bungalow for the weekly convoy of lorries escorted by armoured cars to Razmak, 60 miles away on the Afghan border.

While I was away on the course, the battalion had moved to Gardai, a tented camp for two battalions surrounded by a dry stone wall and barbed wire, and manned by sentries at night. It was fifteen miles below Razmak, which had permanent barracks. Here officers were provided with a large tent with furniture and the mess was in a marquee. The meals were simple but good, though as the Hindu cook would not handle beef and Moslem waiters would not handle pork, more often than not it consisted of mutton curry and *chipatis* made from unleavened flour. We suffered none of the food-rationing being endured by everyone in Britain. We signed *chittis* for drinks, usually gin *piaz* with cocktail onions, served by the *abdar*, who was always a Moslem as they do not drink spirits, but there was no standing of drinks. Occasionally we officers were invited to the VCOs' mess, where their aim was to get us drunk on *burra pegs* of Murree whisky.

At Gardai we got a new second in command. He had served in the King's African Rifles and regaled us with tales of flogging troops with rhinoceros whips when on the march. No Indian sepoys were ever beaten or even sworn at by us.
He drank a bottle of gin a night but he was always out on parade at 7.00AM and was outstandingly efficient.

When the elderly Hukm Singh retired, I was promoted 1st Lieutenant in command of the Ahir company and was allotted an Ahir orderly as batman and personal bodyguard. Sections of ten Jawans, commanded by a *naik* (corporal) had to spend a week in *sangars* made of rough stone walls and surrounded by barbed wire on top of several little hills around the camp to prevent the Pathans firing shots into it, which they occasionally did at night. The Jawans stayed awake all night, scared stiff.

All Pathans carried rifles, often a locally made Jezail, to protect themselves, as most, if not every one of them, were engaged in blood feuds that had persisted over many generations. Their chief desire was to get a modern rifle and they were accomplished thieves, and for this reason, every man slept with his rifle in his bed, his leg through the sling, and officers with their revolvers, although Pathans were said to be able to steal arms from a sleeping man.

Apart from some training just outside the camp carrying live ammunition, our only job was to open the road one day each week by putting a platoon on top of each hill along it for some seven miles either side, thereby protecting the convoy of supply lorries, with old armoured cars fore and aft, from being ambushed as they passed along it.

My company had to climb a hill of 1,000 feet at the far end. We waited there until the afternoon when the convoy returned and passed by empty. Then, on receiving a signal to retire, we ran like hell to avoid being ambushed in the scrub bushes until we reached the cover of the rearguard on the road. If anyone were hurt, they could not be left behind as they would be mutilated and killed by local women!

Radios were not yet in service and messages were sent in Morse code by heliograph, reflecting the rays of the sun over long distance, or by field telephone over shorter ones.

The North West Frontier Province was loosely administered by British Political Agents of the Civil Service, who paid allowances to tribal chiefs to ensure their good behaviour. They had some irregular Pathan police called Khassedars, who lived in occasional towers along the road, armed with rifles and vicious daggers stuck behind their collars. However, in the event of any serious misbehaviour, the Agent would send the Scouts, a company of Pathans commanded by a British officer, to arrest the miscreants, or, in more serious cases still, an old biplane to bomb their village or destroy their crops. As all Pathans lived in fortified towers entered only by ladder, they must have been rarely destroyed.

All pilots carried ransom notes in case of forced landing as they could, it was said, be castrated, or worse, by the Pathan women. A Mullah, the Fakir of Ipi from inside the Afghan border was paid by German agents to foment a frontier war but in fact it never happened. No doubt the memory of their villages being destroyed in the last war in the thirties was still fresh in their minds.

In our time, we had only one serious skirmish when one or two men were wounded. On the Frontier we wore pale blue woollen shirts, Sam Browne belts, khaki shorts and Chaplies, which were heavy sandals, as worn by the Pathans. In the evenings we wore service dress and service caps instead of the ridiculous *topees* of the OCTU.

I was granted 10 days leave, and went to meet my friend of the troopship and Bangalor, Mike Brew. We travelled by uncomfortable local bus – a brightly painted Chevrolet – from Rawalpindi to Srinagar in Kashmir.

The country was beautiful, the climate superb and we stayed in a charming houseboat on the delightful Nagin Bagh lake, where, for the first time, I tried water skiing behind a speedboat. I bought some Bokhara rugs which, incredibly, arrived home by post and have graced our drawing room for 50 years.

During 1943, the Russians slowly drove back the Germans after defeating them in an immense tank battle at Kursk, south of Moscow. Somehow the Russians had managed to produce a large number of very good tanks in factories situated behind the Urals, and recruit a great numbers of new soldiers from Siberia, Kazakhstan and Uzbekistan. In April 1943, the Germans announced that they had found mass graves at Katyn, near Smolensk containing bodies of 4,000 Polish officers. The Russians immediately declared that they were more victims of German brutality. It was not until long after the war that the British Government would admit that this crime and the killing of intellectuals had been perpetrated by the Russians when they occupied half of Poland in 1939. It was not until 1990 that a memorial was allowed to be erected to their memory in London.

In January 1942, Himmler, the head of the Gestapo police, had announced the Final Solution, the intention to rid Europe of 11 million Jews, but it was not until 1944 that our Government admitted knowledge of extermination camps, and never ordered their bombing to allow escape.

While shipping losses had continued at an appalling rate throughout 1943, German U-boat losses thereafter became unsustainable and the Battle of the Atlantic was won at last. It seems incredible now, but while thousands of brave sailors died at sea, dockers went on strike for higher wages. I don't know why the leaders weren't shot as traitors.

In July 1943, the American 5th and British 8th Armies landed in Sicily, but the operation was not without tragedy. Firstly, gliders carrying troops and towed by American planes came under fire from a warship and dropped sixty-nine of them into the sea, drowning 200 men, and, secondly, the battleship *Royal Sovereign* shelled and killed many of our troops after they had landed.

In war there are perhaps as many killed by accident, or 'friendly' fire as are killed by the enemy. Survival is largely a matter of luck, depending on where your orders take you at what time. There were always as many men in support services as in the front line, but now it gets ever more impersonal and so, immoral. The only just war is in defence of one's country.

Added to the other disasters on the Sicily landings, British paratroops were dropped 50 miles away from their objective, a railway bridge, and so failed to secure it.

Mussolini had been overthrown in June 1943 and King Victor Emanuel appointed Marshall Pietro Badoglio Prime Minister, in which capacity Badoglio signed and announced an agreement on September 8, 1943 by which Italy surrendered unconditionally to the Allies. Italian troops duly stood down but the Germans in Sicily fought on and most escaped to the mainland after three weeks. The Italian navy sailed to Malta and Gibraltar leaving the Allies in control of the Mediterranean.

More German troops from the north rapidly overran mainland Italy and with their ruthless efficiency seized control. Amid the overall confusion, some British prisoners escaped but most, swayed by the prospects of a quiet life and survival, stayed put.

If only the Allies had invaded mainland Italy immediately after their victory in Tunisia and offered generous surrender terms, the whole Italian army would have come over to our side and we would have secured the whole country, saving us the bloody Cassino and Anzio battles, and the Italians the misery of a year of German occupation. But haggling for four months over the surrender terms and the usual Allied caution lost the opportunity.

In a further development, German paratroopers, commanded by the notorious Colonel Skorzeny, in spectacular fashion rescued Mussolini from a mountain top castle where he had been imprisoned. After his release he set up the Italian Socialist Republic in German-held northern Italy, with himself as leader.

In August the RAF dropped 10,000 tons of bombs on Hamburg, more than were dropped on London during the whole of the Blitz of 1940/41. Seven square miles of the city were reduced to rubble and 40,000 people died. The brave Dam Busters destroyed the Eder and Mohne Dams in the Ruhr but lost many planes.

On 3rd September the British 8th Army landed unopposed in Calabria on the toe of Italy, followed six days later by the 5th Anglo-American Army at Salerno. This beachhead turned out to be very strongly defended by the Germans, who very nearly succeeded in throwing the Allied forces off again. But in late October, the Germans retreated to Cassino, where they were to hold out for seven months during a very severe winter.

In November 1943, our battalion moved to Wana in South Waziristan, where two battalions lived in permanent barracks. Though the Wazirs were less warlike, we could not train outside the camp without a full company armed and though we did not have to open the road, a supply convoy still came up each week 40 miles from Mir Ali, escorted by armoured cars.

The country was rugged but, at 5,000 feet, very healthy. Today Osama bin Laden is said to be hiding out near there but the Pakistani army have been unable to locate him and have suffered many casualties in the search. I passed the time there playing squash with our very good, one-armed Brigadier Campbell. Another diversion was provided when I had toothache. There was no dentist for 200 miles so I went to the Indian doctor who offered gas to pull it out, but his cylinder was empty and I yelled like hell. There was also a pack of hounds which met on Sunday mornings and hunted jackals. The Pathans did not normally molest the hunt but I remember a few shots one morning from one who evidently didn't know the rules. The master was an eccentric character, Rudge Humphries, whose home was Usk Castle in Monmouthshire and who commanded the transport company of mules and ponies. He had a heavy moustache and, aged about 40, to us seemed old. He stayed at Wana until the end of the war and in 1945 planted a great forest of trees. There are now said to be 100,000 people living there. We were much out of touch with the wide world as newspapers arrived over a week late and we never had a wireless. There were no books so drinking and the occasional drunken mess party provided the only amusement.

I also once rode in a point-to-point race across open country but, when leading, my horse fell jumping a *nullah* and tragically broke a leg. I now think steeple-chasing should be banned. Too many horses finish up broken down.

We went on a practice column to 'show the flag', as would happen if we needed to destroy a rebellious village. Several days were spent sleeping under groundsheets, though we took a mess tent, picketing the hills as we went along.

Our supplies and equipment were carried on camels, mules and ponies, accompanied by a mountain battery with their dismantled guns carried on fine, 14-hand mules, whose drivers led on narrow tracks or hung onto their tails when going up or down hill.

In our Battalion we had 30 mules, willing, sure-footed beasts who carried the Vickers machine guns, and three horses. As transport officer I had the privilege of riding, which I did, and enjoyed. In fact, the only other officer who rode was Bill Wilson, a fine company commander and horseman, so we could always get horses delivered by their *syces* each evening.

In January 1944, I took the motor transport of eleven lorries and two fifteen cwt trucks down to Dera Ismail Khan on the plains, where drivers could be instructed for a month, and in May went on ten days leave to Kashmir with my friend, Ben Brocklehurst of the Frontier Force Rifles, the other battalion in Wana. The intention was to shoot bears and we trekked into the mountains above the snow line near Nanga Parbat.

It was perhaps as well that we never found one, although the *shikari* several times showed us their droppings; we had only been supplied with 12-bore guns and solid ball shot, in which I did not have much confidence. Ben, who had transferred from the British army, later managed to get himself moved to the Frontier Force Regiment in Burma and finished up as Lt Col, commanding an island off the coast.

He was a very good cricketer and, after the war, captained Somerset, married and bought a farm in Berkshire. After the tragic death of his wife, he became bored with farming, joined a publisher in the city and edited the "Cricketer" magazine, which later he bought.

He then took a team to play in Corfu where cricket had been played ever since it was occupied by Britain for a short period during the Napoleonic wars and, having married the charming and efficient Belinda Barneby, started an upmarket travel company called Cricketer Holidays. They let villas in Corfu and a yacht in Turkish waters and eventually expanded their activities worldwide. The company is now managed by his sons. Ben is also a very accomplished artist.

The battalion spent the summer of 1944 in Landi Kotal, on the Khyber Pass, the route of the Mongol invasion into India and of many disastrous British punitive expeditions into Afghanistan during the nineteenth century. Since then the Durand Line had been established as the border and the British occupied the mountainous tribal area all along the Frontier, with army camps and five companies of Scouts of the Frontier Corps, in all about 40,000 men. Their purpose was to prevent the Pathans raiding into India to rob, but it also provided an excellent training ground for the army which lasted fifty years, a period during which there were three or four real frontier wars.

There had been a railway and a good road built by army engineers up through the pass and by then the area was peaceful. Afghan camel trains would pass through, their women heavily veiled and every man carrying a rifle, but they would never exchange any word or greeting.

My only memory is of a *Khud* race over the hills around the cantonment that I was foolish enough to take part in. It was won by a Gurkha from the other battalion. They are good on hills. Since the British defeated Nepal in 1840, Nepalese Gurkhas had been recruited into the Indian Army. They were almost insanely brave and delighted in chopping off heads with their murderous *kukris*. When, years later, it was rumoured (falsely, as it happened) among the Argentinian forces that a detachment of Gurkhas would be joining the British forces already in the Falklands during the early '80s conflict, the South American soldiers were reportedly gibbering with fear, such was the reputation of these Nepalese fighting men.

From the Khyber Pass, I was sent on a motor transport course at Ahmadnagar, where a British warrant officer instructed us on the intricacies of the internal combustion engine. The only useful thing I can remember is his party trick, which was to stop an engine by shorting out all the sparkplugs with his fingers. I have never had the courage to try it!

On the way back with a friend whom I had met on the course, we stayed two nights at the Taj Mahal Hotel, then commandeered for British officers. On his suggestion (he was older and more worldly-wise than me) we visited a brothel on the notorious Grant Road. It proved to be a most tasteful establishment with music and a small dance floor where one could dance with good looking Anglo-Indian girls. After we'd been there a while, the madam, no doubt sensing that I was a bit shy, encouraged me to choose one who took me to her room for an hour of enjoyment. I must say, I've never understood why we can't have such establishments in this puritanical country, as they do in France and Germany where prostitution is legalised.

After the Japanese had captured Singapore in February 1942, they invaded Burma and our small forces were driven back into India. There followed a stalemate for twelve months as the Japanese built a railway from Thailand to supply their troops, using British and Australian prisoners as labour under appalling conditions. Some 15,000 died and a much greater number of local people who had been pressed into service as coolies.

The British meanwhile sent supplies over the very mountainous Burma road to China which, under General Chiang Kai Shek, was also fighting the Japanese. The Americans also flew Dakota planes over the 'hump' of high mountains to the Chinese.

In 1943, the 14th Army, commanded by General Slim, probably our best GOC, launched offensive operations into Burma, in the Arakan near the coast. Progress was slow. The Japanese rated death higher than dishonour and would never surrender. They also used prisoners for bayonet practice and, if captured themselves, committed *harakiri* with a knife in the stomach.

In March 1943, a force of 3,000 men, commanded by the charismatic General Orde Wingate was carried in gliders over the Chin hills and dropped 200 miles behind the Japanese front line. Known as Chindits, they attacked communications and had some considerable success, being supplied by air for three months before marching back to India, leaving behind 800 dead or wounded. Soon after Wingate died in a plane crash.

In January 1944, when the American 5th Army was bogged down before Cassino on the Garigliano river, a large force of 70,000 men with 18,000 vehicles landed at Anzio, 30 miles south of Rome, with the intention of taking the Germans in the rear.

The landing, commanded by the American General Mark Clark, succeeded unopposed but instead of advancing inland quickly, Clark decided to hold up when the bridgehead was twenty miles wide but only six deep. The beaches there were persistently under fire as the efficient Germans brought down forces from the north and contained Clark's men in a small perimeter for four months and very nearly drove them back into the sea. Casualties were vast: 27,000 Germans, 22,000 Americans, 22,000 British and 7,000 French. It was also about this time that my younger sister's boyfriend, Roger Harrison, a captain in the Welsh Guards was killed in Italy.

It was not until May, after the great monastery on top of the hill overlooking Cassino had been destroyed by bombing (an unnecessary war crime as it was not in fact occupied by the enemy) that, following a winter of very heavy fighting, the monastery hills were captured by troops from the 8th Army, including two battalions of my regiment, Gurkhas, Poles, the Essex Regiment and the Free French.

Even then, with the Germans in full retreat, instead of cutting off their withdrawal, the prima-donna General Mark Clark took his troops into Rome on 4th June for his personal glory, thus allowing the Germans to escape north to their newly prepared fortifications on the Gothic line in northern Italy.

At the same time, in the Pacific, the Americans had established naval superiority and progressively recaptured the islands occupied by the Japanese who fought suicidally in defence.

In June on the island of Saipan, 21,000 Japanese soldiers and 8,000 civilians were killed, many jumping off the cliffs to their deaths to avoid capture. Only 800 prisoners were taken, and the operation cost the American marines 3,500 lives.

Meanwhile, the Russians had driven the Germans out of the Crimea and in the course of huge tank battles, pushed them back to the Polish border, with heavy casualties.

On 6th June, D-Day, the immense Allied invasion forces, commanded by the militarily inexperienced but diplomatic American General Eisenhower, landed on the beaches of Normandy, the Americans and British both on two and the Canadians on one.

Under Eisenhower, the Allied air force was commanded by British Air Marshal Tedder, and the Allied armies by General Bernard Montgomery, efficient but cautious, frequently finding himself at loggerheads with Eisenhower and General George Patton, who believed he was a reincarnation of Julius Caesar. He died in a suspicious Jeep accident in Mannheim, just after the end of the war.

Despite the extensive defences of the Atlantic wall which the Germans had constructed along the whole of the French coast, the Allies gained the shore with surprisingly few casualties, except on the American Omaha beach, where some 2,000 men died, largely because their thirty swimming tanks had been unloaded several miles out at sea and all but three sank in the rough water.

The Americans had also suffered a disaster in a practice landing at night on Slapton Sands, Dorset. This occurred 10 days before D-day, when German E-boats found them and sank three landing craft, drowning 700 men.

Fortunately, the German armoured divisions were all back in France as Hitler had vetoed Rommel's wish to place them along the coast, and were prevented from arriving by the complete air superiority of the Allied bombers and by sabotage effected by French resistance fighters.

The German commander, General Rommel was actually at home in Germany as he had considered the possibility of an invasion, but thought the weather too rough.

American and British parachute divisions landed too far inland, as a result of which many Americans were dropped into flooded areas and drowned. The glider-borne Oxford and Bucks Regiment secured Pegasus bridge, although this is always claimed by the Paras.

Inexplicably, the British failed to push ahead and secure the important junction of Caen ten miles inland, allowing German armour to get there first. Thus, it was not until three weeks later, after very heavy fighting and complete devastation by bombing, which left 2,000 French civilians dead, Caen was finally taken.

German forces, which held the Pas-de-Calais and represented by the 15th Army, remained in position, their High Command being persuaded by a clever British Intelligence coup and a large number of dummy tanks on display in Kent, to expect the Allies to launch an attack via the short sea crossing of the Strait of Dover. They were not prepared for a major landing in Normandy, then controlled by the German 7th Army, which on account of its topography, typified by the patchwork of small fields that comprise the Bocage country, was assessed as highly unsuitable for mechanised warfare, as indeed it proved to be.

The massive new German Tiger tanks proved almost invincible, with their guns easily penetrating the British and Canadian Sherman tanks which readily exploded, as they ran on petrol where the Tigers used diesel. The Germans called our tanks 'Tommy Cookers'.

When Montgomery launched a massive attack in the open country beyond Caen, 400 tanks were lost in two days before Allied fighter bombers established superiority.

Had I been GOC, I would have chosen the Pas-de-Calais route, and I am certain a German general would have done so, because the coast in that region, although more heavily defended, was dotted with launch sites for Hitler's new weapons of terror, the V1 flying bombs, nicknamed doodle-bugs, which were to terrify London.

Furthermore, the flat open countryside of Flanders was suitable for mobile armoured warfare and provided little cover for defence, which was exactly opposite to the situation in Normandy. In addition, being so much closer to Britain, the supply of equipment, and particularly fuel would have been considerably easier. It was also 200 miles nearer Germany.

But caution prevailed and prolonged the war to the benefit of the Russians. It would take five months to get to Calais, by which time the V1s and V2 rockets fired from Germany would take the lives of 7,000 Londoners, and wound 20,000 more.

Curiously the Channel Islands which had been occupied by the Germans in June 1941, fortunately commanded by an aristocratic German Wehrmacht General with over 10,000 troops, had been left aside, and would not be liberated until the end of the war, a year later, when they were near starvation.

It was the end of July before the Germans had been driven out of Normandy and not until August 25th that the Free French, led by de Gaulle, were able to enter Paris. They did so amid scenes of wild jubilation, the German commander having disobeyed Hitler's order to blow up the city.

Also in August, an attempt by German generals to assassinate Hitler with a view to suing the Allies for an armistice, failed. The brave Count Stauffenberg had left a bomb beside his chair, which injured but failed to kill Hitler. There were too many plotters and the Gestapo found and brutally hanged twelve generals. Rommel was implicated but allowed to commit suicide, as Stauffenberg had done.

Again, in August, an uprising of Polish partisans in Warsaw took place. They wanted to help the Russians, now nearby, liberate their city. But the communist Russians sat tight on the other side of the Vistula river and refused even to allow our planes, flying supplies and Free Poles to the aid of the partisans, to land and refuel behind their lines.

Long afterwards, I met an airman who told me that he had flown in one of 21 planes out of 24 shot down attempting to drop supplies into Warsaw. He was fortunate enough to have been picked up by the Polish partisans and to have survived. After three weeks of desperate fighting the Germans prevailed, having destroyed the city.

It was also in August that Romania and Bulgaria changed sides to join Russia.

On 23rd July, 3,000 French Maquis (resistance fighters supplied by us by air) had risen in the Massif Central but were overcome by 15,000 German troops who, in reprisal, burnt the village of Aradour, killing all the inhabitants.

The far-sighted Churchill now saw Russia becoming a greater menace than Germany. He had wanted Allied forces in Italy to go on to seize Yugoslavia, Austria and much of the Balkans to save them from Russian occupation, but the naive Roosevelt, always hostile to British imperialism in the Near East, believed he could trust his 'good friend' Stalin, and insisted on removing 100,000 American and French forces from Italy, who then became part of the 400,000 strong American 7th Army which landed unopposed – and unnecessarily – on the south coast of France on 15th August and rapidly moved north, as had been demanded by Stalin.

The reduced 150,000 British Empire and Polish forces left in Italy were unable to defeat the Germans on their formidable defences of the Gothic line until shortly before the end of the war, by which time the Russians had occupied all the Balkan countries except Greece which the British liberated in November 1944.

On September 4th, the British Airborne Division landed at Arnhem to secure the bridge over the Rhine. Overcautious as usual, they landed eight miles this side and although they reached the bridge, they couldn't secure it because two German tank formations refitting nearby, spotted by reconnaissance aircraft, had been disregarded. In fact they were two of their best SS divisions.

The Polish parachute brigade landing two days later were shot as they landed, and supplies dropped from aircraft mostly fell into German hands. The Guards Armoured brigade coming from the south, 40 miles away, had to keep to one road to cross two rivers at Grave and Nijmegen, and were supported by an American parachute division, which also landed on the wrong side of the bridges. They never got through and after eight days of fierce fighting only 2,400 of the 10,000 troops who had landed at Arnhem made it back. 2,000 had been killed and near 6,000 taken prisoner. Sixteen planned airborne operations had previously been cancelled; this time they had to go disastrously wrong. A brave effort lost by inept planning.

In October the Americans, under the flamboyant General MacArthur landed in the Philippine Islands, inflicting a heavy defeat on the Japanese navy at the battle of Leyte Gulf, and the British 8th Army landed in Greece to great rejoicing. In the latter case, however, peace soon gave way to civil war when left wing and right wing supporters turned against each other in their respective efforts to take over the country.

Just before Christmas the Germans launched a massive attack with 24 divisions through the Ardennes, their route in 1940, pushing the Americans back 30 miles and capturing 10,000. Fog prevented Allied aircraft from flying and they very nearly broke through to the Channel ports. Three weeks later, and after the skies had cleared, the British 2nd Army closed behind them and they ran out of fuel. The crisis, known as The Battle of The Bulge, was over, but it had been a very close run thing, with 80,000 American & 100,000 German casualties. It was to be Germany's last throw.

On 28th April 1945, Mussolini and his mistress Clara Petacci, were arrested by Italian partisans by Lake Como while attempting to escape to Switzerland. Their fate was soon sealed. Both were shot and their bodies strung up for all to see. Soon afterwards the German army in Italy surrendered.

As the Allies advanced into Germany, the horrors of the concentration camps were discovered and, in Poland, the extermination camps which massacred six million Jews. Two hundred and twenty thousand Poles had also died in the Warsaw uprising and the city was virtually destroyed.

In autumn of 1944, we left the Khyber pass and went into tents in jungle country between Rawalpindi and Murree, a hill station above. We were to train in jungle warfare preparatory to going to Burma. As vehicles could not get there I had the motor transport a few miles away in empty featureless country, which is now the capital city of Pakistan, Islamabad.

At a riotous party in Faletti's hotel in 'Pindi I met British paratroop officers, who had come out to train an Indian battalion at nearby Chaklala airport. Indian Paras were not volunteers as the British were but whole battalions were detailed for the job.

I enquired about joining but was told I was too tall. Enthusiasm somewhat dulled later when I heard that the chutes were being packed by Indians and that some were 'Roman-candling' down. They later brought out British packers.

I would drive once a week to have dinner in the mess and drive back pretty sloshed, but fortunately always made it. I kept a horse there and my orderly brought me the boys' food. They always had only two meals a day.

To our disgust we were told in the spring of 1945 that we were not going to Burma – because, I think, we had a very weak CO – and were to be posted to Nowshera, near Peshawar on the Great North Road, a tree lined highway across open country with bullock carts the only traffic, as in Kipling's day. Now it is a continuous bazaar traversed in either direction by a stream of heavy lorries.

I was promoted captain and given the Administration company. Only the company clerk, derogatorily called Baboo spoke English. All orders and talk were in Urdu.

It was very hot in the summer, 120 Fahrenheit by day and 100 by night. Fortunately, our rooms were fitted with *pankas*, large ceiling fans. Nevertheless we played hockey in the evenings on dirt grounds. Indians are very good at hockey as they hook the ball and keep it mostly in the air. I rode regularly and played a few games of polo on my army charger with some civil service officers who lived there.

Before the war life had been good for an army officer in India, having about two hours work a day and otherwise able to devote his energies to the serious matters of polo, shooting, pig sticking and frequent evenings at the British only club.

The British and Indian 14th Army endured the longest sustained fighting of any allied force, under the most unpleasant conditions and during which no less than 29 soldiers, almost all Indians or Gurkhas were awarded the Victoria Cross.

One of our officers, Major John Ashworth, who'd won an MC when in the 1st Bn in Libya in 1940, surprised us all by marrying one of the Anglo-Indian nurses from the cantonment hospital known as Chee-Chees. She claimed to have been born in Liverpool Cantonment and was keen to return to the Home Country. She was also very good looking but she was never brought to the mess. After the war he transferred to the British Army, divorced and married again, having a son, Jonathan, who kindly gave me some of his father's photos.

My orderly offered to get me a 'bed warmer', but I thought better than to accept. Ever since seeing my orderly, Mohamed Arfan pray to Mecca three times daily, I have been unable to believe in the exclusivity of the Christian religion.

I had a month's leave with another officer, Major David Foskett, and we trekked 300 miles through the Himalayas from Mussorie to Naini Tal, with our orderlies, three ponies and a cook. It was beautiful country up to the snowline at 13,000 feet, near the spectacular Nanda Devi Mountain. We were the first up in Spring to the celebrated Hindu shrine of Badrinath near the Tibetan border but it turned out to be only a cave with a rather poor statue in it. We met no one *en route* but today Tehri Garhwal is a popular tourist trekking area.

In March 1944 there had been another and larger Chindit operation of 9,000 men behind the Japanese lines in Burma which, again supplied by air, achieved considerable success but at a high cost in lives.

In April the Japanese launched a major offensive against the frontier town of Imphal, but it was repulsed after two weeks desperate fighting by British and Indian army troops.

Thereafter the 14th Army, under the popular and efficient General Slim, slowly advanced over mountains and through the Burmese jungle, hampered by serious monsoon weather, where all roads in the valleys ran north and south. Their aim was to rout out suicidal Japanese, who would not surrender. Had we got there I would probably not have survived to enjoy a long life. The casualty rate among British company commanders in an Indian infantry regiment was quite high; if the Japanese snipers didn't get you, malaria or worse probably would.

In February, 1945 all South American countries, Argentina being the last, had declared war on Germany. Those of the Middle East, anxious to get in on the act, followed suit.

At last the Germans started to crack and the allies pressed on from both sides. The Russians entered Berlin on 30th April. Hitler named Grand Admiral Karl Doenitz to succeed him as Chief of State and shot himself in his bunker on 30th April.

For Doenitz, surrender was the only possible course of action and he duly accepted the inevitable. Early on May 7th, General Alfred Jodl, his representative, signed an unconditional surrender of all German armed forces at Eisenhower's headquarters in Reims, and May 8th was declared by Britain and

America VE (Victory in Europe) Day.

The Allies could have entered Berlin first as the Germans, terrified of Russian troops raping their women, would have made way for them. It did not happen because the gullible American president Roosevelt refused to deny his 'good friend', Josef Stalin the honour. Thus Berlin fell into Russian hands and part of it was to remain so for the next forty years. The country was divided into four occupation zones Russian, American, British and French, and Berlin likewise.

Had it not been for the demand for unconditional surrender agreed by Roosevelt and Churchill at the Casablanca conference in 1942, the Germans would have surrendered to us much earlier in 1945, and we could have occupied more of Europe. There was no doubt that communist Russia was now the new menace.

In 300 raids the R.A.F. had dropped 17,000 tons of bombs on Berlin but 800 planes and 3,000 airmen had been lost. Of Germany's sixty cities, forty-five had been practically destroyed. In February, 1945, at the request of the Russians and when the war was drawing to a close, the RAF and the Americans had wiped out the beautiful city of Dresden, killing 35,000 people. This disgrace had at last provoked public revulsion to terror bombing. In all 600,000 German civilians were killed during the war – ten times our losses – while the RAF lost 9,000 planes and 56,000 airmen. The British Avro Lancaster, the heaviest bomber of the war and introduced in 1942, flew only night-time raids, whereas the faster and more heavily armed American Flying Fortress flew only daylight raids. In 1944/5 they lost 5,000 planes and 47,000 airmen to the highly efficient German ground defences and fighter planes.

The Germans had produced an incredible 1164 submarines, of which 784 had been sunk and 75% of the crews. Of British submariners 38% had also died. Half the U-boats were sunk by Catalina flying boats of Coastal Command, which lost 11,000 airmen in the war. Only bomber crews lost more, at 50%. The latest U-boats were so efficient that we won only just in time. At the same time, the Germans were very close to producing atom bombs.

But the war with Japan went on as the British and Indian 14th Army fought across Burma to Rangoon, through jungle and monsoon, wiping out Japanese forces who preferred to die than to surrender.

In June, after two months' bloody fighting, the Americans finally conquered the island of Okinawa but, in the process, lost 12,000 men; 110,000 Japanese died. The US Marines who achieved this were by far the best of the American troops. Nevertheless, although the Japanese navy had been destroyed, their suicidal kamikaze airmen carried on crashing their planes into American ships, 1,100 of them dying in their attempts.

On 9th August, faced with the prospect of appalling losses if they invaded Japan itself, the Americans dropped the newly invented atomic bomb on Hiroshima, killing 70,000 civilians, and two days later, though the Emperor Hirohito had ordered his generals to surrender, they dropped another bomb on Nagasaki, killing an equal numb of people. Sqdn Leader Leonard Cheshire, who flew in the American bomber as an observer, founded a series of hospices for the terminally ill, which now operate worldwide.

The atomic bombing of Japan brought instant surrender and finished the war. I never understood why the Americans didn't drop the bombs on top of a mountain, which would have achieved the same result without the casualties caused by this war crime.

Subsequently, as Thailand, Malaya and Singapore were recovered, we discovered the appalling treatment inflicted on 40,000 PoWs by the Japanese. Of these, 25% died overall, including 12,000 British and Australians on the infamous Burma Railway. Many of the Japanese generals and camp commanders responsible for this cruelty were hanged once the Americans had occupied Japan under General MacArthur. The Americans were to remain there for several years.

After this occupation, Japan went on to embrace democracy and effected a stupendous revival, so that within a few years, she was the biggest shipbuilding nation in the world.

Germany by this stage was a seething mass of refugees, many of whom would come to Britain or go to America. The German leaders were put on trial at Nuremberg, convicted of war crimes and hanged, as were the commanders of concentration camps.

The war had cost the lives of 350,000 British servicemen - about half the number lost in the Great War – and approximately 150,000 drawn from the Empire and the Indian army. France had lost 600,000 men from their army, including resistance fighters and two divisions fighting with the Germans on the Russian front. 200,000 Frenchmen had been voluntary or forced labourers in Germany. The Soviet Union had lost 13m soldiers and 8m civilians; Germany, 3.5m soldiers and 1m civilians; Japan, 2m soldiers and 500,000 civilians; China, 3.5m soldiers and 10m civilians; Poland, 600,000 soldiers and 5m civilians, mostly Jews in the German extermination camps of the 'Final Solution' - the Holocaust.

Immediately after the end of the war the Russians and the Americans competed to employ German rocket scientists for development of their own missile armaments. The Americans also recruited German intelligence agents in their efforts to find Russian spies. It has only recently been disclosed that the British followed this practice and, in fact, disgracefully employed one named Kopkow, who was known to have been responsible for the deaths of 100 British SOE agents in France.

Another hundred brave agents dropped into Holland had been immediately picked up as German intelligence had broken our radio code. Through gross incompetence, a warning sent by the first agent, compelled to send a signal under duress, had been dismissed as a mistake and disregarded by our SOE directing staff.

The charismatic General de Gaulle, who had so often fallen out with the British and Americans when defending the honour of France and had proclaimed himself leader of France, resigned in November 1945, but was later to be recalled as President. I think he was the equal of Churchill.

In Autumn 1945, my battalion was posted to Malakand at the top of a pass 30 miles north of Peshawar. I was promoted major and given command of the Punjabi Mussalman company at - Chakdara, a small fort 1 mile into the mountains on the Swat border. There I spent an enjoyable few months, keeping a horse on which I would ride once a week to have lunch in the regimental mess.

Nearby was a little hill where the celebrated water carrier, Gunga Din, of Kipling's poem had done his act during the Mohmand campaign of 1897. It is now named Churchill picket as he was there as a war correspondent, where he claimed in his memoirs to have run an Afghan through with his sword.

The area was peaceful in my days. One evening a local brought me some stone figures from Takti Bahi, a ruined city of the ancient Gandwara Buddhist civilization. With the permission of the political agent who provided an escort of two Khassedars, I rode out to see it. There was not much left but I picked up one or two bits of carving. Years later, after I got married, I sold my Buddha at Spinks for the princely sum of £80, which bought us a washing machine, and shortly after saw the same piece advertised in Country Life for a much larger sum.

While lonely in Chakdara I read the books of Adrian Bell that romanticised life of British farming and confirmed my inclination to take it up after I was discharged from the army.

At about this time we got several Indian subalterns from the professional class. At the beginning they would all go on to achieve high rank (one as general) in the new national army. Only a handful of senior British officers were able to stay on for a few years.

My elder sister Sylvia, a Queen Alexandra nursing sister came out to India in 1944 to a hospital in Bengal. After the defeat of the Japanese she was posted to Java, where the Indian Army were engaged in putting down a serious insurrection. The partisans, who had been supplied by air with arms to harass the Japanese, were now fighting for self-government against the return of the Dutch colonial power.

My younger sister Rachel was a nurse at Great Ormond Street children's hospital from 1942-46.

Finally - incredibly, it seemed at the time - as a war service officer, I was offered a month's home leave and flew to Britain from Bombay in a Dakota transport plane, spending nights at Cairo and Malta *en route*. It was a pretty uncomfortable journey and no better on the way back, this time stopping a night at Haifa in Palestine, which, as the Jewish Stern Gang was causing trouble trying to drive the British out, was under martial law.

England was pretty grey, still under food rationing. My mother still worked part time as a Red Cross nurse in the local hospital.

In the spring of 1946 the Battalion moved to Ambala in the Punjab and my company had the job of defending the Government's radio masts at Simla, a charming little hill station 6,000 feet up in the hills, 60 miles to the north. It was normal practice in peacetime for the Government to move there at that time of the year to avoid the heat of Dehli.

Considerable civil unrest had begun to stir and there had been serious rioting in several cities to get the British out of India. The country had been promised self-rule the year before but the Congress party would not wait. As a precaution, we had long traveled everywhere with a .45 revolver on our belt.

In summer the Battalion moved to Allahabad and I took my company to keep the peace in Benares, now Varanasi, a teeming city of several millions where the dead were cremated on the river banks and their remains thrown into the sacred river Ganges.

There were several British police officers there but in the event of rioting, my company would be called upon to restore order. The drill was to read the riot act to the crowd and order them to disperse. If that had no effect we were to order a sepoy to shoot the ringleader and if this was ineffective a volley would be fired into the crowd.

Thank goodness it never happened but it caused me no worry at the time, aged 24, as I knew my Moslem Jawans would shoot rioting Hindus quite readily.

In October I said a moving goodbye to my company who had been a delight to command, always cheerful, keen, and uncomplaining, and took the train to Bombay. I had loved all my time in India, although I was disappointed not to have got into the serious action, yet lucky to have survived.

The 1st and 4th Battalions of the Rajputana Rifles in the

celebrated 4th Indian Division of the 8th Army had won 2 VCs, 10 DSOs, 36 MCs, 29 MMs, 71 IDSMs and 37 IOMs, as well as 230 Mentions in Despatches in North Africa and Italy. 23 officers had been killed, and 44 wounded. 24 Viceroy's Commissioned Officers had been killed and 30 wounded, 547 other ranks killed and 2,257 wounded. The 7th Battalion, overrun by the Japanese in Malaya, was reduced to 120 men.

This time, I sailed home in considerable comfort, two officers to a cabin and very well fed, in a troopship to Liverpool. I took a train to Bedford where at some depot I was given a demob suit and later received a gratuity of about £200 and a proforma letter from the King, thanking me for my services and granting me the honorary rank of Captain for life which was published in the London Gazette.

I was also entitled to two months' leave, which enabled me to go into an RAE hospital in Wilmslow to be operated on for a small hernia. I had disclosed this to a bored army doctor, whose medical examination was limited to asking me how I felt and signing me off as fit, which was even more cursory than the traditional short arm inspection of other ranks.

I considered transferring to the British Army but this would have meant reverting to the rank of lieutenant and I didn't think I could stand the boredom of peacetime soldiering.

I was to regret this later when I heard how enjoyable life in a cavalry regiment in Germany had been with plenty of riding, skiing and sailing, though not quite so good as for Household Cavalry officers before the war. They were free to go home during the hunting season, taking a horse and groom, without suffering any loss of pay.

I also thought of the Colonial Service but reckoned I had spent quite enough of my time on my own and didn't want to spend years as a district officer up-country in some colony.

When in hospital I was visited by Dennis Midwood, who inexplicably brought me a copy of *The Farming Ladder* by George Henderson. Starting out with nothing but a brother and a supportive mother, Henderson, by sheer hard work and employing pupils for labour, had built a large farming enterprise. This book was to inspire me to give myself fifteen years hard work!

At first, I had floated the idea of going out to Kenya, where there was a settlement scheme for ex-officers, but this one (unlike those that became available after the Great War with rights to extensive bush land) required a deposit of £5,000, a lot of money in those days, and a year at an agricultural college in Kenya.

The idea went down like a lead balloon with my parents, as Kenya was then a four week sea voyage away, and I had only £1,000, saved while stationed on the NW Frontier, where there'd been a complete absence of anything to buy. I thought it would be a mistake to be a poor white in Kenya and ten years later found that I was better off than settlers who had been dispossessed after Kenya achieved self-government, having already suffered three years of Mau Mau rebellion.

As usual, I fell in love with my nurse in the hospital and when discharged took her to a dance but was too shy to accept an invitation to her room afterwards. Life was different in those days. In church, vicars regularly warned against the sin of fornication and getting a girl pregnant compelled marriage. You could even be sued for breach of promise for breaking an engagement. Welsh farmers, on the other hand, had the sensible tradition of 'bundling' – getting married only when the girl had a bun in the oven.

In June 1945, just after the end of the war in Europe, an election had been called and our great wartime leader Winston Churchill was replaced by the colourless but efficient Clement Atlee, a major in the Great War and now leader of the Labour party, which took over Government.

This, I am sure, was achieved because the army educational corps, influenced by left wing philosophy, pressed Socialism on the troops and they and their families thought that a Labour Government would ensure the boys came home sooner.

One of its first acts was to increase the pay of MPs from £600 to £1,000 per year. Before the war, all Conservative and Liberal MPs were virtually independent. Having either inherited wealth or acquired it through business or the legal profession, they held only a loose allegiance to their party. Labour MPs on the other hand were mostly trade union representatives and financed by their union.

It is very different nowadays, when most are professional politicians or lawyers, dependent on the job for a large income and pension, and so constitute lobby fodder for whatever party they may represent. Today, few upper class people will become Members of Parliament; then there was more honest Government. The Labour Government nationalised the coal and steel industries and the railways and formed the National Health Service.

In March 1946, at Fulton, Missouri, in the presence of President Truman, Winston Churchill delivered a famous speech in which he enunciated that an 'Iron Curtain was descending across Europe' as the Soviet Union prevented her people from leaving, or anyone from the West entering countries under their control. This was the start of what became known as the 'Cold War'.

In 1946, the Labour Government had promised self-rule for India and in 1947, appointed the charismatic Lord Louis Mountbatten, who had been Commanding Officer for South East Asia, as Viceroy of India, with instructions to hand the country over to self-government.

Mr Jinnah, the bigoted leader of the Moslems, demanded partition of the sub-continent and the separation of Pakistan, which then included Bengal, or Bangladesh as it was subsequently named. Astonishingly, Lady Mountbatten, was said to be enamoured of the Congress Party leader Pandit Nehru.

In May, an impetuous Mountbatten declared partition of India, and in August the British Raj was terminated. Communal violence on a huge scale broke out as refugees started to cross the frontier between the two states. In the bloodbath that followed some 2 million people are reckoned to have lost their lives, as Hindus attacked Moslems and vice versa. Some 10 million people deserted their homes and fled across the new frontiers to their co-religionists.

Yet the mixed-race regiments of the Indian army remained true to their traditions and did their best to limit the genocide. Only afterwards were these regiments broken up and redistributed to the new countries. Two regiments of those wonderful mercenary soldiers, the Gurkhas, were transferred to the British army to maintain British power in Hong Kong, Malaya and Borneo, and one regiment still serves in Britain today.

In 1947 the Americans announced the Marshall plan, by which they gave 4 billion dollars to Britain and 9 billion to Germany which financed the remarkable reconstruction of German industry. President Roosevelt died and was succeeded by his deputy, Truman. He and Atlee had been no match for Stalin at the Potsdam Conference which sealed the division of Europe.

I wanted to go to America but had no friend to go with. It was very difficult to get a berth and in any case, it wasn't possible to take any money out of the country. Ships to America were full, carrying so-called GI brides, women who had married American servicemen in 1943 and 1944, and one could no longer work a passage on a cargo ship unless one signed on for the return voyage.

That year, Princess Elizabeth married her distant cousin, Prince Philip of Greece, who had been a competent naval officer throughout the war, and would be an admirable and loyal consort throughout her reign as Queen. Prince Charles was born the next year, followed by Anne, Andrew and Edward.

Chapter Four

Europe was in chaos and air travel only existed for the seriously rich. For ten years, no one took holidays abroad until skiing became popular. A future abroad looked only a remote possibility to me, and my father suggested I do a course in agriculture at the Royal Agricultural College at Cirencester but 2 years in classrooms again did not appeal, and I had been convinced by *The Farming Ladder* that the practice of farming was learned on a farm. A college diploma equipped you for a job as an agricultural officer at home or in the colonies, not to be a farmer, although I did take a correspondence course for a year.

So, at New Year 1947, I went as a pupil, unpaid, to George Rutter, a tenant of my father's cousin Captain Ralph Aldersey, who owned a 2,000 acre estate, 10 miles south of Chester at Coddington, where my great grandfather, Canon Coleman Royds, whose eldest daughter married Hugh Aldersey, had been vicar all his life.

The Beachin Farm consisted of about 270 acres, all in grass and low-lying. There was a dairy herd of about 80 cows – a large number for those days – which spent six months of the year in shippons chained by the neck and milked by a bucket machine. Apart from machine-milking having replaced hand-milking, little had probably changed for 200 years.

George's son Eric, one labourer and I carried hay from the barn – where it had been cut in wedges with a hay knife – on pikels (pitchforks) on our backs to be deposited in the bing (Cheshire for feeding passage) in front of the cows. We shovelled the muck into a horse-drawn muck cart, which would carry it out to the field to be dropped in heaps that were later spread by hand. Cows calved where they stood.

The only other winter occupation was hedge brushing (cutting by hand hook) and digging out the ditches beside every

91

hedge, as the land lay very wet. On the 20th January 47, heavy snow fell and it was to be the coldest winter for 100 years, with snow on the ground until mid-March.

It was very cold going out to milking at 6.00AM. John Rutter, George's brother was tenant of the next farm of a similar size where all the milk was made into cheese, as happened on many Cheshire farms in those days.

I had a 250cc motorbike on which I would go for dinner once a week to my cousins. They took me and their daughter, Primula to the Cheshire Hunt ball at Eaton Hall, the home of the Duke of Westminster, then occupied by the army as an OCTU, where their son, my second cousin Michael was a cadet.

The Rutters were both Freemasons, as were very many businessmen in Lancashire towns in those days, and would go weekly by car to their lodge meetings in Chester, taking me so that I could go to a cinema.

The Aldersey family had lived at Aldersey Hall since the Domesday Book, but it had been commandeered by the army for the war and been left in such a bad state that it was demolished, the fate of many country houses around that time. Ralph was a JP and, in that year, President of the Cheshire Hunt Club, which is among the oldest in Britain. He was a horticulturist and sold exotic plaints, advertised in The Times; garden centres did not exist in those days. Otherwise, Ralph shot snipe on the estate

His wife Rachel, née Gaussen, had been brought up on an Australian sheep station. She was very beautiful but tragically contracted cancer and died two years later. They had four children.

Primula, who was a society columnist for a Chester paper, died similarly a few years later.

After the death of their mother, Michael, who had had a short service commission in the Cheshire Regiment, went out to Australia, joined an ex-soldier settlement scheme clearing bush country, acquired a farm and married Sybella McCormick by whom he had a son Shane. Sybella died in 1960. Michael married again and had daughters Katherine, Rachel and Anne. When his father died in 1972, Michael sold the estate and took to property development.

Hugh (REME, Australian army) and Rose were to follow him

to Australia soon afterwards.

Since the war, Australia which then had a 'white Australia' policy had encouraged immigrants from Britain by offering £10 sea passages. Over about twenty years, a million emigrated. After the Vietnam war, Australia started to accept Asiatics, and when Britain joined the Common Market which brought about the end of Empire Trade preferences, the Australians were so piqued, they ended any preferential immigration schemes for the British.

In 1949, Ralph married his secretary, Betty Stonor of the Camoys family and had a son William, of whom I was asked to be Godfather.

William married Sheila Griffiths and had sons, Nicholas and Charles. He was left a farm and became an agronomist.

The Rutters, of sterling yeoman stock, who had probably lived in the same farms for generations, were very kind to me, a complete stranger in their home, but there was little except dairying to be learned there so I left in May. It proved to be difficult, however, to find another place, as farmers were then relatively well off and not inclined to take on pupils unless paid a substantial premium.

I was reduced to spending a couple of months on a Suffolk farm with a most unpleasant farmer, but then was introduced to a gentleman farmer, Gordon Collis, who had a dairy farm of 150 acres and 30 cows near Bridgnorth, where he employed two men and grew a certain amount of corn and potatoes. He also kept a large number of hens, running loose as batteries had not yet come into use, and a Standard Fordson tractor, with no cab of course, but we still spread muck on the field by hand.

From September 1947, I spent an enjoyable year as a pupil – still unpaid – with Gordon and his charming wife Joan, who tragically died of cancer a few years later. They had a beautiful daughter, Phillipa aged nine, who would later marry Geoffrey Rollason, and a son, Nigel, who became a land agent. There, life was quiet and apart from playing bridge with Gordon's brother and a neighbour, I met no one. I have always rather envied the working classes in the country their many local relations and girlfriends from local schools and dances.

In 1948, the Olympic Games were held in London with none of the vast construction, congestion and bally-hoo that attends the Games nowadays.

In 1954, the British runner, Roger Bannister was to break the four minute mile record, which has been regularly been improved on since.

Meanwhile, in the wider world, relations between the Allies and the Soviet Union broke down in 1947, the Cold War started and was to last nearly forty years. In 1948, the communists seized power in Czechoslovakia and Russian tanks moved into Prague soon afterwards to take over the country. In June the Russians prevented the Allies driving across their zone of Germany to divided Berlin and an immense airlift of supplies began, with the Americans and British flying up to 1,000 planes a day for nearly a year until Stalin relented.

It was also in 1948 that the Government of South Africa, led by Jan Christian Smuts, was overthrown by the Boer Party of Hendrik Verwoerd. General Smuts, who had led a commando during the Boer War had then transferred his allegiance to Britain and commanded South African forces during the Great War. Against considerable opposition he led them on our side during the World War.

Under the new Boer government, South Africa resigned Dominion status in the British Commonwealth and declared a Republic. This Government also introduced 'apartheid', or separate development, forbidding interracial marriage and decreeing separate areas in shops, hotels, beaches and other public places for blacks and whites, as well as introducing strict pass laws to prevent the movement of blacks into the towns.

These policies were strongly opposed by British South Africans and most of the world, but were to remain in force for 40 years until dismantled by the Nationalist Government of Nelson Mandela.

That year, the British mandate in Palestine was ended, Jews from all over Europe flooded into the country and the state of Israel was proclaimed, whereupon Egypt attacked and was defeated in a short war.

In May the communists, mostly Chinese, started a rebellion in Malaya, murdering British rubber planters. The Malayan emergency was to occupy a large number of British troops for the next seven years until we pulled out and the country was granted self-government.

In China itself, in 1949, the communist army, under Mao Tse Tung defeated the Nationalist army of Chiang Kai Shek, who fled to Formosa. Despite Chinese demands for reunification, Formosa – now Taiwan – with American support, has remained a separate country ever since.

In the same year, the Russians exploded an atomic bomb, restoring the balance of power with the West and causing fear ever after. About this time Britain also produced its earliest atomic bomb, and France soon after. We also produced our first jet-powered airliner the De Havilland Comet, which led the world for many years, until the occurrence of two disastrous crashes due to metal fatigue. From then on Boeing ruled the skies for nearly forty years until the Anglo-French Airbus arrived on the scene.

In 1950, communists in North Korea attacked South Korea. Before the war, all Korea had been a Japanese colony for 50 years – and the Americans, still occupying Japan, went to their assistance. British troops also took part and when we looked like winning the Chinese came to the aid of the North Koreans. The very fierce war that ensued lasted three years, before an armistice was signed, but a peace settlement not finalised up to this day. 33,000 Americans were killed and several thousand British.

That same year, China invaded Tibet, obliging the Dalai Llama to flee, which he did on horseback to India. No countries in the West nor the United Nations have ever done anything to support the gentle Tibetans, who have had to witness destruction of many of their monasteries and the influx of large numbers of Chinese immigrants, bureaucrats and soldiers, sent in to suppress the people and impose on them a policy of so-called modernisation.

Burma, a British colony for 100 years was granted independence and has been run by tyrannical military governments ever since. The Naga, Karen and Kachin tribes of the north who had helped us against the Japanese were handed over by us to their mercies and have suffered persecution ever since. Neither Britain nor the UN has done anything to intervene.

Also in 1950, a German born scientist Klaus Fuchs, who had been working on the American atom was discovered to have been spying for the Russians enabling them to produce their own bomb.

In October 1948, I took a job as assistant to Charles Meiklejohn at Hoo Hall Farm, Preston-on-the-Weald Moors, near Wellington, Shropshire. He again had a dairy farm of about 25 pedigree Friesian cows and I was paid £7 a week for a 6½ day week, from 6am to 6pm, with an afternoon off from milking on alternate Sundays and Saturdays.

He had two labourers and a modern tractor designed by the brilliant Harry Ferguson, who coupled farm implements with the tractor, an idea which was soon copied by all manufacturers. Nevertheless, the harvesting of corn and hay-making were still done largely by hand, which variously entailed turning the crop, pitching it onto wagons and then into barns, picking up sheaves of corn behind the reaper and binder and putting them into stooks, where they would remain for three weeks before pitching them onto wagons for carriage to a stack.

While there, I met Gilly Morris-Eyton who farmed near Newport and introduced me to the Shropshire Yeomanry, commanded by Colonel Arthur Heywood Lonsdale of Shavington estate. As Lieutenant Troop Commander, I went to a drill one evening each week in Wellington with A Squadron commanded by Mike Sowerby MC, a land agent and 2IC Michael (Lord) Cavan, a stockbroker. All had served in the Italian campaign when the Regiment were converted to field gunners. I also met Edith Cowan, a relation of Maud who had married my uncle Roger.

One of the staples of Shropshire social life was the round of annual balls organised by the local hunts. In those days tickets were two or three quid, with free Champagne, and all men wore white tie and tailcoats. I would get back at 5am in the morning and go straight out to milk the cows. I attended quite a few of these and, at one of them, my eye was caught by a girl called Rosemary Thursby-Pelham, who lived at Meole Grange, near Shrewsbury.

Another person I met was Peter Hallifax, an ex-Major, Norfolk Regiment in Europe and then on a farm near Welshpool. A distinguished-looking man of my height, he always wore a monocle and was a great humorist. We would meet occasionally at the Raven Hotel in Shrewsbury. I regret to say that I would drive home very drunk in a van which I had by then acquired. The breathalyser had not been invented and there was no drink driving law.

On alternate Saturdays in winter, I would take Rosemary hunting with the Shropshire Beagles, followed by a big tea in a pub or a private house at the meet.

In March 1950, I left the Meiklejohns, who had been kind but reserved, determined to farm myself or do something else. In three years I had met only four girls, all of whom were to marry farming friends. Although I loved country life, I found it too quiet and I always wished I had been able to spend a year in London where my son in his time would know dozens of girls.

Peter Halifax had a girlfriend who owned a firm manufacturing a rust remover. In April he and I went in my van across northern Europe to Denmark, camping and attempting to sell the product to pay our expenses. Somewhere in Belgium I remember climbing into a huge-industrial boiler to spray Plus Gas to little effect.

In Hamburg, Peter had a friend in the Control Commission then governing the British Zone. We spent two comfortable nights in their commandeered hotel on the shores of a lake and drank at the longest bar in Europe in another hotel, a survivor of British bombing and the firestorm of 1943, which reduced hundreds of acres across the city to a mass of rubble. The astonishing reconstruction financed by the American Marshall Plan had yet to commence.

We met a sinister looking businessman and appointed him agent for our Wonder Cure, but I'm not sure that it ever came to anything. We then drove on to Lubeck, where Peter had a Danish girl friend from the war; Karen, now working in the UN Refugee Organisation and living in another comfortable hotel. She put us up for three nights.

One evening, with a glamorous Dane called Helen, we were chauffeur-driven to Travamunde on the Baltic sea, where we dined at the Yacht Club. The only guests, we were entertained by a dance band and had an excellent dinner for a few shillings. Next day another member of the staff, who had a reputation for fortune-telling, read my palm, saying it was a very good one and that I would have three children and a long life but one serious illness. This has proved correct if replacement of hips counts as an illness.

We drove on, taking Karen to stay with her parents on their farm in Jutland. Later that year Peter emigrated to New Zealand and both Karen and Helen soon followed him. He didn't marry either of them and became an import/export merchant in Christchurch.

Danish farming was far more advanced and efficient than British, using hormone sprays to give weed-free corn fields, a practice not yet adopted in Britain. Now, of course, this is blamed for the loss of our birds and wild flowers.

We continued to Copenhagen where we camped undisturbed in the Royal deer park and then proceeded slowly home with one or two more sales efforts.

In May, Rosemary and I drove to St. Davids to check on restoration work on a fisherman's cottage that her father had bought some years before on the headland above the harbour at Porth Clais. She was very attached to it and kept a sailing dinghy there.

We stayed with Brigadier and Mrs Pym and were invited to dinner by Colonel Browning, the brother of General 'Boy' Browning, who had commanded the airborne division but fortunately for him not flown with them on the disastrous Arnhem operation. After dinner it was suggested that we go seine netting on Whitesands Bay. Seine netting is – and probably was then – illegal if not officially licensed. Two people would gather up a net fifty yards long and about 5' deep and wade into the sea as far as depth allowed, when they would spread apart and drag the net back towards the shore.

A naval officer from the nearby Fleet Air Arm base at Brawdy and I were detailed and donned survival suits which he had brought. We walked out to sea together in the dark up to our necks, then separated and pulled the net back to shore. In three pulls we caught 13 sewin (sea trout).

In June we drove to London to stay with a friend of Rosemary's. We saw the new American musical, *South Pacific* and dined at the Cafe Royal for £1. I proposed and after thinking it over for a day Rosemary accepted me. I was delighted. Although one quarter Welsh, and brought up in Wales, Rosemary was 5'4", equable, blonde and Anlgo-Saxon in appearance and demeanour, quite unlike the emotional, dark Celts, whose female attributes are said to be: "Thrifty in the market, fervent in the chapel and frantic in Bed." Her good nature has stood the test of time, and fortunately she has always known that the way to a man's heart is through his stomach.

Rosemary Elizabeth Annabel was the great granddaughter of the Rev Augustus Thursby-Pelham, vicar of Cound, his elder brother having inherited Cound Hall, a large Stuart House, and estate near Cressage, Shropshire, which had been in the family since the 17th century. Another family possession was a medieval manor house, Upton Cressett, that included several farms.

Rosemary's grandfather Edward Cressett went to Australia for his health. He had married a widow, born Harriet Billyard-Leake, whose father had been solicitor general of New South Wales and whose first husband George Delves-Broughton had died, leaving a son Frank. After fighting in the Boer War, Frank took to tobacco farming in Nyasaland, now Malawi, and died there, unmarried, of blackwater fever in 1913.

Her father, Neville Cressett was born in 1883 and spent much of his childhood at Cound. He was educated at Blundells school and took up employment with a cable company in the Far East until 1908, when he joined his step brother Frank Delves-Broughton tobacco farming. In 1914 he came home to join the Kings Shropshire Light Infantry, was wounded in France and then transferred to the new regiment of Welsh Guards, in which he continued to serve till he retired in 1929 to manage his wife's estate.

His cousin, Jim Thursby-Pelham who had only two daughters, Audley and Nell, sold the Cound and Upton Cressett estates in 1930.

Rosemary's mother, Yseulte was the only daughter of Sir Mervyn Peel, a barrister descended from Sir Robert Peel, the Prime Minister. He had inherited the Danyrallt estate near Llangadog in 1900, was Conservative candidate for Carmarthen and knighted for public services. He was married to Francis Annabel Assheton of Downham Hall, near Clitheroe, whose nephew Sir Ralph Assheton was Chairman of the Conservative Party in 1945/6 and granted one of the last hereditary peerages in 1955 as Lord Clitheroe.

In 1921, Yseulte married Captain Neville Thursby-Pelham and, on the death of her father in 1929, inherited the Danyrallt estate. They lived there until 1937 when the farms were sold to the tenants and the house to a prep school who managed to burn it down in 1940.

There was little money in owning land then, as rents brought in only £1 per acre and landlords had the responsibility not only of repairing old and building new farm buildings but also of providing gates and posts. There was not enough money in it to keep seven servants and heat a large house. Land sold for £10 to £20 an acre at the time.

Rosemary's elder brother Christopher went to Wellington College and joined the Welsh Guards in 1941, serving with them in Tunisia and Italy. He married Rachel (Ray) Willson in 1943 and had a son, David and a daughter, Philippa. Later, he commanded the Regiment, being appointed Brigadier Commanding London District, and then OC military forces on Gibraltar. In retirement he managed the British Heart Foundation.

Rosemary was born 1923 and had a happy, albeit very quiet childhood in London, and then at Danyrallt where she had a devoted governess, Pussy Wells. There were no friends within reach and life was enlivened only by relations coming to stay and summer holidays at Tenby. At eleven she was sent to Mrs Harrison at Mathon Court near Malvern, who taught a few girls and, when thirteen, to Brondesbury School at Cranleigh, a rather Victorian establishment for educating young ladies; my cousin Lynette was also there.

In 1942 she went back to the Harrisons, who had moved to Ludlow to work as a land girl until 1946, and then took a flower arranging course with Constance Spry in London. After that she assisted Stella Harrison, who would later marry Sir Charles Mott-Radcliffe MP, in arranging flowers for weddings, and in 1948, went home to Meole-brace to drive for her parents as her father had fallen and broken his hip and her mother didn't drive.

This gave her the opportunity to acquire a horse and occasionally she rode with the South Shropshire Hunt.

When Rosemary and I returned from our visit to London, I asked her father's approval of our plans to marry, which he gave and disclosed that she had £200 a year invested income. My own father was far less understanding, demanding to know how I could be married when I had no job or income.

In June, now promoted to Captain, I went to the annual camp with the Yeomanry at Hunstanton and while there heard that her father had gone into hospital for an operation for a hernia, when he developed a blood clot – a frequent occurrence in those days – and died.

To keep myself busy while I was waiting for the right opportunity to present itself, I bought a Ferguson tractor and hedge cutter and cut hedges on Cheshire farms. I also for a while looked after Brian Midwood's farm on the Wrekin while he was on honeymoon after his marriage to Jean McConnell, of Hampton Hall, near Minsterley.

Brian was a childhood friend who, due to his asthma, had been an agricultural officer during the war, and Jean was the daughter of a director of Booker McConnell Ltd, which owned sugar plantations in the West Indies. She was an accomplished horsewoman and rode at point-to-point meetings. They would have children, Peter, Joanna, Roger, Sue and Mary, to whom I was asked to be godfather.

In September 1950 Rosemary and I were married at Meole Brace by my Uncle Jack Gamon and her Uncle Hal Thursby-Pelham. Due to the recent death of her father it was a small wedding of about a hundred guests and I had to forego a guard of honour of Yeomanry officers with swords on coming out of the church. My brother, Mark was best man.

Petrol rationing had ended at last so we could spend two weeks' honeymoon driving around Scotland in my mother-in-law's Wolseley car, which she had given to us. We returned to live at Meole Grange for four months as Rosemary's mother had moved to a small house at Church Stretton. For the time being, I continued hedge-cutting on local farms.

Mrs Morris-Eyton very kindly offered us the tenancy of a farm she had inherited on the Cumberland Blackcomb Mountain, close to the Windscale atomic processing plant which had recently had a disastrous leak.

However, we turned it down as I knew nothing about sheep, the principal enterprise, and labour was impossible to find up there. Moreover, it was far from our friends and we were discouraged by my godmother, Elsie Grice, a top amateur golfer who lived nearby. She was later to leave a sizeable farm to the vicar and an antique table to me.

I therefore accepted an offer by Quentin Thomas, a Yeomanry officer, to take over the tenancy of a 60-acre farm, Hanbury Park Gate on the Needwood estate near Burton-on-Trent which he managed as agent for the Duchy of Lancaster.

We took possession in January 1951 of the small house with no bathroom and an outside loo. A tin tub in front of the kitchen range served as a bath. Heated with water from a kettle, Rosemary had it clean and hot; I had it colder!

As Rosemary's mother, had sold her house she gave us all the furniture we needed. Wedding presents were all utilitarian. Only seconds of china could be bought as all the best was exported. In those days the invidious habit of displaying presents in a room at the wedding reception still persisted – to encourage generosity perhaps! But at least the practice of circulating present lists hadn't been started. For our first three months at Hanbury Park Gate, we lived on a £50 wedding gift. Clothes rationing had only ended in 1949 and meat was still rationed. Bread rationing, though never imposed throughout the war, was introduced in 1951. It was only after the next election, won by the Conservatives under Churchill in October 1951, that rationing was abolished for everything except meat.

The following winter, London was enveloped for four days in what was termed 'smog', a thick fog which caused the deaths of 12,000 people. Thenceforward, the burning of fossil fuels was banned in the capital.

My father had lent me £2,000; I still had the £1,000 I had saved while in the army and banks were keen to lend. However, whereas young men had been able to start with very little before the war when farming was so depressed that landowners were offering farms rent free for several years, during the war farming had prospered and now tenancies were hard to get. I had bought my first Ferguson tractor for £330 and now acquired a plough and other machinery and cultivated two fields for corn. Under the aged tenant before me the land was all in grass, so had not been robbed.

Rosemary used to listen to *The Archers* on the radio each

evening. Then it was a realistic tale of a farming family so convincing that some people sent Christmas presents to the characters in Ambridge. People even ordered their Christmas turkeys from the young Philip Archer. The first ever 'soap', *Mrs Dale's Diary* which had started just after the war was still being broadcast but losing ratings to Dan and Doris Archer and their daughter, Grace who died in a fire.

In March I went to Ayrshire and came back with 20 Ayrshire heifers. Our landlord finished modernising the house and put in a milking parlour. This allowed for milking two cows at a time using an American Surge Machine whose units hung on a strap under the belly of the cow. The milk collected in these units was tipped into a churn which was taken down to the farm gate on the road, put on a stand and collected by lorry. Ayrshires, red and white, gave good milk of 3.5% butterfat, although no premium was paid. Since then, Ayrshires have been almost universally replaced by Friesians who give a higher yield, but poorer milk.

I always enjoyed ploughing – about two acres a day – and took pride in leaving straight furrows with tidy cops and reans between each land of 20 yards, which the neighbours could see. Gulls followed behind picking up worms.

In today's chemical farming, powerful tractors plough up to 20 acres a day and there are no worms in the sterile soil and no wild flowers either. When the cows were due to calve I would be up in the night because occasionally one would develop milk fever, from which it would have rapidly expired if not injected with a pint of calcium water into the milk vein. This got them straight back on their feet.

All the cows were individually named and an inspector visited each month to record their milk yield. I also kept their pedigrees, though to little purpose.

We had a beloved Wessex sow called Eve, who produced litters of about ten piglets twice a year. These we fattened and occasionally killed one for the house. The sides of bacon and hams were salted and hung in the kitchen for months to cure. The man who came to butcher it tactfully suggested that the wife should have nothing to do with the process, because, if she was pregnant, the meat would not keep. However, she made brawns from the head, trotters and bits without any obvious ill effects.

Among the many and various artisans on whose skills it was necessary to call from time to time was the mole catcher. He came round once a year to deal with the small beasts that could play havoc with a field of pasture in just a few weeks. The delicate task of correctly setting a mole trap is just one other of the old country crafts that will be sorely missed. We never had to pay the mole catcher; he simply took the skins, which he then sold.

I mowed the fields with a finger mower, as had been used for the past 70 years, although now tractor mounted. A finger mower was good if the crop was standing well but if it had been knocked down by rain it had to be mown one way and if they tangled, they could be the devil. I got a newly invented buck rake which was mounted on the back of the tractor. With this I would carry the grass to a pit to make silage and, in winter, carry it to the cows lying loose in a barn, or, after turning it to make hay, would sweep it to a stack in the field. Later a contractor would come round with a stationary baler.

For harvesting the corn, which was a mixture of oats, barley and peas – called dredge corn – I got an old reaper and binder, converted from horse-drawn, on which I rode while Rosemary pulled it with the tractor. To clear a way for the binder, I first had to cut round the field with a scythe and tie the corn in sheaves by hand. It worked admirably for four years until we used a contractor with the newly imported combine harvester, which deposited the corn in sacks around the field.

A binder cut, tied and dropped sheaves on the ground. These had then to be put into stooks for three weeks to dry before being hauled on a trailer to a stack in the field. Building a stack was quite a skilled job as the middle had to be kept high so that any rain ran out. It was also a matter of pride that it had a good shape which the neighbours would note. Later a contractor came with a threshing machine driven by a single cylinder Marshall tractor, which put the corn into 2 cwt sacks and the straw into boltings. Wheat was always put in sacks of 2½ cwt which men would carry on their backs up granary steps. Nowadays no sacks above ½cwt are allowed. Rosemary looked after a productive kitchen garden.

In October, our first child, Teresa Margaret (Tessa) was born at the hospital in Burton-upon-Trent and after two days she and her mother came home to be cared for by my elder sister Sylvia, who besides being QA commissioned nurse, was now a qualified midwife. Brian Midwood accepted to be her godfather; with Sylvia, and Joan de Hamel as godmothers.

I was on my own, working 12 hours a day for the first year, after which I took on a 16-year old boy, Brian Cooper, whose father had been killed in a huge explosion in a gypsum mine near Hanbury. It left a hole in the ground of several acres. Brian took on the morning milking, an excellent boy.

Later, I took on a pupil Henry Koestler, who lodged in the village, and I bought the new Ferguson diesel tractor for £400. The first one had been started on petrol and then turned over to paraffin, as all tractors were up to that time.

We made friends with John and Ann Penrose. John was a brewer in Trumans Brewery. Due to the very hard water from gypsum deposits, Burton-upon-Trent had five breweries, one of which also made Marmite, and still does. Other friends we made were Pat Featherstone, a gentleman farmer who commanded the Staffordshire Yeomanry and his wife Joan; Mary and John Williams-Ellis, ex-RNR and nephew of Clough, celebrated architect of Portmeirion. He was land agent of the Meynell estate nearby and they asked Rosemary to be godmother to their daughter Susanna. We later asked him to be godfather to our son Julian after he had gone to Ulster and developed a larger practice there.

Remarkably, and sadly, all except Ann were to die of cancer in their fifties. With them we went each year to the Meynell Hunt Ball which was always held in a private house. One year at Keddleston, the home of Lord Curzon, all the lights failed and his lordship was running round distracted for some time.

We shopped in Burton and occasionally went to the cinema there, or out for dinner at a pub either in Tetbury or Uttoxeter. I remember feeling bad that dinner cost 25 shillings each – the sum I paid Brian for a week's work. We also attended a couple of point-to-points each year and drove to London for two or three nights. The car was then useful as there was still little traffic and you could park anywhere. We would stay at the Basil Street Hotel in Knightsbridge which didn't even seem expensive.

It was about this time, in 1952, that a very high spring tide, driven by an easterly gale, caused the worst ever flooding of the Norfolk coast and the land around the Thames estuary, drowning 200 people. Large areas of Holland were also inundated drowning 1,800 people and 50,000 cattle. The Thames barrage was built years later, but is now said to be too low due to global warming and higher sea levels.

I bought a horse from Sheringham in Norfolk and hunted a few times with the Meynell Hounds when they met within hacking distance – there were few horse boxes around in those days. In the evenings, I would ride in the nearby park of Lady Burton, a Labour peeress.

I couldn't, of course, attend weekly drills with the Shropshire Yeomanry but went on the odd weekend exercise and to the annual camp where we acquired armoured cars. A Shropshire landowner, John Kynaston, had taken over command from Colonel Heywood-Lonsdale and the regimental honorary colonel was General Sir Oliver Leese who had taken over command of the 8th Army in Italy from General Montgomery in 1944.

In 1954, we had a charismatic training major, 'Loopy' Kennard, of the 4th Hussars who would later command his regiment and when retired developed a business selling cooked chicken on racecourses. The son of a baronet, who gambled away a fortune, he married two heiresses and wrote an amusing autobiography. Cavalry officers tend to despise those career soldiers who go on to become generals.

I remember well playing poker in the mess and some jolly parties in one of which I rode a cow into the mess and another where some ass discharged a large fire extinguisher that proved to be expensive.

We never took a newspaper for the first two years or more at Hanbury, nor had television become the universal object it is today. It's true to say that, for most of the time then, I simply worked, slept and read the *Farmers' Weekly*, in which AG Street wrote a regular column.

In February 1952, King George VI died, and Elizabeth

became Queen although the coronation did not take place till June 1953. Quentin Thomas acquired some seats for tenants of the Duchy of Lancaster and kindly gave us two, so we saw the procession from an open stand on the Mall in showery conditions. The immensely fat Queen of Tonga smiling from an open carriage got the greatest cheers.

During the procession it was announced on loud speakers that Mount Everest had been climbed by Edmund Hillary and his Sherpa Tensing. The Mau Mau rebellion of the Kikiyu tribe in Kenya had begun in 1952 and was to last three years. It eventually resulted in the country achieving self-government under their leader, Jomo Kenyatta and corruption ever since.

Two diplomats, Burgess and Maclean, who had been spying for the Soviet Union for years, skipped the country in 1951, tipped off just before being arrested. A 'third man' was later found to be Kim Philby, almost the top man in the secret service, who similarly scarpered just before being arrested in the Lebanon in 1954.

Later, when Anthony Blunt, knighted Keeper of the Queen's pictures, was unmasked as a former Soviet spy in 1979, it became obvious that the secret services had been a very effective cloak for homosexual activity which, in those days, was illegal. America exploded a hydrogen bomb many times more powerful than the atom bomb over an atoll in the Pacific.

In March 1953 the greatest tyrant of all time, Joseph Stalin died in his bed. Born the son of a Georgian priest, this clever, ruthless, often drunken sadist had caused the death of 20 million of his own people and deported 28 million from their homes - 18 million of them, so-called dissidents – to the slave camps of the Siberian Gulag, and the whole Tartar population of the Crimea to central Asia when the German army approached.

Show trials of unfortunate victims, whose confessions had been tortured out of them, continued to the end under the appalling Vyshinsky, and only Stalin's death saved his doctors, who had been accused of participation in the so-called 'Jewish doctors plot', although his wife had been Jewish. He was followed by joint leaders, the toadying Malenkov and Marshall Bulganin. They were to be overthrown in 1956 by the Secretary of the Communist Party, Nikita Krushchev, who had supervised the massacre of the Ukrainian Kulaks in 1932, yet who now denounced the barbarities of Stalin and hung the blood-soaked head of the NKVD Lavrenti Beria. The sinister Molotov continued as Foreign Secretary and spokesman at the United Nations. Those few Russian prisoners of war who survived to be repatriated from German camps in 1945 were also sent to the Gulag as punishment for surrendering.

In 1954, the French army were defeated at Dien Bien Phu by the Vietnamese under Ho Chi Min and had to leave French Indo-China.

While, in the English countryside, the virulent Myxomatosis disease had been introduced from Australia and wiped out most of the rabbits, which, in some parts of the country, had become almost a plague, although it's worth bearing in mind that in the depression of the 1930s some small farmers almost lived off their rabbits.

At home, in October 1953, Fiona was born at home under the supervision of a delightful midwife, who stayed for 2 weeks. Nick Assheton, Betty Aldersey and Ray Thursby-Pelham accepted to be her godparents. To help Rosemary, we took on a charming girl called Joan from the village as nursemaid and all went well. When the babies woke at night, Rosemary would put a tot of whisky in the bottle, which worked wonders. And, in 1954 when meat rationing was ended at last, things could only get better.

Rosemary had inherited the cottage at Porth Clais and let it to Nancy Howell but always took the children down there for summer holidays.

I won 2nd Prize in a county competition for small farms. This was very encouraging to me, and I felt that perhaps I was beginning to know what I was doing. Rosemary had been given a marriage settlement of £10,000, so it became possible to buy a farm.

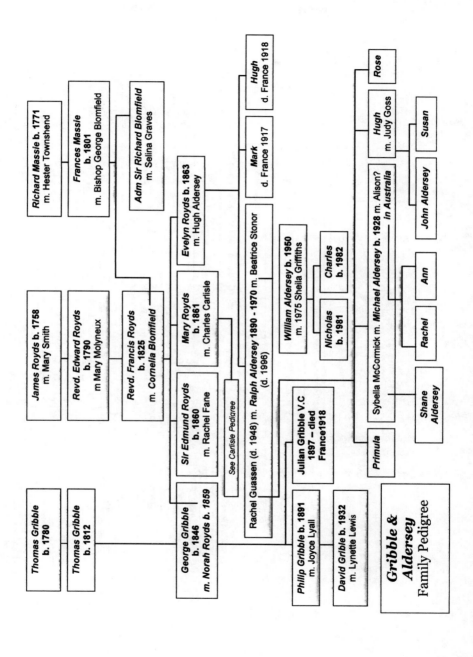

Gribble & Aldersey Family Pedigree

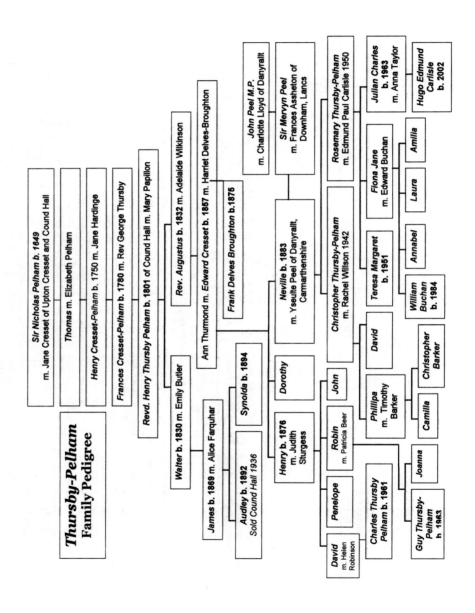

Thursby-Pelham
Family Pedigree

Sir Nicholas Pelham *b. 1649*
m. Jane Cresset of Upton Cresset and Cound Hall

Thomas m. Elizabeth Pelham

Henry Cresset-*Pelham* b. 1750 m. Jane Hardinge

Frances Cresset-*Pelham* b. 1780 m. Rev George Thursby

Revd. Henry Thursby Pelham *b. 1801* of Cound Hall m. Mary Papillon

Walter b. 1830 m. Emily Butler

Rev. Augustus *b. 1832* m. Adelaide Wilkinson

Ann Thurmond m. *Edward Cresset* b. 1857 m. Harriet Delves-Broughton

James *b. 1869* m. Alice Farquhar

Frank Delves Broughton b.1876

John Peel M.P.
m. Charlotte Lloyd of Danyrallt

Sir Mervyn Peel
m. Frances Assheton of Downham, Lancs

Audley b. 1892
Sold Cound Hall 1936

Synolda b. 1894

Dorothy

Neville b. 1883
m. Yseulte Peel of Danyrallt, Carmarthenshire

Rosemary Thursby-Pelham
m. Edmund Paul Carlisle 1950

Henry b. 1876
m. Judith Sturgess

John

Robin
m. Patricia Beer

Christopher Thursby-Pelham
m. Rachel Willson 1942

Julian Charles
b. 1963
m. Anna Taylor

David

Phillipa
m. Timothy Barker

Teresa Margaret
b. 1951

Fiona Jane
m. Edward Buchan

Hugo Edmund Carlisle
b. 2002

David
m. Helen Robinson

Penelope

Charles Thursby Pelham b. 1961

Camilla

Christopher Barker

William Buchan
b. 1984

Annabel

Laura

Amilia

Joanna

Guy Thursby-Pelham
b 1963

Chapter Five

In September 1955 we bought a Standard Vanguard station wagon for £700 and drove across France to the Spanish Costa Brava, then a collection of small fishing villages, where we camped on the beaches. Tourist development was only just beginning – now there are high-rise hotels in every bay.

On our way home we took a detour to look at Greenway Manor, near Llandrindod Wells in Radnorshire, which I happened to have seen advertised for sale. We both liked what we saw, and eventually Rosemary's trustees bought the property, a mock black and white manor house of eight bedrooms, with 450 acres of land and four cottages, for £18,000.

When we asked the agent for the Agricultural Mortgage Corporation, Ralph Woosnam, for 75% mortgage, he would only give us 50%, saying we had paid too much for it! I paid rent for it as a tenant of the trustees.

I took on three men who were each paid £7 a week, with a free cottage. Eric Price milked twenty cows in a parlour in the buildings above the house. Bert Watkins was the tractor driver and shepherd of the 200 sheep I'd bought. Stan, a general labourer, left after six months and was replaced by the 18 year-old Ken Brown. They all worked short hours in the winter and long days at harvest time but were paid no overtime.

The farm actually comprised four small ones, plus a small holding. Overall, it was three miles in length with seven miles of boundary and 97 small fields divided by overgrown hedges that had been acquired by our predecessor Colonel Phillips, a director of Wolseley Sheep Shearing Co. Ltd, who shared the belief of others that I could not make a living from it.

All the lofts in the farm buildings were full of loose hay so a contractor came with a stationary baler and I sold most of it, delivering it with an ex-army lorry, which I had bought for £70 at a sale of surplus army vehicles at a depot near Peterborough. It had done only 1,000 miles. I later converted it to carry livestock. No farmers then had LandRovers and trailers. Although there was a local livestock haulier most farmers still drove their cattle and sheep on foot to the market at Pen-y-Bont. Tessa, the more serious of the two girls, would often come with me to the market, and she loved to poke around the farm buildings. Fiona always stayed at home with her mother.

In the market, deals between farmers were always cemented with a handshake, the seller usually spitting on his hand first (although I've never understood why), and the seller was expected to hand over 'Luck money' of £1 or so. Once a deal was agreed, I never found them to be dishonest or back out.

In 1955 Winston Churchill retired as Prime Minister and was succeeded by Anthony Eden. The Greeks started a rebellion in Cyprus that was to last several years. Colonel Nasser overthrew the King of Egypt and most of the British troops on our huge army bases in the Suez Canal zone were brought home.

In the following year, Nasser nationalised the Suez Canal, owned up until then by an Anglo-French company. After several months of delay, negotiation and secret talks, the Israelis attacked the Egyptian army in Sinai with devastating efficiency and completely destroyed it. After heavy bombing, Anglo-French forces landed at Port Said to reoccupy the Canal, claiming to be separating the belligerents.

The Americans, who had always opposed colonial empires, exerted very heavy pressure and the pound was collapsing. Eden suffered a nervous breakdown and after two weeks, when within sight of success, the whole operation to secure the canal was called off. It was a complete fiasco, which damaged our country's reputation for many years and assured Nasser's. Eden resigned and was replaced by Harold Macmillan, all as a result of removing British troops from the canal zone the year before.

Russia, which had recently invented their own hydrogen bomb, invaded Hungary and, after a week of bloody fighting in Budapest, installed a communist regime accompanied by the uttering of warlike threats.

Many thousands of Hungarians had fled their country and I employed one on the farm, putting him and his family up in an empty cottage. He was a very good worker but left for America within a year.

In 1955 Princess Margaret was dissuaded from pursuing a relationship with the handsome divorcee and royal equerry Group Captain Peter Townsend, and ended up in 1960 marrying a commoner, Anthony Armstrong-Jones, who was made the Earl of Snowdon. They had two children, a son, Viscount Linley, and a daughter, Lady Sarah Armstrong-Jones.

1955 also saw the arrival in this country of six hundred black men from Jamaica. They were permitted to enter the country to work on London buses and the underground, and were followed soon afterwards by large numbers of immigrants who came from India, Pakistan and Bangladesh to work in the cotton and woollen mills. It was then that Liberal do-gooders demanded that immigrants be allowed to bring their families, and a multi-cultural society in Britain was born, with ever more disastrous results.

In farming, a wartime grant of £10 was still paid for ploughing up grassland. Bert used a two furrow trailer plough with an old Standard Fordson tractor, started by handle. I planted 40 acres of barley and a lime subsidy, the only good subsidy ever, paid all the cost of lime spreading.

When harvest time came the season was very wet and the combine harvester contractor, having taken on too much work, was very late, the inevitable result of which was trouble for our crop.

I had a large barn built in the middle of the farm where I kept about 40 dry cattle which self-fed from a silage bunker down the middle. The silage was harvested by a Cut Lift on to a trailer and carried on to the pit with a buck rake. We built a road 400 yards down to the new barns, hauling gravel from the station as most of the country railway lines were shut down at that time.

I retained my tenancy of Hanbury for a year and a half and would go over there once a month, taking Joan, our nursemaid who had come with us to Wales, back to see her family. Brian Cooper and another boy managed Hanbury very well, so I tried to persuade the Duchy to take on Brian as tenant but the agent, Quentin Thomas refused. When we pulled out, Rosemary went over and drove a tractor and loaded trailer the 120 miles home, stopping overnight with the Collises at Bridgnorth. I drove my lorry.

About this time I was asked to be County Commissioner of the Radnorshire Boy Scouts, a position which I accepted and held for 10 years. One of my commitments in the summer was to inspect any scouts from elsewhere who were camping in the county. Later Rosemary became treasurer of the Guides, and Gwenllian Philipps, who was Chief Guide for Wales would invite us to dinner with her parents, Lord and Lady Milford, and to accompany her to the Brecon Hunt Ball. A horse belonging to her father had won the Ascot Gold Cup, which sat on the dining-room table.

Her eccentric brother, Wogan, married to the author Rosamund Lehmann, had long been a communist and was disowned by his father, and yet went on to sit for many years in the House of Lords as Lord Milford. His delightful and more conventional son, Hugo inherited the Llanstephan estate in Radnorshire, and the title.

We became close friends with the Thompsons, who had a farm at Nantmel. Ronald was a major in the parachute regiment during the war and Val was to have seven children. In 1960 they moved to a large house and 100-acre farm in Devon but he got tired of farming and managed to go to Cambridge, where he got a degree and became a don at Bristol University. He had affairs and Val divorced him. She spent all her inheritance on educating the children and had to sell Millom in about 1970. By then, Ronald was growing apples with a French woman in Normandy. He succumbed to the effects of Calvados in 1984. Val, who has suffered several tragedies in her family has remained a friend for life.

Tessa went daily on a school bus to a private teacher in Llandrindod Wells. I bought an old army Jeep, and a County crawler tractor with bulldozer with which Bert pushed out hedges reducing the 97 fields to 25. In those days farmers were paid to pull up hedges, now they're paid to put them back again. I also got a trailed combine harvester which, in a wet harvest, we had to tow with the crawler.

One year we were even harvesting in November and I eventually turned 50 pigs into the field for some weeks. The farm was really not suited to growing corn. I should have kept it all in grass and carried more sheep. Eric Price left and I decided to sell the dairy cows and keep beef cattle, rearing their calves.

In February 1957 we went by train to Klosters with Ted and Rosie Thomas and John (Lord) Swansea under the auspices of the Army Ski Scheme. You could only take £70 out of the country which had to pay for accommodation, ski and boot hire, lift pass, instruction and *après* ski teas and dance. The Swiss must have done it at a loss to encourage tourism and the food was pretty basic. But the snow was good and the holiday marvellous.

The High Sheriff, Ted Thomas invited us to his luncheon at the annual assize court in Presteigne. It was said that a Radnorshire jury would never convict and they maintained their reputation on this occasion. The court moved to Brecon the following year.

I was also appointed vice-president of the Radnorshire Agricultural Show, but it closed two years later when the Royal Welsh Show settled at Builth Wells. In summer we had a Young Farmers' club rally on the farm. The Lord Lieutenant asked me to be Chairman but I thought it was a job for a Welshman.

In the autumn I started a dining club with Ted Thomas, Mervyn Bourdillon and Charles Woosnam. We called it the 'Radnorshire Gentlemen's Dining Club' and soon had twelve members, all landowners, who would dine each month in the winter at an hotel chosen by the presiding member, who had to bring a guest speaker or introduce a topic for discussion. Dinner, including as much wine and port as you could drink, cost about £1.50. It continued so for about ten years when members were introduced from Breconshire. It then expanded rapidly and is still in existence today with about forty members, though dining only four times each winter. I must here record our gratitude to Norman Tyler and Tony Laurie-Chiswell, who have each acted as honorary secretary for over fifteen years.

Our super nursemaid, Joan had left when I gave up Hanbury, being replaced by young live-in nursemaids and dailies. In 1958 Peggy Jones came to live in the annexe to the house and would be with us for many years. I was never a hands-on father, as many are today, believing that children and cooking were the province of women, while men dealt with boilers and fires.

We were lent a wonderful 29 year old Welsh pony, Tassle who would later be followed by Micky and Bimbo. I had sold my horse, Flash, which I'd brought from Hanbury as Rosemary wouldn't ride him – he was too strong – and bought a young mare called Petula at a sale in Llanybyther. At the sale a girl was riding the horse, which afterwards we discovered had a cold back and would rear whenever you mounted her. However, she had a tremendous spirit and was with us for many years. I took Tessa hunting a few times with the Teme Valley hounds when meeting nearby but we had no horse-box and I begrudged the time. Nevertheless, for many years, the girls rode on the farm and attended pony club rallies.

We always kept Welsh Mountain ewes – a breed considered so hardy that they did not need any supplementary feed during the winter. In fact, there had been a tradition among hill farmers that these sheep wintered and lambed on the hills, so taking them hay or silage weakened their instinct to forage for themselves. Wether (male) sheep were stronger and kept because they would lead the flock out from snow drifts when they sheltered under bluffs. The market for wether mutton had gone as everyone now wanted lamb, and the wethers with it.

However, I was told that the very hard winter of 1947 had found them out and thousands of sheep died on the mountains and were not found till the snow melted after two months. Since then, nearly all hill farmers had built barns (with 50% grants) to lamb indoors.

Shearing had always been done by neighbours gathering together on each farm in turn, as they had done for haymaking before mechanisation. Farming was a more companionable job in those days. They shore using blades or hand driven machines and a man would shear about 50 a day, holding them on a bench.

By this stage shearing machines were driven by a small petrol engine or electricity. Australian and New Zealand farms with far bigger flocks used contract shearers. Some came to Britain and a New Zealander called Geoffrey Bowen amazed everyone by being able to shear 400 sheep in a day.

The day before shearing we drove the sheep into the river to wash out the dust and oil (lanolin) and raise the wool to make it easier to achieve a close cut. Matthew Price from Hundred House would bring a New Zealander to shear ours while Bert and I wrapped the fleeces. Welsh boys soon learnt the technique of turning the sheep on the ground between their legs to meet the blades and my man, John Greenow now shears and wraps the fleeces of 200 sheep a day. No one washes them any more and the wool mill extracts the lanolin for face creams.

The Clewedog river ran along the farm boundary and in front of the house. There were a few trout in it, up to half a pound. In autumn, salmon swam up it to spawn and a bailiff walked it to protect them but I once caught a poacher walking up it at night with lights and gaffs to spear them. Penalties for poaching used to be very severe but nowadays few do it; there are fewer salmon, which anyway have been devalued by the introduction of farmed fish onto the market, and the poverty which led people to poach has been alleviated by tax credits and supplementary benefits.

I was for several years President of the Rhayader Ploughing Match Society which held a competition on a different farm each year and a dinner in Rhayader. It was wonderful to get most of our ploughing done for nothing one year.

In the outside world, in 1957 the Russians startled the world by launching a dog into space in their Sputnik rocket. France and Germany had already formed the Common Market. This was essentially a free trade agreement but with greater pretensions. Two years later, Britain and the Scandinavian countries formed the European Free Trade Area, which, after a time, disintegrated. But in '57, France, Germany, Holland Belgium, Luxemburg and Italy formed the European Union with Headquarters in Brussels.

At last the Malayan Emergency was ended and the country achieved self-government.

Also in 1957, homosexual acts by consenting individuals ceased to be a crime punishable by imprisonment. Gradually thereafter the word 'gay' was usurped to describe a homosexual and gays began to find themselves under pressure by their like to be 'outed' (revealed as gay). Until then, they had been known more offensively as 'poofs' or 'queers'.

Divorce would be made easy and the stigma of illegitimacy removed as single mothers proliferated, heralding the moral degradation of society that has continued ever since.

Life peerages were introduced to increase Labour representation in the House of Lords. Ever since then they have been given to retiring cabinet ministers and can virtually be bought by large donations to party funds. Incredibly, their children presume to call themselves 'honourable'. In these democratic days, it is ridiculous to ennoble men as lords when they have nothing to lord it over, and even have to borrow or hire their outdated robes. Now most hereditary peers have been deprived of their seats in the House of Lords, it should be renamed the Upper House, and its members referred to as senators, or something similar.

In 1958 Rosemary regained possession of her Porth Clais cottage near St David's and was very keen on holidaying there. I was not keen on lying on beaches.

When I started farming, I had set out to achieve 1,000 acres within ten years, so, as Rosemary had a few shares in Gratton Warehouses that went up spectacularly in value, we bought Castle Farm (120 acres for £7,500 on mortgage) at Roch nearby. We would stay there in an old caravan for the next three years sowing 50 acres of barley, haymaking and harvesting, the previous owner doing the ploughing and looking after cattle for me.

The Royal Welsh Show, which had previously moved to a different county for each year, had settled on a permanent site at Builth Wells and I was appointed to the Council as representative for Radnorshire. They had appointed professional fund-raisers for the purchase and I donated £250. To my surprise, some sharp member spotted that this sum entitled a donor to a Vice Presidency for Life, which turned out be one of the best investments I ever made.

At home, a governess, Miss Cogswell, came each day to teach Tessa and Fiona. We had always played card games in the evenings but now succumbed to television with a black and white set.

For many years I received a free monthly magazine, *The Plain Truth*, published by an American evangelist. He even ran a 'university' in Hertfordshire, but the whole organisation fell apart when his son, who was being groomed to succeed him, left his wife for a younger model. Many such evangelists seem to have ended their careers in scandal. But I did learn from him to give 10% of my income to charity, which I have tried to do ever since.

That winter we went skiing again with friends at Kitzbuhl in Austria, travelling by train. No one took children in those days and anyhow we couldn't have afforded it.

I was offered command of the Hereford Squadron of the Shropshire Yeomanry but as I had now become heavily involved in farming in Pembrokeshire, and Hereford was 30 miles in the opposite direction, I turned it down and resigned from the TA. Later I regretted this but as things turned out I think it would have proved to be impracticable to continue.

I suppose I must have been living under considerable strain, as for several years I had been taking Purple Hearts, a barbiturate, but the doctor had recently prescribed a new and better pill. Soon after that, the press was full of reports of babies being born with appalling deformities to mothers who had been taking Thalidomide. Fortunately I did not suffer any harmful effects, though I do have restless calves which might date from that time.

Rebellion had broken out in Algeria and a very brutal civil war ensued for two years. De Gaulle had been recalled as Premier and, to the fury of the large French settler population, pulled the French army out of Algeria and granted them self-rule. Most French residents had to follow.

The Campaign for Nuclear Disarmament was in top gear with thousands of its supporters marching between London and the atomic bomb development centre at Aldermaston, which they continued to do for many years.

In 1959, my brother, Mark, now a barrister aged 30, married Sandra Joyce de Voeux, aged 24, at St Marks church, Chester Square. Also that year the Russians landed a rocket on the moon, which stirred the Americans up and, to their fury, Fidel Castro invaded and took over Cuba.

From 1959-61, in China, the megalomaniac Chairman Mao Tse Tung pursued The Great Leap Forward, which resulted in some 40 million Chinese starving to death.

On a lower-tech level, we called in a water-diviner to find water for the new buildings we had put up. He asked Rosemary to rub his rods between her hands and then walk up the field while he held the rods in his hands, pointing upwards. After she had walked 150 yards, the rods turned down sharply, and he shouted at her to stop. We dug a hole where she was, and, incredibly, found water at about 10 feet.

For a long time I had used a Massey Harris pickup baler,

which had an engine mounted on the drawbar for hay and straw harvesting. But I now got an Allis Chalmers PTO-driven Rotobaler, which made round bales, which were impervious to rain so they could be left for days in the field. It was all right when the crop was really dry and they were very popular in Kenya but if the hay was a bit damp it wrapped around the rollers and they were devilish trouble. I remember fighting with the damn thing with Bert till 10pm some nights. I then bought a Danish Combine harvester called Aktiv, which had a canvas pickup and delivered the corn into bags which a man tied and dropped to the ground. This was also fast if the crop were clean, but if there were any grass in it which got under the canvas, it would foul up in the most provoking way.

I did a bit of contracting with this machine and then drove it to Pembrokeshire where we used it for many years, until employing a contractor with a tanker combine, which handled the corn in bulk into trailers. At about this time roll-bars became compulsory for tractors, except for the owner, and soon after, cabs were fitted, giving protection from the weather for the first time. Repairs to machinery were done by Tom Price, the blacksmith at Penybont, who shod the horses and was the most delightful man; he would send his bill in only once a year.

There were a few wild pheasants on the farm, so, in another once-a-year event, we held a shoot party to which we invited 3 or 4 friends who would claim a mixed bag of about a dozen, plus pigeons and a hare. I was invited to shoot by Mike Lewelyn Bt, Brigadier, Grenadier Guards and Lord Lieutenant, by John Walsh (Lord Ormathwaite), and by Mervyn Bourdillon, later appointed Lord Lieutenant, where we would get a bag of 30 or 40, but there were no syndicate shoots rearing thousands of bird, as is common practice today.

1959 was a very dry summer and the reservoirs in the Elan Valley almost dried up, revealing the house under the water about which a well known book was written in 1900. The water from the reservoirs, which crossed our farm in huge underground pipes, went 80 miles to Birmingham by gravity, falling only about 70 feet, without any pumping.

In 1960 the girls went as weekly boarders to Anne Dearden at Hay-on-Wye whose governess taught about six girls.

We took the family to Crossgates church every Sunday. When the excellent vicar retired, theoretically the parish could choose his successor. I was asked to accompany the church warden to meet the bishop, who simply produced two names and more or less dictated to us which one we should choose. The appointed man proved a disaster and only lasted two years, to be succeeded by another, much more suitable vicar.

National Service ended, which was a pity. In my view, every man and woman should serve their country; it is the only way to teach discipline and manners to the young. In Switzerland every man is on the reserve for most of his life and keeps his gun at home. The country has never been invaded as a result

John Kennedy became the first Catholic to be elected President of the United States and his brother Robert was made attorney general. Their father had made an immense fortune by dubious means and had been American ambassador to Britain during the war.

I heard that my Aunt Rosie's husband, Ralph Barbour, who owned an electrical switchgear company, had bought a large farm in Shropshire, which he gave to his sons. It was a good way of avoiding death duties, and he let it to the son of a farmer living next door. He had earlier promised to let a farm to me but had turned down Greenways, as his estate agent appointed to survey it, had given a discouraging report, saying it was too wet. I wrote to say that I was disappointed he had not let it to me and he replied that he would buy another one for his daughter, Lynette if I put forward a suitable proposition. I suggested a farm of 200 acres, Honey Hook, 5 miles west of Haverfordwest, which he bought for £16,000. The agent then offered another of 30 acres about 2 miles away, near Broadhaven and asked if he wanted to buy that. I said it wasn't worth bothering with as I had just seen a farm of 300 acres, Treseissyllt at St Nicholas, near Fishguard advertised for sale. This had high cliffs above the sea along a third of its boundary and accessible bays at each end, and I thought it would be a wonderful place for summer holidays for the children. Ralph also bought this for Lynette for £20,000 and let it to me for a rental of 5% per annum, a good return on agricultural land in those days. It had been owned by a delightful bachelor, Lloyd Perkins, who'd been born there but spent his life as a solicitor in Cheltenham until he retired. Like many gentleman farmers, he was too easy-going and keen on a tipple to make a go of the farm, and it was pretty run down.

I employed Septimus Lloyd to manage Honey Hook, milking 30 Friesian Cows and growing 50 acres of barley, and at Treseissyllt employed a German ex-PoW, who was said to be something of an expert at growing early potatoes, then a very profitable crop in Pembrokeshire. Part of Tresiessyllt was in a bad way so I had it repaired, put in another bathroom and divided it into two, with three bedrooms in each half.

Farm workers were almost impossible to find. There were always few in Wales as, unless they inherited a farm, sons always took to education. No Englishman could be attracted to the tip of Wales. Since the war there had been full employment in England, although there was always a considerable number of work-shy on the dole.

In February we went skiing again to Kitzbuhl with the same party. Currency restrictions had at last been removed so we stayed at a better hotel and could afford lunch on the slopes. On our return we went down to Treseissyllt, taking two pupils, Raymond Taylor and Peter Firebrace. The German had ploughed 100 acres but then left. We lived in the back half of the house and Patrick and Joan Westmacott, who had sold their hill farm at Abergwesyn the year before and spent the winter in our cottage at Porth Clais, moved into the better front half.

Patrick had been working on Christmas Island, near Indonesia, and spent nearly 5 years in a Japanese prison camp in Sumatra where, fortunately, he had not been as badly treated as some. He had a beautiful daughter, Caroline who was then a top model.

We had to plant 40 acres of potatoes by hand, for which women or men on the dole were collected from Fishguard each morning. Then we sowed 60 acres of barley there and 40 acres at Castle Farm, Roch, 15 miles away, and 40 acres at Honey Hook.

Went home for April and May, and in June returned to lift the potatoes with casual labour again. In August we took the girls down for six weeks by the sea while I combined the corn on the three farms. Patrick had looked after a small flock of ewes and I bought store cattle.

In September Patrick left, having bought a small farm near Fishguard where he kept a few thousand hens under contract in batteries, then a recently introduced idea. On his departure we transferred ourselves to the front house and Raymond Taylor who married a local girl moved into the back.

In 1961, the Russians built a wall in Berlin to stop the Germans on their side escaping from communist rule to the free West. Many would be shot trying to escape over this wall, which remained as a barrier between East and West Berlin for 35 years until it was abolished by the Russian leader, Mikhail Gorbachev, under his policy of *glasnost* (openness) in 1989.

The Belgians suddenly pulled out of their vast colony of the Congo, despite that country's vast mineral wealth, including the principal source of uranium needed for atomic bombs and power stations. It had been the worst run colony ever, the natives kept in subjection by the most appalling brutalities. Now they turned on any Europeans, including many missionaries.

Mercenary forces, mostly South African, went in to stop the murders and looted the country. When at last the United Nations sent troops there, they eventually installed the appalling General Mobutu as President in 1965. He was to rule as a corrupt and brutal dictator for 30 years.

South Africa left the Commonwealth under the Boer leader Hendrick Verwoerd and introduced much stronger racial discrimination known as *apartheid* (separateness).

The Russian cosmonaut, Yuri Gagarin became the first man in space, and the contraceptive pill – which led women to become as promiscuous as men – was invented.

The Algerian insurrection against French rule had lasted about three years, with increasing brutalities on both sides. In 1962, de Gaulle pulled the army out and survived several assassination attempts. 500,000 had been killed and a million French inhabitants had to return to France. Forty thousand Algerians who had collaborated with the French were left behind and subsequently murdered.

Britain, under Harold Macmillan ('SuperMac') tried to join the Common Market but was rebuffed by de Gaulle.

In 1962 the Russians attempted to put atomic rockets in Cuba causing the Missile Crisis and posing a threat not only to America, but of another world war. Determined counter threats by President Kennedy, however, were sufficient to warn Khrushchev off and he took his rockets back to Russia, yet America had long kept planes of the Strategic Airforce in the air, carrying atomic bombs at the ready, for use if provoked by Russia.

In the summer 1962 the most prominent Old Radleian so far, Ted Dexter, was made captain of the England cricket team and the annual match of Gentlemen (amateurs) v Players (professionals) was abolished. From then on, all county cricketers were paid employees.

The following winter, we went skiing in St Moritz, travelling by air this time. Although we stayed at a modest hotel we could go *Thés Dansants* in the posh Palace Hotel. Kit Inglis and I tried to ski an Everest – 27,000 feet in a day. I'm not sure if we ever achieved it but on the last day I fell, breaking my fibula, and dislocated my ankle. I had to be brought down the mountain on a 'blood wagon' – a sledge pulled by the resort staff. The short ski boots then gave little protection to your ankles and the skis supplied were far too long. With my leg in plaster I was able to fly out the next day and for a month got around with a rubber tyre on my foot.

We went up to London for a coming out ball for Rosemary's niece Phillipa at Claridges Hotel. Back in Wales each year, dances in support of various organisations, such as Guide Dogs for the Blind, Red Cross and the Teme Valley Hunt, were held at the Metropole Hotel in Llandrindod Wells, owned by the ebullient Spencer Miles and later most successfully managed by his nephew, David Baird Murray. I often drank there of an evening.

The Gibson-Watts, Woosnams and Barstows also gave several dances for their daughters. David Gibson-Watt, a descendant of James Watt, inventor of the steam engine, won an MC and Bar as a major in the Welsh Guards and then became MP for Hereford. He was later offered the post of Welsh Secretary but, surprisingly, refused it.

When Rosemary had come out in 1942 she attended a Queen Charlotte's Ball, where all debutantes wore long white dresses, and was presented at court at a Buckingham Palace garden party in 1948.

In a London showroom I saw a nearly new Alvis drophead coupé which I bought, and ran for many years and was a delight in the summer. About that time also we bought a 16-foot sailing dinghy, *Whiffenpuff*, which we sailed around the coast from Aber Bach bay by Treseissyllt and also towed to Norfolk where we sailed all round the Broads.

On Boxing Day 1962 heavy snow fell. Rosemary suspected she was having a miscarriage so I drove her to London – just getting through the snow on the Cotswolds – where she spent several weeks in bed in the care of friends, Doctors Humphrey and April Kay, and could be seen by her gynaecologist.

That winter was to be the hardest since 1947. All the pipes at Treseissyllt froze and I had to reopen an old well to draw water with a bucket. I took Rosemary back to London at the end of June and Julian was born without complications in Guys Hospital.

Tessa went away to Lawnside School in Malvern. This was a rather old-fashioned establishment of about 80 girls, conveniently near, where she was happy enough. Incredible as it now seems, they didn't even sit A-levels for university entrance, which has been a cause of complaint for Tessa ever since. Of course, Rosemary had not been to university and, up until that time, few girls had.

I had now been farming 1,000 acres for three years but was over-stretched, so I sold 5 building plots at Castle Farm in Roch for the then good price of £250 each, although today they sell for 100 times that sum. I let the farm itself go for a reasonable profit to John Whitfield, who already had a large farm the other side of the castle, where his father, Lord Kenswood, a blind Labour Peer, lived. It had previously been owned by Lord St Davids, brother of Lord Milford and Lord Kilsant, all the sons of the vicar of Roch in the 1890s.

As nanny for the newly born Julian, we took on a delightful Danish *au pair*, Lone.

In 1963 a gang held up a mail train, getting away with a million pounds in the Great Train Robbery. Most were caught but little of the money was recovered. There was also a huge scandal when the War Minister, John Profumo, was found at his cottage at Cliveden with call girls Christine Keeler and Mandy Rice Davies, who also shared their charms with a Russian naval attaché, Ivanov. The girls' future was made, Macmillan nearly had to resign and the brilliant socialite Dr Stephen Ward, who had introduced them all, shot himself. Profumo has devoted his life to good works ever since.

A Liverpool pop group, the Beatles, took the country by storm, unfailingly attracting a mass of screaming adolescent girls wherever they went. Incredibly, in due course, one of them was knighted.

President John Kennedy was shot while being driven in an open limousine through Dallas and was succeeded by his deputy, Lyndon B Johnson. Kennedy's death was originally blamed on Lee Harvey Oswald, a former US Marine who had been apprehended not long after the assassination in a nearby cinema. He was killed two days later by a Dallas night club owner, Jack Ruby, while being moved from the city to the county jail. There has been speculation ever since as to who really did kill Kennedy. Among possible perpetrators were the mafia, Cubans, or Texan oil magnates in a conspiracy to murder the promiscuous Kennedy for hostile policies. His brother, Robert Kennedy, Attorney General, was also assassinated shortly afterwards. Later, the film star Marilyn Monroe, who was said to have had affairs with both John and Robert, committed suicide, or was done in.

The communist state of North Vietnam had invaded the south and American troops were sent to support the king, Norodom Sihanouk. This would lead to huge American involvement and the most appalling bombing and deforestation by chemicals of Vietnam and Laos over the next seven years.

In 1964 there was a general election, which was won by Labour under Harold Wilson, ending fourteen years of Tory rule. My brother Mark became Conservative MP for Runcorn and made his maiden speech in favour of the abolition of hanging, which has proved disastrous and led to all the armed robbery and huge number of murders today. He later recanted.

In 1965, India and Pakistan went to war over Kashmir, which had wrongly been incorporated in India at partition in 1947 –

it was governed by a Hindu Maharaja, yet practically all the population was Moslem. They have been in dispute and sometimes actively fighting over it ever since.

The Central African Federation of North and South Rhodesia and Nyasaland, which had lasted six years had broken up with the North as Zambia and Nyasaland as Malawi gaining self rule.

Southern Rhodesia, our last African colony, led by Prime Minister Ian Smith, who had been a British bomber pilot during the war, also wanted self rule and declared UDI – Unilateral Declaration of Independence. In my view, the Queen should have granted it but Harold Wilson vehemently opposed the idea and initiated economic sanctions. This actually achieved little because South Africa still traded with them and their manufacturing developed tremendously over the next few years.

In 1966, Indira Gandhi, daughter of Pandit Nehru, followed him as Prime Minister of India. Mao Tse Tung started the Cultural Revolution in China, in which fanatical young communists indoctrinated by his *Little Red Book*, attacked the intelligentsia, driving them out of the towns to work on farms faraway in the countryside. This madness lasted several years and led to the massacre of thousands, perhaps millions, caused famines, and set China back many, many years.

Oil was found in the North Sea, making this country rich ever since and probably saving it from revolution as it has enabled a vast number of unemployed to be sustained in idleness.

We had now entered the Swinging Sixties when sex was invented. The trial of the publishers of DH Lawrence's novel, *Lady Chatterley's Lover* had removed the ban on obscene publications; the American Kinsey's Report told us that everyone was doing it, or should be, and there were rallies of the young proclaiming the new utopia of Flower Power, Free Love and psychedelic drugs. The country was pervaded by rival motorcycle gangs of scrapping Mods and Rockers.

In Wales, the Forestry Commission were planting many thousands of acres of mountainsides with conifer forest, cutting drains to take the rainwater away. As a result, the rivers suffer flash floods, and serious flooding downstream in wet weather, with much reduced flow most of the time, which has ruined the fishing on many Welsh rivers.

In 1965 Fiona went to Lawnside and I became the representative of the Radnor and Brecon Country Landowners Association, to attend meetings at their HQ in London, and became Chairman of the branch. Only I and the member for Cheshire spoke against the general enthusiasm for joining the Common Market. Ever since, I have subscribed to the Campaign for Independent Britain, displaying Anti-EU posters on my vehicle and stickers on my correspondence,

Each August, I would buy about 300 Welsh lambs from a farm on Plynlimmon for £2.50 and send them down to Tresiessyllt where they grew well on grass, the climate was mild and the land dry. I would sell them in March for £5.

Colour television had been invented, introducing more programmes which effectively stopped all game playing and has undermined childhood ever since.

In 1962 we took the ferry to Cork and drove round Kerry in a hired car. At Kinsale we went shark fishing, picking up about a dozen mackerel in a few minutes at the harbour entrance and then out to sea for about 5 miles, where the boat stopped and we were given rods and harnesses. The wind started to get up and Rosemary felt very seasick. Another man and I caught a shark each of about 7 feet. Shark fishing turned out to be rather dull as they didn't put up a fight and were easily pulled alongside where they were gaffed and hauled aboard by the boatman.

At about 4pm the boatman started the engine, the boat mounted a roller and as it crashed down the other side there was a bang and a large crack opened at the front of the wheelhouse. Thereafter we corkscrewed over the waves and were massively relieved when land came in sight and we reached port.

When the new Austin Gypsy, the first diesel four-wheel drive came out, I bought one, and the local agents asked me to help with a promotional advertisement. The Gipsy was parked in a field with Rosemary perched on a shooting stick nearby, while I stood, gun raised as if shooting a pheasant, with Bert Watkins behind, as loader. I thought it was only for local advertising but it appeared in all the national papers; I should have demanded more than the £50

I was paid. The vehicle didn't sell well and was discontinued after a couple of years when Land Rover introduced their diesel model.

That summer, we went camping in the Gypsy in Ireland, carrying a dinghy on the roof. We drove around the spectacular country of Donegal and Connemara and sailed across to Achill Isle for two nights. We also visited the astonishing rock formation of the Giants Causeway.

In Belfast, the IRA were just beginning their reign of terror. It's interesting to note that all our best generals have been Ulstermen, descended from the Scots who settled there in Cromwell's time.

In January 1965 I went to Dublin to buy cattle at the sales and had arranged to get a day's hunting with the local hunt, of which Christopher T-P's brother-in-law, Jim Willson, who had married the daughter of Lord Curzon, was master. Tragically their son was to be drowned a few years later when canoeing on the Liffey. Unfortunately it snowed and I never got the hunting.

In 1966 the breathalyser test was introduced and has blighted entertaining in the country ever since. Amusingly, the only dining club member to be caught was a judge who sloshed a policeman, got arrested and had to resign from being a QC.

Throughout the sixties British racing drivers won all the championships but strikes by car workers and dockers ruined their industries and foreign cars flooded in as the British manufacturers went out of business.

That year we took all the family camping to the French Riviera. There was still not much traffic on the roads and we returned through Switzerland. This was the only time we ever had a family holiday abroad.

In 1967, a large oil tanker, the *Torrey Canyon*, ran aground off the North Cornish coast, spilling several hundred thousand gallons of oil. I never understood why they couldn't pump her out right away. Instead, incredibly, they spread many thousands of gallons of detergent on the oil, which only increased the pollution. After many days, when 25,000 dead birds had been picked up off the beaches, the vessel was bombed to set her on fire, but much too late. Many miles of beach remained polluted for several years.

That same year, abortion was made legal and women no

longer had to resort to back-street abortionists which had often ended in their deaths. That year also, professional tennis players were allowed at Wimbledon which had previously been amateurs only and de Gaulle again rebuffed Wilson's attempt to join the Common Market.

Supported by a vast arsenal of American tanks and planes, Israel launched the 6-days' war against Egypt, Jordan and Syria, who were preparing to attack. It was a dramatically successful counter-attack. From then until the present time, Israel has been the base of American power in the middle east, manipulated by the votes of Jewish financiers and politicians.

For the past seven years, Rosemary and I had stayed for five months each year at Treseissyllt. February was spent sowing early potatoes, April, with the children, sowing corn, June lifting the potatoes – always a traumatic time with prices altering overnight and the uncertainty of getting pickers – and August to September, with Rosemary and the children picnicking on the beach and bathing, while I harvested 100 acres of corn there and at Honey Hook. The price of barley was £18 per ton; with an average yield of 30 cwt per acre, there was not much profit in it.

During the rest of the year, I drove down to Pembrokeshire for a couple of nights about every fortnight to keep an eye on things. Regrettably, I'd had too puritan an upbringing to keep a mistress there. Besides, mistresses are expensive, and there's never enough surplus money in farming. Country life also demands respectability.

Chapter Six

For a long time, I'd had the feeling that a colonial life would suit me much better then farming in Britain. It had none of the labour problems and lonely life that were the lot of most British farmers. From my Indian days, I'd been left with a taste for a hot climate and it would be good to have a club within reach where one could play polo. And perhaps it would be possible to teach modern farming techniques to Africans.

I enquired at the Rhodesian embassy, but it was too late to get any kind of sponsored start. I then tried Nyasaland and was put in touch with Rolf Gardiner who owned an estate, Springhead, near Shaftsbury in Dorset. He was half German and before the war ran Anglo-German holiday camps to promote good relations. He owned a very profitable tea estate at Cholo and a rundown dairy farm near Blantyre, the capital of Malawi.

He was also something of an ecological nut. His son Christopher worked in a finance company in London but devoted most of his time to fund raising for Subud, a fringe religion started by an Indonesian mystic. They offered me the opportunity to go to their farm, managed by the elderly George Dow, now due for retirement. No doubt they were hoping I would buy it.

I sold my tenancy of Honey Hook for £11,000 to an early potato tycoon, Henry Beer, who would later go bankrupt, as did several other growers of earlies. I arranged with a neighbouring farmer for him to grow the potatoes and sow the corn at Treseissyllt. I also took on an Italian ex-POW, called Victor to look after the sheep and cattle, managed by a friend, Robert Thomas, who ran the local agricultural merchants. I flew out to Malawi in September 1967.

Before I had even arrived, George Dow had died and I found myself managing the farm, which had a dairy herd of 25 cows, and not much else. I was sharing the house with George's widow, Connie, who was an illegitimate daughter of a Bowes Lyon – an uncle of our Queen mother – who later visited her at Michiru farm near the airport. Connie was a neurotic who kept her storeroom locked from her houseboys.

There were about 15 African employees who did very little for very little pay, but were always cheerful. If an animal died they got it for meat but had to pay a small sum for the carcass to discourage them from killing others. In Blantyre, a pleasant colonial town at about 3,000ft, built around Livingston's mission, a supermarket sold meat for Europeans on one counter and meat for 'boys' and dogs on another.

There was a long-unoccupied house on the farm in the middle of the bush on a dirt road to Blantyre. I got this done up and in February, Rosemary flew out in a new VC10, bringing Julian, aged four with her. Mlombwa House had a fine view to the hills, and the brilliant stars in the clear African nights were a wonderful sight.

I had an Austin Minimoke, which I once drove 80 miles on dirt tracks to lake Nyasa, re-named lake Malawi. I realised afterwards that this had been a pretty risky thing to do as I had no telephone or help if I broke down, although I did carry a small pistol in my pocket in case of a hold-up.

I also climbed Mlange on the Mozambique border and was surprised to find Portuguese and Africans dancing together in the hotel where I stayed. The Portuguese, like the Dutch had always integrated more than the British but it did not do them much good in the end. Staying with Jimmy Trotter, the manager of the tea estate at Cholo, I was given a copy of the new, revolutionary Playboy for night-time reading. At that time it was banned in Malawi, as were mini-skirts, by the puritanical dictator Dr Hastings Banda, once a British GP, who was to rule increasingly dictatorially for 30 years.

Mlombwa house was surrounded by exotic birds and we occasionally heard leopards at night. The rainy season had started and each evening there were spectacular thunderstorms which turned the road to very slippery mud. This made driving home after drinking or dinner in Ryall's Hotel in Blantyre a nervous business as I did not fancy walking home in the dark with leopards about.

Being near the equator, days and nights were of equal length and there was practically no twilight. At about 6pm it suddenly fell dark. We had a house boy who cooked quite well, a night-watchman and a garden boy who, when the rains had finished, would collect the bathwater for the vegetables, which practically grew overnight.

The boys lived nearby in mud huts with no amenities. There was also a half-caste, Ivan, who was tractor driver/mechanic and looked after the generator, which provided electricity and pumped water from the well.

I had divided the house in two and an Irish woman lived in the other half with two grandchildren who were playmates for Julian. She drove them to a multiracial nursery school in Blantyre and we collected them at midday, often having a swim and lunch at the European club.

A Catholic priest visited her occasionally, for the good of her soul, she said, but we suspected more earthy reasons. The capital Zomba, thirty miles away at 4,000ft, was cooler. All the Government administration lived there, at the foot of Zomba mountain, which was covered in fine fir plantations planted by the forestry service. There, Rosemary had a friend from childhood, Robert Garnett, who had a comfortable and I should think undemanding job as military attaché.

When we went there for lunch we swam in the high Commissioner's swimming pool. We also made friends with old colonial residents Robin and Esme Thornycroft and David Henderson, who had tobacco farms nearby.

And we visited the tobacco farm where Rosemary's father and half brother, Frank Delves Broughton had lived until Frank died of blackwater fever in 1913.

Her father had come home in 1914 to join the army, leaving the farm in charge of an agent, who managed to lose it all. Malawi was the biggest recipient of British aid funds but, as was often the result in Africa, little reached the poor – everything was spent on armed forces, a football stadium for parades, a palace in Blantyre for Dr Banda, and a new capital city built at Lilongue. Africans would pass our house staggering down from Mlombwa mountain with loads of charcoal on their backs. Rolf Gardiner considered this wicked deforestation, and I started to fall out with him when I said that it was the sensible way to collect timber for firewood as the trees grew again from the stumps.

In the evenings we went to the club – white only members, and by election – near Chileka airport two miles away, where we would play tennis, swim and have supper. Twice we drove the 100 miles to the lake and camped on the shore at Monkey Bay.

At nearby Cape McClear, the flying boats of British Imperial Airways had touched down en route to South Africa before the war, when only the rich could fly. The road was tarmacked down the middle with graded dirt each side. When meeting a vehicle it was a matter of brinkmanship as to who would blink first and leave the tarmac.

Apart from tea in the Cholo hills, tobacco was the only profitable farming but the life was free and with labour so plentiful and cheap, it seemed possible to do anything.

I made bricks, formed in a wooden frame, dried in the sun and then built into a kiln of several thousands, covered with earth and fired by wood for a couple of days. It was profitable as there was a building boom on.

The population was then four million, poor but reasonably self-sufficient. Now it is twelve million, and the people are much poorer, many suffering from famine. No birth control was practised as Dr Banda, like many African tyrants, considered contraception a European conspiracy. Now about 20% have aids or are orphaned. When Dr Banda drove by in his limousine with outriders, everyone, including Europeans, had to remove their hats or risk being beaten up. Fortunately I never faced the situation.

In April, we drove in a large old Dodge car 300 miles over dirt roads through Mozambique, where we were warned not to stop, to Salisbury, the capital of Rhodesia, prosperous under the illegal rule of Ian Smith, who had locked up African opposition politicians.

We looked at two girls schools and visited a farm where we bought eight horses for a modest sum as a widow wanted to get rid of them. Then we drove to the Western highlands around Umtali, where we looked at the Eagle Boys School, which, in a few years, was to be destroyed when the whole area became a battleground against Mugabe's insurgents.

I had come to Rhodesia to buy cattle as there were none to be bought in Malawi. With a serious drought going in, cattle there were very cheap. We drove on south to Fort Victoria where we were chased by a white rhinoceros in a game park.

We also visited the Zimbabwe ruins. Large rough stone buildings of unknown origin but not, as claimed, evidence of an early civilisation. Julian and I slept in the Dodge, Rosemary on a camp bed outside. She was disconcerted to be told later that she was bait for a leopard.

We spent a couple of nights in the Low Veldt of sugar plantations, which was very hot and the home of the warlike Matabele. The majority of the country was High Veldt and, at about 4,000 ft, it was too cold for the natives. It had been very thinly populated by the Shona tribe when the visionary Cecil Rhodes acquired it by treaty and British settlers moved in about 1890.

It was very similar to the empty Kenya highlands where British aristocrats, seeking a free life, settled after the Great War. Rhodesia had been run for many years as a model and fairly liberal colony, where another 240,000 less aristocratic Europeans then lived. Once we crossed Beit Bridge over the Limpopo river into South Africa we found strict racial segregation, with 'Whites Only' notices in the parks, on the beaches and in trains. There were separate counters in the shops and banks. Though there was a large Indian and mixed race population, all were registered by race and any intermarriage was forbidden by law.

We stayed several nights in Johannesburg with my younger sister Rachel, who had been a nurse at Great Ormond Street Children's' Hospital during the war, then Sister at Westminster Children's' Hospital and afterwards ran a nursery school. In 1955 she went out to Rhodesia, became an air hostess with Central African Airways, which at that time was quite a glamorous job, and married Barry Crewe Sloane, the manger of a civil engineering company with whom she had three children – Jane, Christopher and Nigel. Rachel devoted much time to working for the Red Cross and a charitable hospice.

My elder sister, Sylvia, also lived in Jo'burg. At the beginning of the war she had trained at St Thomas's Hospital, my father paying a premium of £70 for the privilege, and became a sister in the Queen Alexandra Nursing Service in England. Later she was posted to India and then, after the Japanese surrender in Singapore, to Sumatra.

After the war she joined the Colonial Nursing Service and was matron of hospitals in Zambia and Rhodesia, where she married Jack Knowles, who had served in the South African army in North Africa and was then managing a holiday camp near the Victoria Falls. They had a daughter Elizabeth and Sylvia was Sister at a hospital.

Jack had been married before and had a young daughter Maureen. He was then Bursar of St. John's College. The attractive and capable Maureen is now tragically incapacitated, as a result of a lifetime of smoking.

I was taken by Barry Sloane to the prestigious Rand Club, which at that time did not admit blacks or ladies, and we spent a day at a country club which was the centre of their lives.

We drove on east to the Kruger National Park for two days' game watching, and thence back to Beit Bridge and Rhodesia. Near Bulawayo there was a huge ranch owned by Leibigs Meat Co Ltd. of which my cousin, Kenneth Carlisle, was Managing Director in London. The ranch was called Fray Bentos after their Argentinian base.

Here, all the cattle were living on the leaves of the bushes and the manager was happy to sell me 40 of them. He gave us a bed for the night and sold us a Weimarana puppy which we called Fray. Next day we climbed up to Cecil Rhodes' grave on top of a hill in the Matopo Hills.

When we reached Tete in Mozambique, on the Zambezi river, cars were queuing for the ferry and moving on slowly. I allowed a gap to open in front and the car behind jumped the queue. I got out and angrily expostulated with the Portuguese driver. There was a policeman standing nearby and somehow he managed to claim that I had hit him and I was taken to a court where, incredibly, a prosecuting lawyer and a magistrate soon appeared and I was convicted, with a small fine.

There was not much love lost between the British and the Portuguese, but we could certainly take a leaf out of their book on how to administer summary justice, instead of the appalling rigmarole, delay and expense of justice in this country.

Meanwhile night had fallen and Rosemary had taken the car across on the last ferry. She was very relieved when I was carried across in a launch after threatening them with the retribution of the British Empire, but we had a nervous drive of 200 miles on a road through the bush.

Arriving back at Michuru after three weeks away, we found the horses had been delivered by rail. Several were not yet broken in,

Kingston Russell House
Home of George Gribble 1908 - 1927

Henlow Grange, Herts
Home of George & Norah Gribble 1890 - 1908

Mary Carlisle née Gamon
1894 – 1985

Philip Edmund Carlisle
1889 – 1980
Cheshire Yeomanry 1915-1917

Edmund Paul Carlisle
Rajputana Rifles 1942-1946

Julian Royds Gribble V.C.
Captain Royal Warwickshire Regiment
1897-1918

Capt. E.P. Carlisle in India

Trekking in Himalayas 1943

Wana, South Wazirstan 1943

Author in centre

Rajputana Riflemen

On Column 1943

Road to Wana

Only 8 officers in Bn –
Author right front

Rosemary Carlisle
Born: 1923
née Thursby-Pelham

Danyralt, home of
Rosemary Thursby-Pelham

Wedding Day 1950

so I got to work on them with a friend from Blantyre. One evening, when Rosemary and I were riding in the bush on the two quietest animals, we found ourselves on a very narrow path in a gully and Rosemary's lost its footing, rolling down the bank. She came off, of course, and her head was bleeding profusely. Worried that she would faint and with darkness coming on, I just managed to get her up to the dirt road and ran to get the car to take her to hospital where she required about 10 stitches.

The cattle had also arrived but, disgracefully, had not been watered in transit and had been left standing in the wagon in a siding for a day. Three of them had died. I found the Government veterinary department, which had a large farm, had also followed my advice and bought a large number of cattle from the same ranch. In fact, I'd been offered the job of managing their dairy farm at the new capital Lilongue, but politely refused it.

Rosemary went home in July. About that time Christopher Gardiner came out and I agreed to buy the Michuru Company but, shortly after, his father said he would only give me a tenancy of the farm. This was useless because only as the director of a British company did one have any security against arbitrary ejection from the country and I only had a temporary employment visa, so I turned it down.

The principal expatriate company in Malawi was Lonrho, run by the buccaneering "Tiny" Rowland. He had bought tea estates, a clothing factory, a brewery and car dealerships and had a large sugar plantation in the Lower Shiree Valley. I was friendly with their manager, Jack Wemys and, as Michuru farm was very bare, arranged to send about 50 young cattle down to graze the waste sugar leaf with an educated boy, Cyrus, to look after them.

In August I flew home for the Harvest at Treseissyllt. At Greenways, Bert Watkins had managed very well looking after 20 suckler cows and a flock of 250 ewes. Much of the summer he was engaged in making silage using a tractor mounted forage harvester. Grass was first blown into a trailer and then transferred to a pit with a buckrake. We sold him his nice bungalow for £1,500. It would sell for 100 times that sum today.

We had also sold off 80 acres at the far end of the farm to make it more manageable and to pay the school fees, then about £600 a year each.

Meanwhile in the wider world, in 1968 there had been a serious outbreak of foot and mouth disease in Cheshire and Shropshire which was kept under control. There were violent student riots in Paris supported by communist workers and anti-American Vietnam war protest marches, which were brutally suppressed by the police.

The Russians sent tanks into Prague and took over Czechoslovakia after an anticommunist government had elected Alexander Dubcek Prime Minister. In America, Tricky Dicky Nixon become Republican President after the Democrat LB Johnson.

Biafra tried to secede from Nigeria giving rise to a vicious civil war that was to last three years until the Biafrans were defeated by famine with the loss, it is said, of over a million lives. The United Nations did nothing to intervene.

British troops were pulled out of Aden after four years of insurrection.

The brilliant MP, Enoch Powell finished off his political prospects by a speech predicting 'Rivers of Blood' if immigration was allowed to continue unchecked. He may well be proved right yet.

Tessa had left Lawnside where she had been unable to take the A-level exams which would have enabled her to go to a university. On the advice of Gabbitas and Tring Educational experts we sent her to a finishing school at Paddock Wood owned by a French woman. There were many foreign students there and she got good French but no qualifications, so it was something of a disaster about which she later complained.

Meanwhile Julian was going to the local school by bus.

In September I flew back to Malawi to find the Gardiners had had the dairy herd and also a very good road grader, which I had bought at a sale, removed from Michuru to their tea estate and Mlombwa house was barred to me, so I went down to the lower Shiree Valley and lived in a tiny hut having meals in Lonrho's mess. It was very hot indeed, over 90°F during the day and sticky at night as I had no fan.

At the sugar factory, chain hooks swung through the air unloading the cane and the Africans wore no safety helmets until I complained. Life was cheap!

I managed to get about 20 acres of land and planted cotton which did very well. The Dodge had been changed for a Land Rover and occasionally I would go up to Blantyre where I would stay with Gerald Acton, the elderly District Commissioner. He said I had the distinction of being known as the last of the gentlemen farmers, but I was certainly not living a very gentlemanly life then.

One night I went out with a crocodile hunter, which was illegal, as most had been shot out and they were supposed to be protected. The motor boat had a searchlight which reflected their eyes in the reeds at the side of the river channels. He shot one, but it was very small. Someone had obviously split on me, as driving to Blantyre next day I was stopped and questioned by an officer though, fortunately, I was carrying nothing.

Lonrho had experimented with growing 50 acres of wheat and were using a trailed Massey combine harvester, like the one I'd first had at Greenways, but they couldn't make it work properly. I was fool enough to show them how when I should have bought the crop as it yielded well.

Dr Banda was becoming increasingly megalomaniac. He had formed a corps of Young Pioneers, commanded by his principal lieutenant and suspected mistress, who terrorised the population. He had also imprisoned any politician who opposed him.

I was getting a bit reckless and in March wrote to the Rhodesian newspaper which was sold in Malawi, protesting about detention without trial. I was called for an interview with the head of security – incredibly, an Englishman – and was told my work permit would not be renewed after it expired in September. It is astonishing how tuppenny ha'penny countries can say who can come in and freely deport people when this country allows in hundreds of thousands of immigrants uncontrolled and is unable to deport any when defended by crooked lawyers.

I bought an old Minimoke and had a guard fitted under the sump, intending to drive across Tanzania and on through Kenya to the Sudan, then still peaceful, but in May, Rosemary begged me to come home as she did not trust the man growing early potatoes in partnership at Treseissyllt.

I therefore tried to sell the cattle to Lonrho but the manager would only offer a very low price so I rashly sold them to an African on credit and flew home intending to return after the potatoes were lifted. I did get paid in the end but it took a long time and the help of a Blantyre solicitor.

During the past winter, the Prime Minister, Harold Wilson had announced that British troops would be pulled out of our bases and airfields in the Persian Gulf. This was disastrous and even against the wishes of the small Gulf States which had always been under British protection against Iran and Iraq. It removed British influence and later resulted in the unnecessary Gulf War after Iraq's invasion of Kuwait. Two Labour MPs, Woodrow Wyatt and Desmond Donelly resigned from the party over the issue and Donelly, MP for Pembrokeshire, formed a new Social Democratic Party. I hoped to stand as a candidate for him at a bye-election in Stoke-on-Trent but was not chosen.

They made a fair showing but the seat was won by Nicholas Winterton for the Conservatives, a right-wing MP after my own heart. At a general election a year or so later Donelly put up three candidates but they had little success after which he inexplicably and tragically committed suicide. Without proportional representation, fringe parties never get anywhere and are really only pressure groups, as most notably has been the Green Party, whose policies, nevertheless, have been adopted by all parties.

Ever since the war British politics have been bedevilled by the Liberal Party, which has meant that Governments are elected by less than half the population and in practice we have had Socialism from all parties.

If only we had two parties, as the Americans do, the Government would represent a majority of the population and we would be free of tactical voting.

During that year, my brother, Mark and his wife Sandra produced a baby, Vanessa Lucy, who was to be their only child.

In 1969, the Americans at last pulled ahead of the Russians and put men on the moon in two trips. It turned out to be a fairly useless achievement whose only purpose was prestige, at vast expense when so many people in the world were near starvation.

Anglo-French aircraft companies produced the brilliant, supersonic Concorde, which made its maiden commercial flight to Bahrain on 17th January 1976 carrying a full complement of 100 passengers. Fares in Concorde were always high, but it never operated profitably. However, it was to remain in service until 24th October 2003, its last flight taking it from London's Heathrow airport to Airbus UK at Filton, where it is preserved.

The Americans approach to the future of air travel was orientated towards low cost, subsonic travel, which gave rise to Boeing's wide-bodied 747 with a capacity of 385 people. Known as the Jumbo Jet, it went into service in 1970 laying the foundation for cheap mass tourism which has bedevilled the world ever since and led to uncontrolled immigration.

The admirable Prince Charles, who had endured a Spartan education at Gordonston when he should have been sent to Eton, was now in command of a navel vessel. He was invested as Prince of Wales by the Queen at Caernarfon Castle. However, the Welsh people showed little enthusiasm for their new prince and the Free Wales Army protested by burning down a few holiday cottages belonging to English ex-pats.

About the same time, the Welsh Nationalist party were making ever more vocal demands in defence of their language. As a result, to placate them, all place names and road signs were duplicated in English and Welsh, to the confusion – and even danger – of motorists ever since. Also since then, all official and many commercial documents, regulations and accounts have been duplicated in Welsh at vast expense, and completely pointlessly as there are no Welsh speakers who are not totally bilingual. In any case, Welsh is only spoken regularly among farming communities of the coastal counties and Carmarthenshire since the language was outlawed in schools during the C19th.

The death penalty for murder was abolished and the carrying of guns – never known before – by robbers and violent criminal gangs has flourished ever since.

This also encouraged the IRA to attack Protestants and the British Army in Ulster when they knew they would not swing for their murders. As a result nearly 1,000 soldiers have died and at least as many police and civilians, the total now some 3,500.

In May 1970, we drove across Europe to Austria, staying in Vienna and visiting the famous Riding school of Lipizzaner dressage horses. We reached the Hungarian frontier at dusk and handed in our passports for transit visas allowing us 48 hours stay to cross the country.

This was part of the Iron Curtain dividing free Western Europe from the communist East, whose people so loved their regime that they had to be prevented from leaving! A grim border post beneath a tower was manned by gun-toting soldiers. Here we waited and waited, getting increasingly worried that they had found we had given shelter to a refugee family after the bloody rebellion in 1956 against Russian domination. Not another car appeared travelling either way. At last, after two hours, we were allowed to proceed to a small town just across the frontier where we intended to stay the night, only to find that we could not get a bed there, so had to drive on about 80 miles to the provincial city. The journey, over rough roads, took us through villages where there was no light of any sort to be seen and was marked by a total absence of any other traffic. We arrived at about midnight. In the large hotel, dinner was still available and a few party officials were there, dancing with their young mistresses.

Next morning, a Sunday, we walked around the town and came across a large church filled to overflowing. Communist police stood outside, no doubt watching for dissidents.

Our next stop was Budapest where we went to the tourist office and asked to stay in a pension to meet some local people. This turned out to be a flat in a tower block where we found an elderly couple in obvious poverty and very reserved – or suspicious. Budapest is a fine city with the Danube flowing through the middle and fine parliament buildings, a copy of Westminster, beside the river. After dinner at a good restaurant, we took a bottle of Slivovitz back to our host and the atmosphere changed completely.

He had been an officer in the Austro-Hungarian army during the Great War, spoke good English and bemoaned the fact that since the last war he was unable to get *The Times*.

In the morning, after eating, I fear, their only two eggs, and bidding a touching farewell to our hosts, we departed for Belgrade where we also stayed with families and, at breakfast, had to drink toasts in Slivovitz to Marshall Tito and Churchill.

Yugoslavia was mostly a wild mountainous country and still communist although Tito had distanced himself from the Soviet Union. All factories and services were nationalised but free enterprise prevailed in smaller businesses, and the country was fairly prosperous. Hotels were basic. They had extensive menus but practically all the dishes were off, except omelettes. We drove up the Dalmatian coast to Dubrovnic, which is a quite beautiful walled city, where young people paraded along a street in the evenings, bedecked in their best clothes looking for mates. Most of the tourists we saw were German. I was amazed that any German could show his face there after the atrocities of the war only twenty years before.

We had a night at a casino in Slovenia, which had been on the German side during the war and whose Ustazi had been as vicious as the German SS, running similar concentration camps. At Trieste at the end of the war, one of the most shameful episodes in our history had occurred. The British Army, having accepted the surrender of the Cossack corps of 40,000 men – with some women and children – who had fought for Germany, hoping to liberate their country from the communist Soviet Union, packed them onto trains and transported them back to Russia, where they were all shot or imprisoned in the Gulags. It was claimed that our Government were fearful that the Russians would hold hostage British prisoners they had liberated in East Germany but this was most improbable. The truth of the matter was not disclosed until many years later in a book by Count Tolstoy who blamed Brigadier Toby Lowe, now Lord Addington for the atrocity. Addington sued for libel and won ruining Tolstoy. Never trust the British courts!

Bavaria was quite beautiful; I should say the nearest thing to fairyland. And Munich was a beautiful town where we went up to Bertesgaden, Hitler's mountain retreat. I also visited Dachau concentration camp. It was set up in 1935 as a camp for political prisoners and, though never an extermination camp, was found to contain many thousands of dead or dying inmates when liberated by the British in 1945. Typhus had broken out and the bodies were bulldozed into mass graves. Local Germans were compelled to walk round and view the atrocities. We also visited the Ruritanian castle of the eccentric king Ludwig of Bavaria.

Having seen the success of Lonrho in Malawi, I entrusted my African money to Tiny Rowland with excellent results. Somehow I never got back to Malawi and had had to leave behind an old hammer gun of my grandfather's, which I had taken out without trouble in 1967 but could not then be taken on an aircraft. Today you can hardly even carry a pair of scissors onto an aeroplane.

Chapter Seven

Our ex-POW farm-worker, Victor had gone back Italy and not returned. His place at Treseissyllt was taken by another Italian, Rafael Colella – the son of a POW – who was accompanied by his wife Rosy, two girls and a Mongol son. Rafael was to work loyally for me for thirty years and Rosy was always the best potato picker of all.

We bought a half-ton sailing yacht, Lara, which we kept at Lawrenny and sailed in the Milford Haven estuary. We had evening parties on the beach at Aber Bach and occasionally tried seine netting for sewin but never with the success of the first time at Whitesands. Later we sold Lara and bought a Dory with outboard motor for water skiing.

In those days I always kept a sheep dog as well as a Labrador. One was very wild and chased some sheep over the cliffs above the sea and we had a spectacular rescue by a helicopter from the Fleet Air Arm base at Brawdy. Fortunately, I never got charged for it. Most of the sheep dogs got run over as they *will* bite at the tyres of cars. We took Petula and the ponies down for summer holidays and Julian's godmother, Katherine Lloyd, would also often come with a horse. Her husband, Grouse, of Cynghordy – Rosemary's second cousin – was for many years Master of the Towy hounds and their son, John later inherited the estate near Llangadoc. The girls were always keen on riding but Julian never took to it.

In 1970, the Conservatives won the election and Edward Heath became Prime Minister with Sir Alec Douglas Home as Foreign Secretary. To my mind it should have been the other way round but Home was tagged with the 'Grouse Moor' image, wrongly considered unacceptable in these democratic days.

Heath was a good musician and sailor, winning the Fastnet race, but a disastrous PM. He appointed my brother, Mark as Parliamentary Secretary at the Home Office and Anthony Barber as

Chancellor of the Exchequer, who, saying he was going to stimulate the economy, encouraged the banks to lend, allowed the creation of several fringe banks, and let inflation rip.

In 1971, ex-King's African Rifles Sergeant Idi Amin seized power in a coup in Uganda, and ordered out all Indian tradesmen, of whom 50,000 came to this country. Amin inaugurated in Uganda a reign of terror and destruction in what had once been the jewel of Africa under our colonial administration. The premature end of the colonial regimes in Africa has resulted in appalling corruption and millions dead through war and starvation.

On March 26th 1971, East Pakistan declared itself an independent nation, Bangladesh, thereby triggering a bloody conflict with the forces of the Central Government of Pakistan that was to end after India stepped in (the third Indo-Pakistan war) to support Bangladesh. Thus, on the 16th December 1971, a new country, Bangladesh was born and was soon recognised by most other nations.

In Egypt, Colonel Nasser died and was succeeded by the more moderate General Sadat. The Americans now put a vehicle on the moon at astronomical expense and without any useful purpose. The Rhodesian government, under Ian Smith was being heavily attacked by 'freedom fighters' based in Mozambique and Zambia under the command of Robert Mugabe.

At home, Fiona left Lawnside in 1971 and went to the grammar school in Llandrindod Wells where she could take A-levels. Julian went to Abberley prep school near Worcester. This was a very happy school, but it didn't do to be seen to be trying too hard and he just scraped through common entrance to Radley.

That winter we gave a dance for the girls with about 120 guests in a marquee at Greenways. Tessa had gone to London in a secretarial job and was living with her friend, Barbara Kreiser. I went up to London and bought a small house for the girls in Kilmaine Road, Fulham with no bathroom and an outside lavatory, for £7,500. A generous council offered a grant of £2,500 towards modernisation and I set to work with the help of a mason, adding two rooms in two stories at the back with a bathroom, and central heating throughout.

Rosemary reluctantly agreed to sell her Porth Clais cottage at

St. Davids for the modest sum of £5,000. It had been earning only £200 per year in holiday lets and we had had to do some decoration and attend to the garden each year. It appeared on television this year being sold to some lunatic for £230,000. Admittedly, it had been extensively renovated and has a prime position overlooking Porth Clais harbour.

The girls would sell their house ten years later for £130,000; today it would fetch nearer £250,000. Such is the crazy price of housing through so many in the countryside being bought for second homes by overpaid city slickers, that the young cannot afford to buy them, and a shortage of housing in the towns because so many are occupied by single mothers married to the state or men with no intention of getting married. The situation has been aggravated by a flood of immigrants from all corners of the world, encouraged by liberal politicians, who have turned this once proud country into multicultural Britain.

In 1972, the PM, Edward Heath traitorously railroaded this country into the European Community, without consulting the people by election or referendum. It was a move opposed by the Labour Party and against the wishes of a majority of the population. It is incredible that the Queen allowed it.

Decimalization of our currency was introduced; 1p replaced 2½d, with the effect of putting up the price of everything. The ensuing shambles over decimalising weights and measures still goes on. Kilos are only just being accepted, and farmers still prefer acres to hectares. Kilometres are still rejected, because we have kept the mile, like the Americans, and measure speed in miles per hour. Absurdly, though, we buy petrol in litres, and measure a car's economic performance in miles per gallon.

My brother Mark was made Minister of State at the Home Office with responsibility for the police. He also approved the building of new prisons, which has increased ever since, now so comfortable with televisions in every cell and such good food that many inadequates re-offend simply to return. Except for dangerous criminal lunatics, shutting people up in prisons is disastrous as they only meet more criminals and many come out worse and with a chip on their shoulder. It also disrupts their families and is hugely expensive. If they were birched in the town square there would be no more crime wave. Alternatively, as many of them are just bored and would make good soldiers they could be put in the army, following the practice of National Service.

Mark invited us to watch the Armistice Day parade from the window of the Home Office. There was a drinks party afterwards, which I thought most unsuitable. It was there I met Mrs Thatcher, who was then Minister of Education and asked her why she did not introduce loans instead of grants for university education. She replied because it would lose the party votes! Such is the weakness of democratic government.

After many years of terrorism by Greek inhabitants, our colony Cyprus was granted independence under Archbishop Makarios. A United Nations force moved in to protect the Turkish minority and has been there ever since. Nevertheless, we kept our military base, our most important since evacuating the Suez Canal bases.

In 1973, accompanied by Fiona and Julian, we took a long wheel-based Land Rover by ferry to Bilbao and went camping across Spain, visiting the Prada in Madrid and the Moorish city of Toledo, then on to Algeciras and over to Morocco.

We drove over the beautiful Atlas Mountains to the desert, where there were Touaregs on camels, and then by rough tracks to Casablanca, finally taking the coastal route to Tangier. It had been our intention to go on to Gibraltar, but the Spanish had shut the frontier, so we left the car in Tangier and took a ferry across.

In Gibraltar we spent three nights with Rosemary's brother, Christopher, who was then a Brigadier in command of the garrison. I flew directly home from Gibraltar to lift the early potatoes at Treseissyllt, leaving Rosemary, Fiona and Julian to return to Tangier to collect the car and drive to Ceuta to take the ferry to Algeciras. Rosemary was worried that drugs might have been hidden in the Land Rover but got through customs without trouble and drove back across Spain and France to Le Havre.

Meanwhile in 1973, the Americans negotiated a peace in Vietnam. In fact, after dropping more bombs than during the whole of World War II and suffering casualties that amounted 57,685 killed and 153,303 wounded – not to mention forests destroyed by chemical defoliants – they were forced to withdraw.

An army coup by colonels had usurped the Greek Government.

The socialist president of Chile, Salvador Allende, had been overthrown and murdered by General Augusto Pinochet, who was supported by the American CIA under the direction of the megalomaniac Henry Kissinger. The CIA had disgracefully trained the intelligence services of the South American countries in brutal interrogation techniques.

And the Israelis launched a pre-emptive strike against Egypt, Syria and Jordan, gaining victory in six days in the Yom Kippur war, again armed by Americans directed by the Jewish Kissinger. As a result, the Arab states introduced an oil embargo, which increased the price of oil four times and led to massive inflation.

Princess Anne unwisely married Captain Mark Phillips. Subsequently she had two children, rode in the Olympic team, was divorced from Mark Phillips and married a naval officer. If the monarchy is to survive, it is fatal for members of the Royal family to marry commoners.

The coal miners called a national strike, which stopped supplies to power stations. The Prime Minister, Edward Heath weakly failed to confront them and placed all industry on a three-day week. This stemmed from fatal acts of nationalisation imposed on the mining industry and railways by the Labour Government after the war that, whilst they favoured the owners of the mines and railways, who were delighted to be bought out, put power into the hands of the unions to hold the country to ransom ever after.

The strike finished Heath and saw the Conservatives lose the next general election in 1974 to the Labour party, led by Harold Wilson, PM once again.

In America, Richard Nixon was forced to resign as President, over the Watergate scandal and was succeeded by Gerald Ford.

The flamboyant Lord Lucan shot his children's nanny – mistaking her for his wife – and disappeared. Despite many reported sightings of him, he has never been found.

Death duties, which had been raised to the punitive level of 80% by the labour government after the war and resulted in the sale of many landed estates, were now reduced to the more reasonable figure of 40%. Now called Inheritance Tax, it is just state robbery, and encourages intricate evasion schemes by the less scrupulous.

We were invited by Shirley and John Wilson to stay in Lisbon, where he was British Ambassador. His father had been Churchill's doctor throughout the war and had been given a peerage, taking the title Lord Moran. They took us to the harbour to see a Polaris nuclear submarine; it was surprisingly spacious inside.

We hired a car in Lisbon and drove around Portugal, which then was mostly cork trees. These, however, are now fast disappearing as many products once exclusively made of cork, are now produced from synthetic materials.

At Oporto we stayed a night with a director of Cockburns Port Co, who took me to the weekly lunch at the factory house.

That year early potatoes had really come good and I had made about £10,000 on them – serious money in those days when a workman was only paid £16 a week. Instead of going round the world and enjoying it we decided to start a pedigree herd of beef cattle

The Hereford breed of cattle, which had been exported to much of the world over the past 200 years, was out of favour as they had been over-bred for the pampas, got over fat with a yellow fat and often produced insufficient milk to rear their calves well. Foreign cattle were all the rage.

I was interested in the Murray Grey breed, which had swept Australia, the result of crossing a white Shorthorn bull with black Aberdeen Angus cows, and bought two heifers and a bull, for about £3,000. I also bought 20 Aberdeen heifers from a farm in Wiltshire to grade up over two generations by mating with the bull.

Charolais, Simmental and Limousin particularly, imported about that time have largely replaced the old British breeds as they have less fat on the carcass but the Murray Greys proved disappointing, being slow growing and I and most other enthusiasts gave them up after a few years.

We went up to Scotland for two weeks in a camper van to visit the principal importer near Perth and met Lord Inchcape's factor who took me deer stalking in Glen Isla, where he and a ghillie were shooting hinds. I was allowed to shoot a stag and we had the antlers for a hat rack thereafter.

Gone were the days of walking up mountains with ponies, we drove up on a halftrack and there was not much hard work to it. We also drove round Mull and camped in a valley with rutting stags roaring all round us.

For several years Tessa and Fiona had worked during winter months as chalet girls in skiing resorts as, having a house and one or two lodgers, they were fairly independent. Otherwise, Tessa worked mostly for travel agencies and Fiona did lunches for company directors. The charming Katherine de Courcy lived with them. Her father, Kenneth published the Intelligence Digest, full of articles on how the Russians were plotting world domination from behind the Iron Curtain, which used to scare Rosemary when we were at Hanbury.

He also used it to promote a property company in Salisbury, then capital of Rhodesia – now Zimbabwe. It was declared to be fraudulent and the poor man went to prison. I suspect he was fixed. Nowadays fraudulent prospectuses are common enough, but the directors are very rarely prosecuted.

In 1975, my cousin Jim Gamon, who had become disillusioned with life as a prep school master, came to work for us. The same year Rosemary went to Persia travelling round by car for three weeks with her friend Elizabeth Beazley, an architect and writer who specialised in old houses. They also had a holiday in Iceland the following year.

Also in 1975, the appalling tyrant Pol Pot seized power in Cambodia and proceeded to drive all the people out of the towns to the villages. Over three years he succeeded in massacring about two million people. Yet, incredibly, his regime was recognised by America and Britain, as they thought he was not a communist.

The Americans finally left Saigon in chaos to the Vietnamese who, having suffered about two million dead over seven years, started to rebuild their country, becoming gradually more capitalist. 56,000 Americans died, out of the 1,250,000 men who had served there during the protracted war.

Civil war broke out in Lebanon between Christians and Moslems. The Suez Canal was reopened, eight years after it had been blocked by sunken ships.

Dutch Elm disease destroyed almost all the elm trees in Britain. Oil flowed from the North Sea to supply all this country's needs and pay the unemployed. Without it, there would have been serious unrest.

The Labour Government now called a referendum on whether or not we should remain in the European Common market, which they had opposed. All the newspapers were in favour and a huge propaganda campaign was launched and financed by Brussels and big business, loudly supported by the Liberal Party. The Conservative Party, except for a few led by the farsighted Enoch Powell, were strongly in favour and a small majority of the people took the view that as we were in, we had better stay in. So we have remained in this bureaucratic, corrupt organisation, later called the European Union, ever since at vast expense and transferring to it many of the powers of our Parliament to govern the country.

The next year, Harold Wilson suddenly resigned as prime minister, for unexplained reasons, although he had become too friendly with his secretary Marcia Williams and there were even suggestions that he had been too friendly to the Russians. It has since been reported that he was under investigation by MI5, as a Russian defector, Anatoli Golitsin had claimed they had murdered Hugh Gaitskell to ensure that Wilson was made Party Leader.

Wilson was succeeded by the more moderate and, in fact, excellent James Callaghan who retained power with Liberal support.

After years of guerrilla warfare, the Portuguese pulled out of Mozambique and Angola, where a vicious civil war was to continue for many years – the Marxist MPLA, supported by Russian arms and Cuban soldiers, being opposed by UNITA, helped by American arms and South African mercenaries.

A few years after he had unleashed the horror of the Cultural Revolution, the Chinese tyrant, Mao Tse Tung died, to be replaced by more moderate, but still communist leaders.

The Democrat, Jimmy Carter, a peanut farmer, became president of the United States – and a very good president he was, too.

Chapter Eight

I happened to see a small classified advertisement in the local paper that, due to the failure of a sale, a farm called Penyrwrlodd, near Hay on Wye, was on the market. Radnorshire had been a delightful place to live in beautiful countryside, close to the mountains, but it was a bit off the map. All our friends were in the Wye or Usk valleys. A new housing estate was being built across the river in front of the house at Greenways, and Bert Watkins who had worked for us loyally for 22 years had retired. I was ready for a move.

Although this would only get us to the border I had always thought myself to be an expatriate Englishman living in Wales and hoped to get back into England, and we would be 30 miles nearer London, where the girls were now living.

So one cold January day in 1976, we went to view Penyrwrlodd and were shown the house by Lyn Hughes. She lived in a bungalow nearby with her husband Philip, who was employed on the farm and I suspect discouraged many prospective buyers by telling them that the house was haunted. The house of six bedrooms, apart from the attics, was half 16th and half 17th century, with a fine oak panelled drawing room with moulded plaster ceiling and a beautiful view across the valley. It was listed Grade II.

It had been acquired by one of Cromwell's colonels, William Watkins after the civil war. He cannot have been one of the regicides who signed the death warrant of King Charles as they were hunted down and hanged after the restoration of James II. On the other hand, as he is not buried in the churchyard, he may have fled, as some did, to America. An enthusiastic Puritan, Watkins built one of the earliest non-conformist meeting houses in Wales across the road behind the farm.

We fell for the house and did not bother to walk round the 250 acres of farmland and 100 acres of woodland, half old oak and half 25 year-old fir plantation, with about four miles of boundary. We simply drove to Hereford and offered £120,000 for it.

The farm was offered with rights to graze 2,500 sheep on the

Black Mountains above it, but as the land was not contiguous and the rights had never been exercised, there was some doubt about it. However, no objection was raised and we have always put 300-400 ewes up for two months between weaning and tupping, which has been tremendously useful as our grass grows up for the winter. All farms around the mountain had registered absurdly excessive rights.

Penyrwrlodd had been bought three years earlier by a city financier at the height of the property boom let rip by Edward Heath's Chancellor, Anthony Barber. Now the fringe banks had collapsed and property prices tumbled. It was said that he flew over it in his helicopter, buying it for his wife, who wanted a place in the country, and appointed a friend who farmed thirty miles away to manage it. Unfortunately, it seems the friend had managed his wife away and his business was in trouble.

Our offer was accepted if we would complete before April 5th, the end of the tax year. We borrowed the money on a mortgage against Greenways, which we put off selling until the following autumn as land prices began to recover.

The house remained empty until January 1977, when Jim moved in and fortunately was not disturbed by the ghost, which has never been seen. It was in a poor state and he and a jobbing builder, Eric Price, spent most of the next year repairing and renovating it, in the process taking down two chimneys and putting dormer windows in the derelict attics which hitherto had been lit by just a few glass tiles in the roof.

To our advantage, the previous owner had installed a central heating system, built a fine swimming pool in the garden and erected a large cattle barn. He must have lost half his money as he sold it to us for less than he had paid and inflation then was 16% pa.

The Greenways land was easily sold to four neighbours but there was little interest in the beautiful house, now a hotel, which eventually we sold in March 1977 for £40,000, when we moved to Penyrwrlodd.

The next year, I saw advertised for sale a small manor house with a tenanted farm of 120 acres, and about 500 acres of ancient woodland, down the Golden Valley in Herefordshire and going cheap. It was just what I wanted so as to give up farming for forestry and get back into England, but Rosemary wouldn't agree to another move so soon and further away from her friends. We missed a great opportunity. Life was much easier before the days of the Married Women's Property Act.

Although we have always lived by farming, expansion always demands more capital, so there is little left for holidays abroad or other luxuries—any serious money we have made has been by sale of land or houses.

This year Julian went to Radley College – the twelfth member of my family over three generation to do so – and I tried to have myself adopted as Conservative candidate for Brecon and Radnor, a seat that had been held for thirty years by the Labour MP, Tudor Watkins. He was put in by the mining valleys in the south of the constituency while the Conservatives and Liberals shared the country vote.

I proposed to stand as an independent Conservative with Liberal support and was nominated by a local landowner Amyas Chichester. The Liberals agreed but the Conservatives turned me down in favour of a farmer from Carmarthenshire. At the adoption meeting I had unwisely said I was against the European Common Market. It is a great mistake for a politician to declare any personal preferences in these days when an MP is ruled by the party whips as lobby fodder.

Labour won again, but for the following election in 1983 the Conservative, candidate was Tom Hooson, cousin of Emlyn Hooson, MP for Montgomery (now Lord Hooson) and Deputy leader of the Liberal Party. He won the seat comfortably, but the poor man died soon after and the seat went to Roger Livesey, the Liberal candidate.

For the next five years I would be more tied to working on the farm than I had been since Hanbury Park Gate days. Rafael Colella managed on his own at Treseissyllt but I went down for a couple of nights every fortnight. Jim lived with us and we employed several young boys and girls in succession on what was called "work experience"

This was the year that Iceland unilaterally extended her territorial waters by two hundred miles, initiating the so-called Cod War. After some protest, we lost some of our best fishing grounds. Meanwhile, in the iniquitous Common Market, other countries fished to within six miles of our coast and the Milford Haven Company disgracefully sold their quota to the Spaniards, who have fished from there ever since. As a result, our once great fishing industry has been largely destroyed, and we now import from Norway, who were sensible enough not to join the European Union.

Before we entered the Common Market land and food prices had been half those in France. Now after several years of gross inflation they were double. Additionally, whilst prior to entry farmers received a "deficiency payment" when the price of fat lambs dropped below a certain level, afterwards a subsidy was paid on every breeding ewe kept, thus encouraging hill farmers to keep too many and sometimes to make excessive claims. Ever since, subsidies have become more generous but more of a bureaucratic racket.

With the lifting of a restriction previously placed on the importation of French new potatoes before the 20th June, there was no longer a profit to be made from growing early potatoes in this country. A levy had to be paid each year to the Potato Marketing Board on the quota acreage planted. I led a campaign in the press against this, refused to pay the levy and, at the annual general meeting of the Board, opposed the salaries of its members.

A vote was taken by show of hands and was obviously won but the chairman declared that it was inconclusive and ordered a paper ballot which would be based on quota acreage. This was obviously unprecedented as it took them two hours to produce ballot papers but growers of main crop with large quota acreages liked the levy because in those years when potatoes were in surplus, the board bought them up and sold them at a loss for animal feed; accordingly the vote was lost.

Thereafter, I could only refuse to pay until they took me to court, a bailiff came to distrain upon my livestock, when I was forced to back down and pay up. Since then all large growers of early potatoes in Pembrokeshire have gone bankrupt.

At the Ascot horse sales, we bought two well bred 4-year old, 16hh mares which had failed as hurdlers. They bred us foals for the next ten years and I would break them before selling at the annual bloodstock sale in Hereford.

Penyrwrlodd was not a great place for riding as there was a mile and half of narrow lanes up to the mountain and the local hunt, with an overage master, a country of small fields and many roads, was not very exciting. Moreover, I begrudged the time and did not want to finish my days in a wheel chair, as the elderly often do. Hunting nowadays is mostly a pastime for townies and children.

Elsewhere, in the open spaces of America and Australia, free of roads and traffic, riding is different. In Argentina, cowboys break a horse simply by jumping on its back and galloping it to exhaustion. I broke in my horses at two years by riding them round a deep muddy pit and then leading them with another horse. Debbie Hughes would get them into the stables in winter nights in return for keeping her horse.

In 1978, Rosemary spent much of the first years there decorating the house, helped by Julia Williams, our faithful 'daily' ever since. It was in that year that Princess Margaret divorced Lord Snowdon and spent the greater part of her life on the island of Mustique with Roddy Llewelyn, son of Sir Harry, who won an Olympic riding Foxhunter. She was a rather sad figure, devoid of occupation.

Oil from the North Sea made this country self-sufficient.

A year after the Shah of Iran had held a vastly extravagant pageant at Persepolis to celebrate the 400th anniversary of the Peacock Throne (although, in reality, he was only the son of an army officer who had usurped it) he was driven out of his country by civil revolution, being succeeded by the Ayatolla Khomeini and a Moslem theocracy, which has kept the country in chains ever since. They turned against America who had consistently armed the Shah against Russian influence. This resulted in US diplomatic staff being imprisoned in their embassy in Teheran. American Special Forces mounted an ambitious operation to free them, which failed disastrously when two of their helicopters crashed. It must have been partially as a result of this that at the following US election, Jimmy Carter lost to the republican ex-B movie star, Ronald Reagan, who was then required to negotiate their release at considerable cost.

In 1979, the Conservatives won the election and Mrs Thatcher became Prime Minister. She appointed my brother Minister of Education but far from replacing grants with loans for university students as I had suggested to her, he introduced an assisted places scheme for children from poor homes to attend public schools. A socialist measure if ever there was one, but welcomed as their numbers were then falling. Mrs. Thatcher also obtained a £3 billion rebate of the funds which we paid each year to the EEC, although it still costs us £10 billion, much of which is lost through corruption.

About this time, County Councillors started being paid. Until then they had been gentlemen or ladies of some distinction in the county who did the job out of a sense of public service. Now it would attract the unemployed. Their emoluments have steadily increased so that now they are even asking for some thousands of pounds to retire and make way for younger men.

Lord Mountbatten and his grandson were murdered by the IRA in an explosion on his yacht – another cowardly crime only committed because of the abolition of the death penalty.

Ian Smith who, after 14 years of independence and guerrilla warfare, had handed over the Government of Rhodesia to the moderate Archbishop Abel Muzorewa the year before, was summoned to a conference at Lancaster House and compelled to hold new elections. These revealed overwhelming support for ex-rebel leader, Robert Mugabe, a member of the Shona tribe who became Prime Minister and, after massacring the minority Matabele tribe with the help of Korean soldiers, eventually, following twenty years of reasonable rule, would dispose of all the white farmers and reduce Zimbabwe to ruin and starvation, which the United Nations have done nothing to prevent.

The Russians invaded Afghanistan, claiming to have been called in to put down an insurrection. The Americans foolishly armed the Afghans and the Russians became involved in a brutal war of oppression for the next seven years, just as the Americans had been involved in Vietnam. When they eventually withdrew the country would be involved in civil war for another several years as three different warlords fought for control of the country, leading eventually to the country being taken over by the fundamentalist Mujahadeen.

In 1980 the 'marsh' Arabs from the head of the Persian Gulf were being oppressed by the Iranian Government. To draw attention to their plight five freedom fighters occupied the Iranian embassy in London, taking hostage the embassy staff. Instead of listening to their complaints and peacefully resolving the crisis, the gung-ho Mrs Thatcher unnecessarily ordered the SAS to storm the building, resulting in the deaths of the freedom fighters and promoting in her favour their commander, Colonel Peter de la Billiere.

This year also saw Ronald Reagan, the Republican President of the United States, put pressure on Russia in the continuing cold war by persuading our government to permit the stationing of cruise missiles with atomic warheads in this country.

Iraq, where the murderous Saddam Hussein had seized power armed by Britian and the US, attacked Iran, now armed by Russia, starting six years of war that included the use of poison gas, particularly directed against the Kurds, who took the opportunity to press for self-government.

In 1979, we spent a holiday in Greece, hiring a car and visiting the ruins at Delphi, Olympia and the Parthenon, whose marble frescoes the British Museum still refuses to return, and driving round the Pelopennese. In fact the ruins of the Greek civilisation in Greece itself are not nearly so impressive as those in Turkey, at Ephesus and other places.

We went on to Crete where we again hired a car and drove all round the whole island and walked up the spectacular Samaria Gorge. We went to the ruins of the earliest Mediterranean civilisation at Knossos and Maleme airport and the British cemetery nearby containing graves of many New Zealanders and British soldiers who fell in the disastrous failure to prevent the German airborne assault in 1941. They suffered so many casualties that never again did the Germans attempt an airborne assault, but they did conquer the Island, and the British, commanded by the elderly General Freyberg VC, evacuated with heavy naval losses. Flying from Greece the enemy had complete air superiority but we had many more British and Greek troops and should not have lost.

That year my cousin, the eccentric Everard Royds, who lived in Glasbury, invited us to stay with some people in Yorkshire. There was a polo match on to promote Everards' phenomenally successful venture, *Riding for the Disabled*, which he started in the 1960s and now has branches all over the country. He hoped I might be able to persuade my brother, the Minister of Education, to grant financial support. I never heard with what success.

In 1947, the Dead Sea Scrolls had been found by an Arab shepherd boy in caves at Qumran. In 1980, they were finally published. They were tattered manuscripts written on vellum and buried by the Essenes, a Jewish sect who inhabited a monastery nearby from 200BC to AD70, when they were dispersed after the Jewish revolt of AD66-70 against the Romans, which resulted in the destruction of Jerusalem and final defeat at the battle for Masada, followed by the diaspora of most of the Jewish people around the Caucusus, later to spread to Europe.

Over thirty years, from the many thousands of often indecipherable fragments, Jewish and Christian scholars have printed 600 pages of psalms, hymns, prayers, garbled instructions and threats to the community, as well as incitement to murder infidels, much as Mahomet would preach six hundred years later. Their god was YHWH, which is what the Freemasons call the Almighty. Christianity, on the other hand, is based on love of thy neighbour. There appears to be little of historical value to justify the vast expenditure of time and money on this study. I could find nothing on skipping through it.

Penyrwrlodd had been bought in 1913 by a cattle dealer called John Jones, known as 'Johnny-go-buy-em', who was said to have paid for it by selling the oak trees. This could still be done in 1960 when the Caerwnon estate near Newbridge was sold. At that time a large house could still be bought for £1,500.

John Jones had the leading Atock herd of pedigree Hereford cattle and was followed by his son Eustace who finished by selling a bull to the Argentine for a record price. Unfortunately, it died before it could be delivered.

Eustace Jones took to the bottle and on the premature death of his brother, Elwyn moved lower down the valley to his farm. Penyrwrlodd had been neglected, the fences and gates were all in a poor state of repair.

I put in the first British made waste burning boiler to burn all the old fence posts, fallen timber, plastic bags, tyres and twine, which accumulate on a farm and saved myself £2,000 a year in heating oil, at the same time keeping the farm tidy.

Livestock farming is a way of life, and a free life, but it requires every day attention, especially weekends when employees don't come in – unlike a job with five days work a week, with two days off at the weekends, plus four weeks holiday a year, or the life of an arable only farmer, who keeps no animals and can take long holidays during the winter. Nowadays, farming is also a lonely life. I have always been inspired by the saying: "It is more blessed to make two blades of grass grow where one grew before than all the politicians."

But, at the same time, you need to be dull, as there is not enough to occupy an active mind. Hence I usually have some campaign on my hands.

However, the price of land, inflated by subsidies and overpaid city slickers seeking country gentility, is now such that no young man can acquire a farm except by marrying or inheriting it. There are practically none available for renting, as a tenant is now granted possession for life and his son after him. Only a small amount of land is let on short term business tenancies at very high rents to existing farmers.

This is very different from the situation in France where young men are encouraged by being able to borrow money at special low rates of interest. In Britain, some farmers won't even marry for fear that, in the event of divorce, the wife will get half the farm.

When we first came to Penyrwrlodd there was a barn owl in the buildings and a covey of partridges in the corn fields. At Greenways we had always heard curlews calling their name to herald spring and a flock of Lapwings (Green Plovers) around in the summer.

At Treseissyllt there had always been larks in the sky in the summers. Now it is even rare to hear a cuckoo in April as our birds have been decimated by appalling chemical arable farming practices, which leave no weeds or worms for birds to eat, and the early mowing of grassland for silage destroys the nests of plovers and larks.

I kept all the land in grass, which we would mow for hay and pick up with a square baler in July or even August, or in June for silage with a forage harvester which we put in a clamp to be self-fed by the cattle.

Since then I have always kept a flock of 500 Welsh ewes

served by Suffolk rams. They are little trouble and lamb outdoors in March unless the weather is bad when we bring them into buildings at night. We have also kept about 20 Hereford x Freisian cows or latterly Limousin served by a Hereford or now Charollais bull and about 40 young cattle.

My father died in 1980 aged 91, an honourable, slightly reserved man with little sense of humour. He took after his Royds mother, as did two of his brothers. The other three Carlisles were much jollier. He must have had a disappointing life. Through the activities of German submarines in two wars, the mighty cotton trade in this country collapsed, giving way to new manufactories in other countries and forcing my father, in 1958, to close the family firm of export merchants to which he had devoted 50 years of his life, except for the Great War, in a dismal Manchester office. He is buried in Alderley cemetery as are my father's parents. There is a plaque in my father's memory in St Philip's church, where he was long a warden and sidesman.

In the summer of 1980, we drove round Scotland in our camper van to Bettyhill on the north coast at the mouth of the Naver, an excellent salmon river. There we found an estate for sale by the executors of the late Arthur Negus, of television antique furniture fame. It comprised a five bedroom lodge, thirteen crofts, a tenant farm of 100 acres and 10,000 acres of barren moor.

We walked it and found only one brace of grouse and no deer but there were plenty over the fence on the estate next door. It did not have fishing on the Naver, which ran along the boundary, but it was tidal just below where fishing is free. I wanted to buy it but Rosemary was dead against the idea. It was 500 miles from home with no motorways in Scotland then. Nevertheless, as there was little interest in the property, which in Scotland is always sold by tender, I put in the very low offer of £80,000.

I believe it was sold for not much more and must have been very profitable as, shortly after, there was a big demand for moorland for forestry by rich men seeking to avoid inheritance tax. If my bid had been successful this would have altered the course of our lives.

In 1981, widespread rioting by Afro-Caribbeans broke out in ten cities, in London and the Midlands, destroying a great deal of property.

The country went mad with enthusiasm as Prince Charles was steered into marrying the spoilt, immature, fragile and unsophisticated Lady Diana Spencer, victim of a broken home and a wicked stepmother. A magnificent marriage service held at St Paul's Cathedral was followed by spectacular parades.

Chapter Nine

In March 1981 I happened to see a small classified advertisement in the *Farmers Weekly* offering a farm for sale in the Falkland Islands. This interested me as it would be an opportunity to travel via South America where my family had been in business for 130 years. The Foreign Office had agreed, after several years of negotiation, a sale and leaseback deal on the islands with Argentina.

I replied to the advertisement and was visited by Colin Smith, a Bradford woollen merchant, who purchased half the Islands wool crop and had bought San Carlos farm of 120,000 acres carrying 26,000 sheep two years before, and I thought I might possibly have some influence towards settlement.

He was apparently overstretched and wanted to sell. After some persuasion of Rosemary, we offered to buy half the company which owned the farm and during discussions with him and his solicitor, a delightful man, heard that there were two other directors of the company in the Islands, Robin Pitaluga and Bill Luxton, Manager of Chartres.

The farm manager, Adrian Monk was retiring and Luxton had appointed, without consultation, his protégé Pat Short as manager, having employed his wife. This was considered to be unsatisfactory.

Eventually the deal was done for £150,000, which I borrowed on mortgage and we took a flight to Buenos Aires in December where we stayed for five nights with my second cousins Anne and Bruce Carlisle, who was managing director of Brookebond Leibigs in the Argentine.

Buenos Aires is a fine city, often described as the Paris of the South Atlantic. From the sixteenth to the eighteenth century all of South America was in the Spanish Empire except for the slave state of Brazil, which was Portuguese. At the beginning of the nineteenth century General Bolivar liberated several states, and General Jose de

San Martin crossed the Andes from Chile with 3,000 men to defeat the Spaniards at the battle of Chacabuco.

By 1830 the Spanish had been driven out of all of South America and San Martin, whose statue is in every town, proclaimed the state of Argentina and opened the country to world trade.

British gentlemen and some Germans including Count Leibig, the first man to can beef at Fray Bentos and manufacture Oxo meat extract, moved in and started cattle ranching on *estancias*, and in the 1930s, there was a flood of poor Italian immigrants. It was said that Argentinians were then mostly Italians who spoke Spanish and wished they were English. The British had also built the railways and public services of Buenos Aires.

Apart from the brutal extermination of the Indian population of Patagonia and Tierra del Fuego in about 1870, the country had been a fairly liberal democracy and in fact tried to join the British Empire at the beginning of the twentieth century. But in 1947 General Peron seized power and nationalised the railways and other British companies.

Peron was governed by his wife, the charismatic Eva, whose socialist policies ruined the country. They were followed by a series of military *juntas*, which brutally suppressed urban revolutionaries and resulted in the disappearance of some 10,000 young men, mostly students. Now, it was peaceful and crime-free.

In 1830, Argentinians had started cattle ranching in the Falkland Islands, which were unoccupied but had been in disputed ownership of Spain, France and Britain since their discovery 150 years before. Two years later, a British naval vessel forcibly transported the immigrants back to Buenos Aires, a Governor was appointed and the land distributed to settlers – mostly Scots – and the Falkland Islands Company, which owned the supply vessel and only stores.

Ever since then Argentina had claimed the Falkland Islands – *Malvinas* as they called them – but was not able to do much about it while the British navy ruled the world and needed them for a refuelling base.

The island's farmers had prospered particularly during the Korean war when the high price of wool made fortunes for them and several had retired to Britain leaving a manager in charge of their properties.

Peron had always pressed the claim and school children in Argentina were taught that the *Malvinas* were part of Argentina. When the *junta* were in trouble at home, they revived the claim – a common political ploy – and our Foreign Office, after several years of delaying negotiations had agreed the transfer of sovereignty, considering the islands to be a considerable drain on the British economy.

The then Secretary for Defence, the arrogant John Nott, had now arranged to sell the naval protection vessel, *Endurance*, which was stationed in the Falklands, to Brazil, and our last aircraft carrier to Australia. This, of course, was a huge come-on to the *junta*. Nevertheless, there was a small, very vocal group in Parliament who raised a stink about these 2,000 innocent British citizens being placed under Fascist despotism. So at the last moment, the Foreign Office declared that the transfer must be subject to the wishes of the islanders by referendum.

The Minister of State at the Foreign Office, Nicholas Ridley (of Nimby [Not In My Back Yard] fame) had also managed to rub the islanders up the wrong way when he went to Stanley and tried to sell them the idea of transfer of sovereignty.

On the day of the referendum, a member of the Executive Committee, our farm manager, Adrian Monk, who had represented the Islanders at the talks made an impassioned plea for them to remain British and the vote for transfer was just lost. This naturally infuriated the *junta*, who now accused the British Government of deceit and threatened to recover the Falklands by force.

Thus, incredibly, the future of this great nation was placed in the hands of a few simple islanders. Such is the lunacy of democracy! And the results were to be fatal.

Until then, the *Palabra de Ingles* – the word of an Englishman – had been famous in South America. This action now justified the old pejorative tag of 'Perfidious Albion'.

On 20 December 1981, we took a plane to Commodoro Rivadavia and from there, a 20-seat Fokker of the Argentinian airforce across

4,000 miles of sea to the airport at Stanley. This had been built by the Argentinians, who also provided all the oil for the islands and fresh food supplies. In fact, over the years, they had done their best to woo the islanders, whose children went to Buenos Aires for secondary education. We stayed at the only hotel in Stanley, *The Upland Goose*, hardly first class – I found a rubber sheet under my bed sheet!

On Christmas Eve, we were invited to drinks by the Governor, unsuitably named 'Rex' Hunt, who emphasised his democratic leanings by having two able seamen from the Endurance playing snooker on his table.

Later, when there was a strike threatened by farm labourers he unwisely disclosed that he was the son of a miner. Though instructed to sell the proposal for transfer of sovereignty to Argentina, he preferred to seek popularity with those opposing it. Hunt's previous appointment had been as ambassador in Malaysia where his secretary, who wrote a letter to me long after, described him as a party loving fool.

Then we attended a dance in the town hall, for which I had been instructed to bring a dinner jacket, the only time I would wear it. For Christmas dinner in the hotel, we were given lamb. The other 364 days of the year, everyone eats mutton! We were invited to stay for a couple of nights by Graham Hardcastle, the manager of the Falkland Islands Company's farms at Darwin to attend the social highlight of the year, the race meeting on New Year's day on the rough racecourse near Stanley, and sheep dog trials of a rather poor standard.

Two days later we flew in a four-seater Beaver seaplane to San Carlos, on the other side of the island. All farms were situated around the coasts of the two islands as transport was entirely by sea in a small cargo vessel. There were no roads apart from an unmetalled one across East Falkland, from Stanley to Darwin, which is the oldest and largest settlement owned by the Falkland Islands Company. However some farms now had their own grass airstrip to which the 20-seat Islander could be summoned when required, at moderate cost, all farms being connected by radio, to which, incidentally all could listen in.

We were accompanied by the delightful Adrian Monk, who had been manager of the farm for several years and was now an agricultural officer and member of the Executive Council under the Governor.

During WWII he had been a merchant service officer and twice torpedoed, then had gone to farm in Radnorshire. He now lived in Stanley with his charming wife Nora, who pined for the UK, where her son was at school. We were to share the house with the new manager Pat Short.

There were another five houses for employees, a school hall, occasionally visited by a teacher and a large shearing shed on the settlement. Out on the farm there were three more houses for shepherds, though no longer occupied, as a Land Rover and tractor had increased mobility.

The farm, covering 120,000 acres, was divided into about ten large paddocks. It was bordered by mountains and intersected by occasional stone runs, which are found nowhere else in the world and whose origin cannot be explained. They consist of rivers of boulders, up to 50 yards wide from top to bottom of a mountain and they are quite impassable. Much of the land was covered by peat bog which provided fuel for the houses. Attempts had been made to drain the peat by cutting ditches across it but these were death traps for sheep because, if they slipped in them, they couldn't get out. Sometimes the peat had caught fire and would burn for weeks, destroying the land.

The whole area was covered by a coarse grass known as White Grass, which when young was good grazing for sheep but then became too coarse.

Attempts had also been made to re-seed one or two paddocks but with little success as the soils were acid and there was no lime or fertiliser available. The obvious solution to the problem was to introduce cattle, as ranched by the original Argentinian settlers, who sold their hides to Argentina. However, when the British settled on the islands they kept only sheep, using Argentinian gauchos to ride down the cattle, which they felled by entangling their legs with a *diabolo*, a weighted rope, and then cut their throats.

A very few wild cattle still roamed the mountains and a dozen or so were kept to provide milk for the staff. The sheep which, originally, had been Romney Marsh were later crossed with a Merino to breed a Corriedale or a Polwarth, that produced finer fleeces. As in Australia, wool was the only saleable product. In all there were about 500,000 sheep on the islands. The old wethers were given to the men at one per week each or fed to the dogs. Twenty thousand old ewes had their throats cut and were chucked into the sea each autumn.

Cancer was common in the islands through the consumption of too much meat and there were strict regulations about worming dogs as hydatid disease can be caught from them. There was recently in the 1990s a scare about that in this country although it seems to have blown over.

A few ponies were kept on the farm for gathering sheep when the time came in the spring to worm and tail lambs, and in the autumn for shearing by contractors when the lambs were weaned.

The only decent fields were just around the settlement. They were mown to provide hay for the dairy cows and grazing but the grass was devoured by flocks of Upland Geese. Although snow fell in winter when the wind was from the south, it soon disappeared when the wind turned to the north, so sheep were never fed.

Life on a Falklands farm was not strenuous. All activity stopped for *Smoko* at mid-morning, and no one worked very hard.

Across San Carlos water stood a slaughterhouse and refrigerated stores at Ajax Bay, which were still in good order. They had been built in the 1950s at the vast cost of £500,000 by the Colonial Development Corporation, to facilitate the export of sheep meat. They did this for two years before going bankrupt – another of their several failures. They should, of course, have sited their operation in Stanley or Darwin where ships could get alongside, and closer to more farms.

There was not even a ferry between East and West Falkland Islands. But the coaster, Monsunem visited each settlement about every three months collecting wool and delivering stores. Although we were there in mid-summer and the islands are on the same latitude as London, the sea was too cold for bathing or seine netting, although we tried netting once or twice at the head of San Carlos water and caught a few bass.

About a week into our stay, I was told by Pat Short that the men were all going on strike, instigated, I imagine, by Short and Luxton, who saw me as something of a new broom and resented a few suggestions I had made. I called the men to a meeting in the school hall but never did ascertain the cause of complaint.

In fact, it all blew over and we got on well with them. A little later, we flew in the Beaver seaplane to spend two nights with Luxton at Chartres on West Island. He was a radio ham, on the Executive Council and virulently anti-Argentinian, even though he had been to school in Buenos Aires, and he was a friend of Hunt. There was a bit of an atmosphere there and I didn't endear myself to him by pointing out that his new hay turner was being used incorrectly and driven the wrong way round the field.

A storm blew up and the plane couldn't fly that evening, so we had to stay another night. That day we helped tailing and marking lambs. When the sheep were released into a cold gale from the south, the flock took off at a mad gallop. This was a danger, particularly after shearing, when a flock could pile up against a wire fence and hundreds get smothered.

We did two drives around East Falkland in the farm Land Rover. One across to Port San Carlos, the next farm, to Cape Dolphin on the north coast, where we spent a night in a hut and walked among sea lions and a penguin colony of thousands of birds which stank to high heaven.

All animals and birds were incredibly tame having had practically no contact with humans. This was the most attractive country we saw in the Falklands. The owner, Mrs Cameron, whose father had been Governor, lived in Ireland and her son, Alistair, was the representative in London and was tragically killed in a car accident when visiting the islands after the war.

We stayed there one night with the manager Alan Miller. Mrs. Cameron's house was the best one on the islands. It had also the best garden, which, as no trees grow on the islands, was surrounded, like all gardens there, by thick gorse hedges.

Potatoes and all vegetables had to be grown as they could not be obtained otherwise. When we were there they were cutting the throats of old ewes and chucking them in the sea.

Alan Miller was to die of cancer eight years later and I tried to buy the farm and get Jim Gamon to manage it. But he had got married by then and his wife Patti was not keen. Also, I was by then *persona non grata* and, incredibly, as in all colonies, the Governor could dictate who could buy property.

The other trip we took was across country to Douglas Station, owned by Harland Greenshields, who had retired to farm in Caernarvonshire, and on to spend two nights with the delightful Robin Pitaluga, another director of San Carlos, and his wife at Gibraltar Station. His family had come from Gibraltar three generations before.

On the way we had to cross a sea creek and got stuck in the middle. Fortunately there was a radio in the Land Rover and we were able to call up the manager at Douglas Station. He came to our rescue with a tractor and pulled us out with the incoming tide washing in above the floorboards. Adrian Monk had lost a Land Rover in a similar creek a year before.

We spent two chilly nights in unheated sheds on the San Carlos and Malo rivers, trying to catch salmon without any success and on our way home got stuck in a ditch across a peat bog fifteen miles from any help. But all Land Rovers carried a couple of planks and a jack which could be attached to the front bumper, so we were able to extricate the vehicle.

San Carlos carried 26,000 sheep. In February they were gathered in by ponies into two flocks in a huge shed when contractors came to shear them. The fleeces were not wrapped as we do it in Britain but pressed by a really antique engine into bales of about 10 cwt, to be collected later by the coastal vessel and shipped to Bradford, where the wool was sold by Colin Smith. The lambs were weaned then, too early in my view, but inevitable as they would have got separated from their dams in the two days it took. Put off in a paddock, they were not fed at all so mortality was high and they didn't breed until two years old.

There was no television on the islands, but videos were in common use. The only entertainment was provided by Radio Stanley transmitting the evening news and BBC programmes, relayed by Eileen to whom I dedicated a poem which was published in the monthly news sheet, Penguin News.

At the beginning of March, we flew to Commodoro Rivadavia and on in an airliner to Rio Gallegos where we stayed three nights. There we met the British Ambassador, a friend of my cousin, who was attending some local Anglo-Argentinian festivity. We also met David Barton, whose family had come from the Falkland Islands and who had a huge sheep farm at Cape Virgenes, the southern tip of

South America. He was very progressive, pregnancy testing his ewes and on many using artificial insemination, a practice unknown in Britain for sheep. There were great numbers of penguins on the sea shore. David was extraordinarily kind in driving us 80 miles to the farm and back in the evening. The next day we visited an Anglo *estancia* inland where we had the usual outdoor *asado* lunch of beef roast on skewers over an open fire. Then we flew across the Magellan Straits to Rio Grande. All the planes in the south were flown by airforce pilots and for about £100 one could fly all over Argentina for a month.

There I went to the abattoir on the coast to enquire the possibility of shipping old ewes and wethers to them for export abroad. The manager was very encouraging. He also gave us an introduction to a very large sheep station owned by the Menendez family, which had managed to acquire the *estancias* of Argentine Southern lands that had been owned by Leibigs until nationalised by General Peron in the l950s.

They invited us to stay on their *estancia* near Esquel, but first we took a bus across the mountainous Tierra del Fuego to Ushuaia on the Beagle Channel, on the way visiting a nature reserve where beavers lived, then taking a trip in a tourist ship down the Channel.

The weather was calm when we started and the mountain scenery on both sides quite spectacular, but after a couple of hours a gale blew up and we were quite relieved to get back on dry land.

Near Ushuaia there is still a British missionary post dating back 100 years, when Fuegan Indians were regarded as subhuman.

Next we flew to Calafate where we took a day trip in a tourist launch to the head of Lake Argentina to see the spectacular glaciers that fall into the lake. From there we went on to the *estancia* near Esquel at the foot of the Andes where the German manager put us up for two nights. His assistant, Peter Faulkner, showed us around his sub-station and gave us the usual *asado* lunch.

Our next stop, to which we flew, was Trelew, where Welsh religious dissidents had settled in 1850. It is the only fertile river valley in Patagonia, which is incredibly barren, and they were near to starvation when they found it after being dropped on the coast at Rawson 40 miles away. There was a large chapel and some of the people were still Welsh-speaking but the small farms were much run down.

From there we flew to Buenos Aires, took a ferry across the mighty estuary of the River Plate to Montevideo and then a bus to Punta del Este, where my cousin Betty, who was married to a much older psychiatrist, Eduardo de Caballero, had a flat.

There are said to be more psychiatrists in BA than any other city in the world and, like all the rich, their principal interest is in transferring their *pesos* into dollars abroad. Hence the deplorable state of the Argentine economy.

When I went to Punta, aged six, when my father had changed jobs with his brother in Montevideo, there'd been nothing but sand dunes. Now it is the playground of rich Argentinians and boasts a world yachting marina. After three days on the beach and driving round some of Uruguay, which had always been a model of democracy until Tuppamaros guerrillas tried to incite communist revolution in the 1970s, as in Argentina, we took the ferry back to BA and Rosemary flew home.

As our farm manager in the Falklands had given notice, I intended to return to the Falklands to run the farm until a replacement could be found. However, three weeks before, a party of Argentinians employed by a scrap merchant had landed on the remote island of South Georgia to dismantle an old whaling station, which their boss had bought from the Norwegian owners.

The island, whose closest neighbour was the Falklands, had long been uninhabited except for a few men of the British Antarctic Survey, who reported that the Argentinians had raised their country's flag there. Since it was still claimed as British territory, the *Endurance* was sent to investigate this trivial provocation.

Our ambassador in BA registered a protest but nothing was done to remove the flag, which the *junta* regarded as another sign of our weakness – even another come on.

The day before I left BA, I went to see the Minister for the Malvinas, the charming Colonel Balcase, a descendant of Prussian nobility, to discuss the possibility of exporting the old ewes and wethers from the Islands. I knew he had visited them in better times, and Des King, owner of *The Upland Goose*, had recommended me to see him. He was encouraging and said that this could easily be arranged as they would be occupying the islands later in the week. I warned him that this would be fatal as Britain would be bound to recover them at whatever cost. He actually rang General Galtieri in my presence but I was unable to understand what was said, my Spanish being poor.

I flew out on Wednesday on the weekly 350 mile flight in a Fokker and found five British journalists on the plane, who obviously also knew that an invasion was imminent. On arriving at Stanley, I was told that an invasion was indeed expected, yet nothing had been done to block the airfield and the *Endurance* had been sent off to South Georgia, presumably to avoid her being involved in any military action! The representative of the Argentinian Airlines in the Falklands was an Air Commodore Hector Gilbert, who had an office in Stanley, where he lived

At 8.00pm on Thursday evening, Governor Hunt confirmed on the radio that an invasion was imminent and, in bombastic fashion, declared his intention to fight 'these Argies', the pejorative term he was wont to use.

At about midnight, some Argentinian oil workers staying in the hotel were arrested, yet Air Commodore Gilbert, who had his own radio frequency to BA, was left loose.

It was then that Hunt announced that the Marines were resisting invaders on the airport road and a hysterical woman came up to say that shots had been fired through the roof of her house, puncturing the water tanks. This must have been done by our Royal Marines, as the Argentinian commando of about forty men didn't land until 4.00am at Mullet Creek to the south west, and approached Stanley from the other side.

At six, Hunt – later reported to have been hiding under a table still shouting bravura – said that water was pouring down through the house, again presumably self-inflicted damage, and the Argentinian commander was killed and two wounded in the House garden. As I observed in the morning, no pane of glass in the extensive conservatories adjacent to Government House had been broken.

There was a pause in the 'bloody' engagement and Hunt came on the radio to announce that the Argentinian Air Commodore had appeared to negotiate a ceasefire. So ended the pantomime battle.

Around 8 o'clock, a transport vessel entered the harbour where some dozen armoured personnel carriers were unloaded and driven off to Government House. General Menendez and his staff flew in shortly afterwards.

There were about 70 Marines on the island, as the detachments of 40 were being replaced and 10 had gone off in the *Endurance* to South Georgia, where they did later shoot down a helicopter. Those remaining in Stanley were disarmed and humiliated by being made to lie on the ground for the benefit of the press photographers, both Argentine and British. This was very stupid of them as, although the photos caused wild scenes of jubilation in Argentina, they raised a thirst for revenge in Britain. The commando had been ordered not to harm any British personnel or property and had behaved with remarkable restraint, despite the loss of their commander.

They had not fired a shot whereas it was later admitted that the Marines had fired 2,000 rounds – the shell cases were all over Stanley. Few of the FI Defence Force reported for duty and took no part in the 'battle'.

British troops should not have been put in this situation. If ordered to fight they should sell their lives dearly, as has always been the tradition. As this stood, however, it would have been perfectly honourable for the Governor to have surrendered without this phoney fight and so avoided the humiliation.

But Mrs Thatcher, who had been given every warning of the impending invasion by our ambassador and military attaché in BA and the reading of Argentinian signals by GHQ Cheltenham, had uttered no warning because she wished to encourage it and needed to claim violent military aggression.

The Argentinian *junta* were in trouble at home and wanted to hand over powers to a democratic Government, reckoning that they could then go out in a blaze of glory and avoid being put on trial for the *desparicidos* – the thousands of revolutionaries who had disappeared and whose parents paraded each week on the main square of BA demanding answers. It was the 150th anniversary of our seizure of the Falkland Islands.

Mrs. Thatcher was also in trouble at home, with inflation out of hand and three million unemployed. She reckoned a little colonial war would restore her fortunes, particularly as some stupid

Russians had christened her the 'Iron Lady'.

Women in power like wars, as did Indira Gandhi, Golda Meir and Mrs Bandaranaika. Male politicians and particularly soldiers, who have to fight them, are more cautious.

The Marines were flown out to Uruguay that morning in a transport plane but the foolish Hunt dressed himself in his Governor's uniform with plumed hat to make a ceremonial departure. He was driven by his chauffeur in his official limousine, a London taxi, to the airport, where he was curtly ordered to change into civilian clothes before being allowed to take the Fokker flight to Commodoro Rivadavia and thence home.

Incredibly, government officials continued to operate as usual under the cultured Anglo-Argentinian Colonel Bloomer Reeve, Chief of Staff. Their officers did not commandeer *The Upland Goose* Hotel but took rooms as paying guests to the profit of Des King.

The Falkland Islands Company also supplied goods to the invaders. All this was, of course, trading with the enemy. Only the pilots of the island planes refused to fly, so I was unable to get out to San Carlos as I had intended.

British newspaper correspondents who were also staying in the hotel were over-friendly with the officers, who all spoke good English. The journalists seemed to take the whole business as rather a joke, instead of a national humiliation.

They penned articles describing in fanciful detail battles on the road to the airport where no Argentinians had landed. When I protested they were not writing the truth, they said their job was not to write the truth but what they thought the public wanted to read.

Only Simon Winchester of *The Times* seemed serious. He told me that he had gone out to the Marines barracks at Moody Brook and found the place wrecked but their orders conveniently left on the table. They had obviously done it themselves before departing but the correspondents were to describe how it had been destroyed in an attack by the Argentinian commandos, who had never been there.

Winchester was later to be arrested for spying in Patagonia and imprisoned for several weeks but when I'd asked him if he had any connection with MI6, he'd said no! He has since become a very good writer, with books on the Yangtsei River and the Krakatoa Volcano Eruption.

I left the hotel the next day as I didn't want to be consorting with the enemy, and moved in with a friend. But the previous night I had met a very Anglo naval officer, Captain Hussey, in the bar and told him they would have to get back home soon. He, like all of them, was convinced they were there to stay and that Russia would prevent any armed recovery by Britain. I heard after the war from my cousin that the poor man later committed suicide.

Next day I found the only policeman, Ron Lamb chatting happily with a sinister Argentinian secret police major and complained to him that their sentries stood with their rifles across their waists intimidating anyone who approached them. The following day I was glad to see them slung on their shoulders.

The invaders behaved well and promised to bring in television. Compensation was also offered to anyone who wished to leave their property. Their only offence was to order all vehicles to drive on the right of the road, and the only islander arrested was the rabidly anti-Argentinian Bill Luxton.

Talking to islanders it appeared they were fairly relaxed about the situation. They had long been ungrateful to Britain, which had recently refused them full British citizenship on the ridiculous grounds that they might have to give it to all the inhabitants of Hong Kong.

Later, all the British officials, except Adrian Monk, wrote to the Foreign Office demanding that they be repatriated before this happened. I went to see the Anglo-Argentinian Chief of Staff, Colonel Bloomer Reeve to suggest that a referendum be held, which might well have resolved the whole situation and prevented the unnecessary war. He, in turn, consulted General Menendez, who unfortunately turned the idea down. So I asked if I could leave the islands, thinking that I could tell the Ministry of Defence about the military dispositions which I had taken trouble to observe and that I might influence the Government towards a peaceful resolution of the situation.

The weekly Fokker had just left so I was flown out in a Hercules transport plane. On arrival at Commodoro Rivadavia I was arrested and interrogated by Major Dowling of the secret police for an hour or so. When released I was seized by the British journalists from the Islands, who sat with me on the plane to BA and generously plied me with whisky, encouraging me to talk. Next day there was a long article by Christopher Thomas in *The Times*, expressing my view that most islanders were apprehensive of a British military re-occupation and wanted a diplomatic settlement of lease-back or joint sovereignty. The best solution of all would have been to have ceded West Falkland Isle, whose people favoured it, to Argentina, while keeping East Island British. I consider this could easily have been achieved.

Arriving in BA, I was again arrested, this time by airforce intelligence officers who seemed to think that I might be in our secret service. However, they were civil enough, even producing tea and biscuits, and after three hours I was allowed to go and get a room in a hotel; it was 4.00am.

Next morning, thinking I might be detained in the country, I reported to the British embassy where I was directed to the Swiss embassy, who were acting for us as our ambassador had left. After some time, their ambassador told me that he had spoken to the foreign office, who wanted to talk to me and that, as he did indeed believe I was at some risk, he would personally drive me to the Airport and put me on a Swissair plane to London, paid for either by the Swiss or the British FO, although I had a return ticket of my own on Argentinian Airways.

Arriving at Heathrow at midnight Saturday, I rang my brother, then Minister of Education in the Cabinet, who said that Cranley Onslow, Minister of State at the Foreign Office, wished to see me next morning.

To my surprise I found that I was *persona non grata*. There had been a libellous letter in *The Times* from the Governor, Rex Hunt attacking me. After the Parliamentary uproar over the Falklands debacle, for which Mrs Thatcher had disgracefully blamed the Foreign Office, Lord Carrington had resigned as scapegoat, although he was soon appointed minister to NATO. The new Foreign Secretary, Francis Pym, although in the building, did not see me.

I was interviewed by the South American secretary, to whom I described the situation in the Falklands, and again suggested that a referendum of the islanders be proposed as this would resolve the situation peacefully. The Ministry of Defence made no attempt to contact me, although I could have given them much information and our forces were later to land at San Carlos.

On Monday I was interviewed on a BBC programme. Several foreign newspapers rang me including the principal Buenos Aires paper, to which I refused to speak as it would have been talking to the enemy. I had a letter published in *The Times*, describing the pantomime battle and urging a peaceful settlement. The editor, William Douglas Home rang me in encouragement. He had been court-martialled and served six months in gaol in 1944 when, as a battery commander, he had courageously refused to shell the town of Le Havre. The German officer Commanding had asked for a ceasefire to enable evacuation of the civilian population, but this was refused, and 2,000 were killed by the British artillery bombardment that then went ahead.

The following Sunday the poisonous John Junor attacked me in his column in *The Sunday Express* about my going to the Foreign Office, who must have tipped him off. I complained to the Press Complaints Committee who turned out simply to be a Press Protection Agency and dismissed it.

But by this time, Rosemary and her brother were urging me not to speak to the press, so I kept quiet, as I did not wish to embarrass the family or risk losing friends. I received a few letters of encouragement but, astonishingly, only one that was abusive.

On the day of the invasion, the 2nd April, an emergency sitting of Parliament had been called and Mrs Thatcher pretended that the Government had been taken by surprise, announcing amid uproar that steps would be taken to recover the islands.

Yet the Secretary for Defence, the arrogant John Nott, reported that the Navy had a fleet of 40 ships ready to sail, which disproved any surprise. The Labour and Liberal parties supported the Government as the *junta* was seen as a right-wing Fascist regime. Had they been left wing, I'm sure they would have opposed.

Only one or two voices were raised in dissent, most prominently the brave Labour MP Tam Dalyell, who would consistently and vocally oppose the unnecessary war.

On 3rd April, the United Nations Security Council was persuaded by Sir Anthony Parsons to demand Argentinian withdrawal, when Russia and China, who could have vetoed it, abstained. The fleet sailed on 5th April. It included the Aircraft carriers *Invincible*, which had been sold to Australia but fortunately had not left yet, and *Hermes*, which had been due for decommissioning. Both ships carried Harrier jump-jets and two Marine commandos.

The liner *Canberra* was converted to troop carrying and would soon follow with two RM Commandos and two battalions of the parachute regiment. A Gurkha Battalion and Scots and Welsh Guards followed later in the QE II. The 1st Sea Lord Admiral, Sir Henry Leach, and Admiral of the Fleet Terence Lewin had encouraged Mrs Thatcher in her warlike intent (no doubt seeing honours ahead), but retired generals and air-marshals appeared on television warning of the great risks of the operation, and would be proved right.

My cousin Bruce Carlisle, who was a friend of the Argentinian foreign minister, Costa Mendes, flew to London to speak to Foreign Secretary Francis Pym, with whom he had served in the 9th Lancers, but without result. His son Nicholas joined the Argentinian army.

Mrs Thatcher wanted war.
The country was about equally divided on the matter but once operations had started, it became unpatriotic to speak against it. Apart from Tam Dalyell, the only man brave enough to do so was the legless air ace, Douglas Bader.

The fleet, accompanied by 60 tankers, troop landing and support ships, assembled for reorganisation at Ascension Island in the South Atlantic, where men were reported to be complaining that they had not joined the army to fight a war and some were taking out insurance, while the American General Al Haig flew to BA trying to negotiate a withdrawal settlement.

But Mrs Thatcher was demanding nothing less than unconditional withdrawal, which would have caused complete loss of face to the Argentinians. It served only to strengthen their resolve to hold fast. This was reminiscent of the stance taken by her hero Churchill and Roosevelt in the last war, when, at the Casablanca conference in 1943, they demanded unconditional surrender by Germany, thereby discouraging Hitler's generals from overthrowing him, thus prolonging the war by another two years, and allowing Russia to occupy half of Europe and emerge as a super power as tyrannical as Nazism. The Japanese had also been ready to surrender 3 months earlier if they had been assured that their God-King emperor would not be tried as a war criminal, and Russia would not have been able to occupy Mongolia.

On 25th April a few SAS men were stupidly landed by helicopter on a glacier on South Georgia. A gale blew up and they called for withdrawal which was achieved with great difficulty after a plane crashed.

Later, on 19th May, while being transferred between ships, a helicopter missed one vessel and fell into the sea with the loss of 15 SAS lives. Next day, a submarine, which had been bombed in the harbour, surrendered and was found to be commanded by the notorious Captain Aziz, who had been in charge of one of the military prisons where dissidents were tortured, among them a Swedish citizen. Sweden demanded Aziz be extradited, but, unbelievably, the British Government insisted on returning him to Argentina.

The British Government had declared a 200 mile exclusion zone around the Falkland Islands. They had, however, never declared war. On 1st May, the atomic submarine *Conqueror* reported finding the aged training cruiser *General Belgrano* and two destroyers 35 miles south west of the exclusion zone.

On the request of the task force commander, Admiral Sandy Woodward, the war cabinet of Thatcher, Admiral Lewin, John Nott and William Whitelaw met on the 2nd and immediately changed the rules of engagement, without publication or informing Argentina, and ordered the Captain to sink her.

The vessels were in fact sailing away from the zone, prompting the Captain Wreford-Brown to query the order but he was told to get on with it.

The Belgrano was hit by two torpedoes. Her watertight doors were not shut as she was not at action stations and she sank within an hour. It was getting dark, a gale was blowing and one of the destroyers was also damaged by a torpedo which failed to explode.

Survivors could not be picked up until next day when it was found that 323 of the *Belgrano* crew had been lost. This deceitful attack was one of the most shameful acts in our recent history.

Challenged on television three days later, Mrs Thatcher

denied that the ships were outside the exclusion zone and sailing away, asserting that they were an immediate danger to our ships and carrying Exocet missiles. This was entirely untrue.

Pursued by the brilliant Tam Dalyell – Labour MP and Scottish laird – the Government was to persist in these lies for a year until a civil servant, Clive Ponting produced documentary evidence. He was sued, dismissed and prosecuted, but exonerated in court.

The President of Peru, Senor Perez de Cuella, had intervened to arrange a settlement and had at last persuaded the Argentine *junta* to withdraw from the Falklands. The British Foreign Secretary, Francis Pym, was in Washington on 1st and 2nd May to agree the final details.

There is no doubt that Mrs Thatcher ordered the sinking of the *Belgrano* deliberately to scupper their agreement and compel a war, as she was accused at the time. Britain was condemned throughout the world, and on the 4th May Argentina took revenge by sinking the destroyer *Sheffield* with an airborne Exocet missile. Our politicians were stunned; it wasn't going to be such a jolly war after all.

Fortunately, the Argentinians had only 12 Exocets and were unable to obtain further supplies. We had bought them up around the world and persuaded France not to make any more available for sale. Some MPs even called on us to bomb Argentine cities. A few days later, in a ridiculous show of strength, Vulcan bombers flew from Ascension, being twice refuelled on the way, to drop bombs on Stanley airport which did practically no damage at all.

A party of SAS was flown by helicopter near to Rio Gallegos on mainland Argentina to radio when planes were taking off. In another cock-up, they landed too near the airport and were seen, so scarpered off across the nearby Chilean border. And Chile, being in a dispute with Argentina over an island near the Beagle Channel, instead of interning them, allowed them to return to the UK.

On 15th May, the Royal Marines Special Boat Squadron landed on Pebble Island and destroyed some aircraft. In a book published since then, the SAS claimed to have had men observing on the islands but they achieved nothing.

On 21st May our troops landed unopposed from the *Canberra* at San Carlos, on the other side of East Falkland, 80 miles from the Argentine garrison at Stanley.

On the 25th, two Super Etendard aircraft sank the container ship, *Atlantic Conveyor* before she could unload any of her supplies and transport helicopters with an Exocet missile, and badly damaged the destroyer *Coventry*.

Days later the destroyers *Ardent* and *Antelope* were sunk by low level bombing. The Argentine pilots were very brave in attacking ships so low and so close that their bombs sometimes didn't have time to fuse and passed through the ships without exploding – unless they'd been sabotaged at home? This error saved several of our warships. If they had attacked the *Canberra* with 4,000 troops on board, the whole operation would have been a disaster. It can only be assumed that they had been instructed not to do so.

The whole force then sat around for ten days, presumably hoping a diplomatic solution would yet make fighting unnecessary, until, under pressure for action from Mrs Thatcher's War Cabinet at home, 2 Para attacked Darwin.

To get his reluctant troops moving, their flamboyant Colonel Herbert "H" Jones bravely charged a bunker and was mysteriously killed, shot in the back. His sacrifice was later rewarded with a posthumous 'political' VC, when an MC would have been the appropriate decoration.

The 2 i/c took command and managed to get his men to advance by the sea shore. The enemy then started surrendering and the paras were able to get on to Goose Green where they unnecessarily fired a Milan napalm rocket into the school building in which many were sheltering. When reinforcements landed on the airstrip, one of our planes decimated many of them with fragmentation cluster bombs, which are outlawed by international agreement. 250 of the enemy had been killed for the loss of 17 paras.

Later the press made much of finding napalm, also outlawed, but the Argentinians used it only for cremating their dead.

The old abattoir buildings on the west side of San Carlos Water were used as a field hospital and such was the improvement in treatment of casualties since the world war and the skill of the army surgeons, that not one of our wounded died throughout the whole campaign, thanks to rapid casevac by helicopter.

It's unclear who chose San Carlos as the site for the landing – the gung-ho Admiral Lewin at Force HQ in Northolt, Admiral

Woodward, commanding the Task Force, or the cautious General Moore commanding the troops. The Chief of the General Staff, Field Marshall Sir Edwin Bramhall appears to have taken no part in the planning.

Any determined commander would have landed on the other side of East Falkland at Berkeley Sound, only 15 miles from Stanley where our ships would have been out of range of aircraft flying from the mainland and we would have had complete air superiority with our Harriers flying from the carriers, which had always to be kept out of range in the Atlantic.

The war should then have been won in a matter of days. But no one had their heart in this 'War of Mrs Thatcher's Succession'. They were obviously hoping that the Argentinians would cave in and that fighting would be unnecessary.

As it was, most of the troops were faced with an eighty mile march across wet moorland in winter without waterproof boots. To avoid this, the Welsh Guards were put aboard the *Sir Tristram* and *Sir Galahad* and carried round by sea at night, to land at Bluff cove on the south coast which 2 Para had now reached.

Due to some unforgivable ineptitude, they were not unloaded immediately on arrival at daybreak and the *Sir Galahad* was hit by a bomb from a Pucara aircraft that caused a devastating fire and the loss of over fifty lives.

In his history of 2 Para after the war, General Frost, of Arnhem fame, unwittingly disclosed that the ship had also been carrying Milan rockets which contained napalm. Of course, no admittance of this disgraceful fact was made at the time, when distress in South Wales was considerable.

At last, twenty four days after the landing and after a very heavy artillery bombardment 1 and 2 Commando and 1 Para overran the half-starved Argentinian conscripts on the hills north of Stanley, and the Scots Guards took Tumbledown Mountain to the West. The Argentinians had heard a rumour that the Gurkhas were to be brought in on the action. They were terrified of the reputation of these Nepalese fighters, but fortunately for them, the Gurkhas weren't deployed in the Falklands conflict.

A Spanish speaking intelligence officer was in contact with General Menendez, who agreed to surrender, and the insufferable journalist Max Hastings set off next morning to walk into Stanley ahead of the troops to gain notoriety.

Ninety percent of the Argentinian troops were conscripts so could have had little motivation for the conflict but nevertheless fought very commendably. Yet they were apparently very poorly treated by their officers, who had remained in Stanley, and were shunned on their return home by an ungrateful nation, since when 300 are reported to have committed suicide.

In fact, the whole operation was a very close run thing as all our artillery ammunition had been exhausted and Admiral Woodward admitted that his ships could not have remained at sea more than a week longer. If their bombs had all exploded we would have lost 16 warships.

After the war, it was reported that one or two of our paras had shot some Argentinians out of hand when they surrendered. An enquiry was launched and police were sent out to Argentina to investigate the position but, as usual, nothing came of it. I complained in a letter to a friend, an ex-para, General Peter Chiswell, but we are friends again now.

At dinner a year later with Peter de la Billiere, who commanded the SAS during the Falklands War, I met General Plant who described how the sergeants had followed behind their men to prevent any backsliding. I can't imagine that happening in the Indian Army.

It's hard not to come to the conclusion that this was the most unnecessary and irresponsible war since the British invasion of Tibet in 1903, under the charismatic and aggressive Colonel Francis Younghusband, to compel their alliance against suspected Russian influence when the pacific Tibetans, armed only with a few outdated muskets, were instructed not to fight, only to demonstrate. Yet about 3,000 were massacred by Maxim guns and horse artillery.

British casualties were 5 officers and 29 Indian sepoys, but a large number of mule drivers and coolies died in the appalling winter snows and there was widespread looting of Buddhist manuscripts and treasures from the monasteries when they reached Llasa.

The only other aggressive war in our history was the Boer

war, started in 1899 when Colonial Secretary Milner demanded the independent states of the Transvaal and the Orange Free State, to which the original Dutch settlers of the Cape had trekked to avoid British control, be incorporated into the British Union of South Africa.

It took a huge army three years to subdue the brave Boer guerrilla fighters, which was only finally achieved after burning many farms in a scorched earth policy and shutting the women and children up in concentration camps in which some 20,000 died of disease.

The Falklands war was a similar charade. Argentina's claim to the islands was better than ours as we had seized them in 1830 and had ever since refused to have our claim to ownership tested in the international court of justice, as they had often demanded.

We would not have tolerated a foreign power owning the Isle of Man for 150 years, which would have been comparable. It could not be called a war of liberation as we had already agreed to transfer sovereignty of the islands to Argentina but had then reneged on our promise, and the islanders were not asking to be liberated.

The only just war is a defensive war in protection of one's homeland.

In this case, Mrs Thatcher had invited the Argentinian invasion for her own political fortunes and the *junta* had achieved it for similar reasons without violence and convinced that they would get away with it.

It only proved that a major power with vastly superior armaments and aided by America can defeat a third rate one — just as Israel can always defeat the Palestinians.

In truth, the Falklands war was very nearly a disaster. We lost five warships, and if the enemy's bombs had all exploded, we would have lost sixteen. Of the 11,500 Argentinian soldiers involved, 655 were killed and 1,100 wounded. British casualties included 255 dead, and 746 wounded soldiers and sailors.

One woman was killed in Stanley by British artillery. Large numbers of land mines were left which, as they are made of plastic, are very difficult to disable or lift.

Without the Sidewinder missiles supplied by the Americans, our Harriers would not have defeated the Argentinians' aircraft, of which 24 were shot down, including some from the ground by Rapier missiles. Our professional troops always used the vastly expensive Milan anti-tank rockets containing napalm to incinerate the wretched enemy conscripts in their bunkers. The cost of the war was never disclosed but it must have been several billion pounds, ours probably ten times greater than Argentina's, which was enough to ruin their economy.

We were left with the cost of building an international airport and garrisoning the islands ever after. What good might have been done with this money to alleviate poverty in the Third World doesn't bear thinking about.

The 70,000 Anglo-Argentinians who had been put at considerable risk had fortunately not been victimised. The *junta* resigned and the new civilian Government arrested the patriarchal General Galtieri and nine other officers, condemning them to some years of imprisonment or house arrest.

Back at home, Francis Pym resigned as Foreign Secretary, or perhaps he was simply sacked. His political career was finished, but he has never written his memoirs.

A knighthood was given to the Secretary for Defence, John Nott, whose agreement to sell the *Endurance* to Brazil had been such a come-on to the *junta*, and a peerage to the bellicose Admiral Lewin, who had encouraged Mrs Thatcher to wage war. The wet Rex Hunt was returned as governor with a knighthood, the only commanding officer in our history to be so rewarded for surrendering his forces, when not one had been wounded.

Lord Carrington, who had resigned as scapegoat for the Government was rewarded by being appointed British representative on NATO. Captain Barker of the *Endurance* was passed over for promotion for having expressed criticism of his orders. He resigned and died not very many years after.

In August, the *News of the World* printed a front page article accusing me of being a traitor. I instructed our London solicitors, Lawrence Graham to sue for libel and found that Patrick Wall, a partner, who dealt with libel, was blind. He instructed a barrister with the unpromising name of Proviti who seemed equivocal about it. It took me two years of pressure to get the case to court but the day before the hearing was due to take place, the paper offered to settle for c.£20,000 and Wall urged me to accept, but I demanded £60,000 plus costs and, after a day of brinkmanship, they paid up. I never heard what the costs were, but probably near as much.

Three months later the Daily Mail published a piece accusing me of being 'The Black Sheep of Goose Green', inspired, I suspected, by Luxton, who had been brought over for the above libel.

For this case, I instructed a firm of solicitors in Cardiff, who were said to be competent over libel. They, too, were pretty dilatory and I had to conduct most of the case myself, eventually getting £30,000 and about £5,000 for the solicitors, who then had the neck to demand a success fee, which I refused to pay.

Looking back, I was taking big risks but then I just didn't believe I could lose. Bringing libel actions is highly stressful and usually just jam for the lawyers and the libel laws are most often used by rich crooks like Robert Maxwell to protect them from the kind of free speech that is legally available in America.

The flamboyant Maxwell had been born into a very poor Jewish family in Czechoslovakia. He reached England in 1939, changed his name and joined the army, managing to end up as a captain in the Intelligence Corps. He gained an MC and secured a position in the Control Commission in Berlin at the end of the War.

He made a clever fortune publishing trade and technical magazines and became a Labour MP. Later, he bought the *Daily Mirror* and helped himself to its pension fund. In the end, he was mysteriously drowned, falling off his yacht in the Canary Islands. It was believed by many that he was murdered by Mossad, the Israeli Secret Service because he was trying to blackmail their government into clearing the gargantuan pile of debt his megalomania had accumulated.

His body was rapidly flown to Israel and buried without proper autopsy. Two of his sons and co-directors were charged with embezzlement of the pension fund and represented by leading barristers in a trial of several weeks. Incredibly, they were exonerated of any blame because they had 'just done what Daddy told them'!

The lawyers earned a million or two; the poor *Mirror Group* pensioners got nothing.

During the Falklands conflict I had appeared on two television programmes, one in Manchester, the other in Leeds, at which I met Colin Mitchell, the brave young Colonel 'Mad Mitch' of the Argyll and Sutherland Highlanders, who had disobeyed orders and restored order in Aden before our evacuation in 1969.

He had been rewarded by being passed over for promotion and so resigned his commission to become a journalist and now an MP, though he was to lose his seat and die young shortly after.

Some months later, I also appeared on Kilroy Silk's programme. I have never acquired the skill for television. Firstly I lose my nerve about being outspoken and secondly I was fool enough to answer the questions when one should ignore the question and just get your message across.

On the 29th September, I wrote to *The Times* demanding that a war cemetery be constructed in the Falklands for the Argentinian dead – their bodies were said still to litter the islands – offering a site at San Carlos where their relations could visit without encountering hostilities from the islanders.

This was taken up by the World Council of Churches and on 21st October *The Times* printed a leading article in support. The Government then sent out undertakers to collect the corpses and perversely made the cemetery just outside Darwin, which meant their relatives could not visit the graves until about 15 years later.

At about this time, I got a notice from the Inland Revenue saying they wanted to come and examine my books. Coincidentally, a Minister at the Treasury was advising the Rossminster Group, which assisted rich men in putting their money in tax havens abroad.

In protest I therefore refused to let the inspector into the house to check whether I was collecting tax from my employees on their overtime or whatever. This led to a summons for me to appear before the commissioners when a barrister, who had been brought down from London to confront me; let out that this was the only such case of defiance they had faced.

I lost, of course, and was ordered to allow the inspection, at which it was found that I had not deducted tax on the tax I had paid on Jim's earnings and that I had paid my wife the tax-free sum she was allowed to earn late in one year and early in the next bringing the two payments into one year and so rendering them liable to national insurance.

Fortunately, no fine or costs were imposed so the whole sum was pretty trivial and cannot possibly have covered the barrister's fee.

In the same year also I got a visit from a VAT inspector who found that I had not collected the tax on irrigation equipment which I had sold to a neighbouring farmer for a few thousand pounds. I pointed out that no tax had been lost as, if I had collected it, the farmer would just have reclaimed it, as farm produce is exempt.

But my argument was to no avail. He insisted that I must pay the VAT concerned, about £800, against which I appealed and was called to a hearing in Birmingham.

I was delayed by an accident on the road but was not concerned as I imagined other cases would be heard first. On arrival, however, I found there was no other case and that the adjudicator and prosecuting counsel had been waiting for about an hour. My appeal was soon dismissed but I told the judge it was ridiculous and that I would just reclaim it in future monthly returns, which, I'm not ashamed to say, I did.

VAT is an absurd tax which was imposed on us as a result of joining the EEC. It must be a bureaucratic nightmare to retailers and businesses and I am sure open to widespread corruption.

A civil servant whom I met recently was sacked for disclosing a racket in Romanian immigrants which resulted in the resignation of a Government minister. Some minor irregularity from his past was immediately publicised – reinforcing my belief that, if you cause trouble to the Government, you are likely to find yourself tied up in enquiries or they try to find something from your past with which to smear you.

I had fallen out with our Falklands partner, Colin Smith, the woollen merchant in Bradford, as he had been persuaded by some journalists to make some adverse comments about me in a newspaper. I threatened to sue him but dropped it and relations were restored after a year. Pitaluga had resigned as a director of San Carlos, as had Luxton with whom Smith also fell out now.

The Government appointed the trusty Lord Frank to hold a

Commission of Enquiry into why they had been caught unawares by the Argentinian invasion. Lasting for six months this, like recent enquiries by the Lords Butler and Hunt into our joining America in the invasion of Iraq, was the usual whitewash to clear Mrs Thatcher of any blame and, against all the evidence, concluded that she could not have foreseen it. One might have thought that she would have known that when in 1977 the Argentinians threatened to take the islands, the PM James Callaghan had despatched a nuclear submarine and two frigates to deter them, but despite ample information, Mrs Thatcher had sent no warships and uttered no warnings.

I wrote a submission but was not called to give evidence, nor was my submission included, even though my name was recorded as a contributor.

It was admitted that our military attaché in Buenos Aires had given prior warning, which was considered by the Joint Services Committee, but this was ignored. Patrick Watts, the editor of *Penguin News*, the island's weekly paper, stated that the people of West Falkland had always been in favour of transfer of sovereignty to Argentina. Such enquiries are always an expensive farce, set up simply to get a Government out of trouble.

It was also disclosed at about this time, that the ship's log of the submarine *Conqueror*, which had sunk the *Belgrano*, had gone missing. The navigation officer was related to a Mrs Murrell who lived near Shrewsbury and was a prominent anti-nuclear campaigner. The poor woman was murdered and her body deposited in a ditch a mile away. There was no sign of break-in and nothing had been stolen from the house. Nor has the log book ever been reported found. It was suspected that MI5 were involved.

In November 1982 Fiona married Edward Buchan at our parish church in Llanigon. We had a reception for about 150 guests in a marquee on the lawn at Penyrwrlodd. Edward – a grandson of the author John Buchan, who was later created Lord Tweedsmuir and made Governor General of Canada before the war – was a junior director of the merchant bank Hill Samuel Ltd, subsequently transferring to Rothschilds to enjoy their generous salaries and to pick up one or two company directorships. They then lived for nine years in London, having children, William, Annabel, Laura and

Amelia.

Tessa, having sold the house in Kilmaine Road, bought one in Wandsworth Road, near Clapham. She was working for Serenissima, an upmarket travel agency, and led tours abroad. Although the most talented of our children, unfortunately she has always been unlucky in love, or too outspoken, which men don't like.

Julian had left Radley and had spent a year working on the farm while we were in the Falkland Islands – an experience which convinced him that he wanted a city life. I had met the commanding officer and Colonel Commandant of the 16/5th Lancers, who said they would take him in the regiment, but unfortunately he failed the Regular Commissions Board, which at that time seemed to have a prejudice against public school boys. I knew of several sons of regular army officers who also got turned down. They and the Army Chiefs were gung-ho paratroop officers who mistakenly thought that officers should be tougher than the men they would command rather than just braver.

Unfortunately, Radley had not pushed him enough and he had not the A-levels to get to a University. So he took a three year course at the City of London Polytechnic, which got him a diploma in business studies, and then spent a further year there, which earned him a degree but proved quite useless, as jobs for graduates were then very hard to get.

He had joined the Honourable Artillery Company Territorials as a gunner, although they were tied to special forces, but he failed again on another attempt at a commission. I wondered at the time whether my appearance on television about the Falklands campaign might have hindered him but when I heard the Shropshire Yeomanry were looking for officers at this time he could not be persuaded to join.

In September 1982 the Israelis, who had invaded Lebanon, allowed the Falangist Christian Militia to enter the Sabra and Chatila camps of Palestinian refugees, where they committed the most bloody massacres, killing many hundreds of men, women and children.

We were asked to give land at San Carlos for an army base and firing range, which we gave free. The Falkland Islands Company on the other hand, when asked for land for a new airport to be built to serve the forces, demanded and got a huge sum at three times the usual price for land in the islands.

Before the war about a dozen Polish trawlers fished the seas around the Falklands. Now licences were offered to all and several islanders and the Falkland Islands Co, with no experience of fishing – there had never been any fishing by the inhabitants around the islands – applied and formed partnerships with Korean and Japanese fishing fleets, which have stripped the seas ever since. The licensees got rich. Incredibly British trawler owners never took any interest in fishing there.

Chapter Ten

During the winter we took the car to Normandy and stayed with our friend Ronald Thompson, where he was still growing apples.

We visited all the D-day invasion beaches and war cemeteries. While British cemeteries have three foot high grave stones the Germans have a bronze plate about a foot square lying flat on the ground. Both are always beautifully tended but the German graves look more severe with little space for putting flowers on them.

In England, Mrs Thatcher had disposed of what she called the 'wets' in her cabinet – generally the more upper class, of more traditionally paternalistic Tory leanings. She wanted only those she could dominate.

My brother had been replaced as Minister of Education by one of her Jewish friends the right wing Keith Joseph, but he did not alter much. She also made Nigel Lawson, another Jew, Chancellor of the Exchequer. Her constituency was Finchley, which had a large Jewish community.

The secret to Mrs Thatcher's abrasive character was disclosed by Auberon Waugh, who claimed that she was the illegitimate daughter of Lord Brownlow in whose house her mother had been a housemaid. This she has never denied so one can only assume that she is proud of her aristocratic, if irregular, lineage.

In June, there was a general election won by the Conservatives with a record majority of 144 seats, though still not with a majority of the votes cast. This always happens under our crazy electoral system, bedevilled by the useless and unstable Liberal party and giving no voice to fringe parties. Either we should have proportional representation – all the continental countries do – or the Liberals should stand down and give us two parties, as in America.

Now there would be no holding the 'Iron Lady' on her

mission to break the great power of the Trade Unions, whose Communist shop stewards had virtually destroyed the British motor car industry and did indeed need curbing.

Incompetent bosses must also have been much to blame, as the Japanese have managed to build cars in this country without such troubles.

In 1984, the most serious riots ever known broke out in Handsworth, Birmingham, and the London suburb of Brixton, caused by heavy-handed policing of the black community. Many shops were looted and buildings set on fire. Disgracefully, the police made little effort to control the situation; they only have the courage to act against peaceful demonstrators.

In America, the ex-film star, Ronald Reagan had become President in 1980 and in 1983 had inaugurated his Star Wars policy of developing missiles able to shoot down Russian rockets carrying atomic bombs in the event of the feared attack.

This was vastly expensive and never successful, yet American planes carrying atomic bombs had for years been flying round the Soviet Union, threatening annihilation.

There was mutual admiration between Reagan and Mrs Thatcher and equal antagonism towards the so-called 'Evil Empire'. Accordingly, she allowed the Americans to base their Cruise Missiles at the aerodrome on Greenham Common and stirred up vehement anti-nuclear feelings which led to huge demonstrations by the Campaign for Nuclear Disarmament in London and at Greenham, where women protesters would remain camped outside for years. Cruise missiles were also placed in Turkey and Germany, again despite large protesting crowds.

In 1984, I went to Russia with Tessa, one of whose friends was involved with an Anglo Orthodox church group. At that time visas were not easily obtained and practically no tourists from Western Europe went there. The visa application for our party of about 15 stated the purpose of our visit as being 'to study Russian icons', but on arrival at the airport (Leningrad, recently renamed St. Petersburg) after a flight in a rather basic Aeroflot plane, the true purpose proved to be the clandestine import of bibles, then banned in the Soviet Union.

The customs officials opened our cases and discovered that Tessa and others had been persuaded to carry them. After some sticky questioning the bibles were confiscated and we were allowed to proceed to an hotel where the food was terrible.

St. Petersburg is the most magnificent city, built by Peter the Great on marshy land divided by the river Neva and interspersed with innumerable canals. A charming In-tourist guide took us to visit the magnificent Hermitage museum and several beautiful palaces. The city was now restored after being much destroyed when the Germans laid siege to it for over a year in 1941/2, when nearly a million people died of starvation. But the post- war tower blocks built on the outskirts were bleak beyond belief.

We then took a train to Moscow, where we stayed in a huge In-tourist hotel, which no Russians, except prostitutes, were allowed to enter. We went to an opera, where it was very hot so I took off my jacket and hung it over the back of my seat and on departure found that it had been stolen. I complained and was interviewed at a police cell in the basement of our hotel.

The city was very bleak, with practically no restaurants and very few cars except limousines for Soviet officials. The people were all ill-dressed and obviously poor. However, the Moscow underground is quite magnificent, with spacious platforms and murals all over the walls. From talking to our guide and others it was obvious that the Russians were just as terrified of the Americans attacking as the West was of them.

Although religion was discouraged, St Basil's cathedral in the Kremlin was functioning and they were re-gilding the domes of some churches. We visited museums where I found icons rather dull and were taken to several derelict churches out in the country around that our guide told us had been destroyed by the Nazis. I protested that we knew they had been wrecked during the Communist Revolution. I must have been reported as a subversive as after this my telephone rang in the night, presumably to check my presence as there was no reply on the line.

In the Falklands, the Government were pressing what they called the absentee landlords of several farms to sell, so that they might be distributed to the workers. This was a curious policy for a Conservative Government, reminiscent of the socialist Allende in

Chile before he was deposed and murdered.

However, these workers were not given the land; they had to buy it with substantial government mortgages. Colin Smith urged us to sell, though the farm had been quite profitable over the past three years, and I reluctantly agreed. As he negotiated a price twice what we had paid for it, and we had borrowed all the money on mortgage, we came very well out of it. Our good relations were now restored and I must say that, despite our disagreements, I always found him very honest.

My brother Mark, who had been made a Queen's Counsel on becoming a Minister (a cosy legal custom) had been appointed a Recorder of the Crown Court on leaving the Government and was also made Treasurer of the Commonwealth Parliamentary Association, and would be Deputy Chairman from 1985 to 1987. This enabled him to attend meetings in different Commonwealth countries each year, usually accompanied by his wife Sandra. He was made a Deputy Lieutenant of Cheshire in 1983.

Jim had left us to take on a job as farm manager and I took on George Griffiths who had a smallholding next to Penyrwrlodd. The woodlands planted in 1950 were maturing and I managed to sell enough timber to produce a profit of about £2,000 a year. People will tell you they can't make any money from forestry, but this is nonsense. It all depends on buying at the right price and watching your costs, and, of course, care in selling it. I sold some oak by tender and found a huge variation in offers. A year or so later the same buyers made offers in opposite proportions. It all depends on whether the merchant has got a customer for it at the time.

I wanted to write a book about the Falklands war but could not risk it until the libel actions were settled. Later I approached one or two people who were associated with publishing but did not get much encouragement, probably because I was going to be controversial. Without certainty of getting it published I was not willing to devote the necessary time to it, possibly without reward, so it was never done.

About this time I gave up smoking a pipe, something which I had done since my Indian days, took to smoking a few cigarettes a day, not then so demonised as now but Penyrwrlodd house was draughty enough not to give offence.

Ever since leaving Hanbury and not working so hard I had had difficulty sleeping but going down from 600ft to Treseissyllt at sea level removed the problem and also removed the stress of worries. I had given up growing the troublesome early potatoes and Rafael managed the corn, haymaking and livestock very well on his own, but I still went down for two or three nights every three weeks or so.

Most years I slipped a disk hauling hay bales and once went to the hospital in Haverfordwest where they stretched me on a table quite uselessly. Driving home by minor roads in my old Alvis I went over a bump in the road which fixed it! Sometimes it caused very painful spasms in my back at night but I found that by sitting on the ground with my legs out and Rosemary forcing my head down to my knees we could get the disc out at home.

For a long time, we were glued to the television each week watching Dallas, where the scheming Texan oil millionaire J R Ewing and his glamorous wife Sue Ellen lived at South Fork with his decent brother Bobby and his naive wife Pammy. When J R was shot, there was such an outcry that he had to be resurrected later. There has never been another television 'soap' to compare with it. Now they are all sex, seamy social problems and miscegenation – terrible rubbish!

In 1983, when the miners were striking, Mrs Thatcher had appointed an American businessman, with a reputation for strike breaking, as Chairman of the Coal Board. These strikes came to a head in 1984 with appalling scenes of violence between pickets and the police. In the end the strikers were beaten and over the next years most of the pits were closed, with power stations being turned over to oil or gas from the North Sea. The number of miners fell from 180,000 to 10,000. Once there were six hundred pits in South Wales; now there is one.

Ever since then most of our coal has been imported from Poland or Australia, which are cheaper sources of supply. But this made no allowance for the unemployment pay of the unfortunate men, the backbone of Britain, who had lost their jobs and self-respect. Such is the immorality of capitalist free trade, although it had never been Labour or Conservative policy, until promoted by Mrs Thatcher, influenced by the American economist, Milton

Friedman, and it has resulted in disastrous globalisation.

It is obvious that if there is to be a higher standard of living in this country than in Eastern Europe or the third world, there has to be some protection from imports. However, the Conservative Government were throwing money at railways and farming!

In October, the IRA blew the front off the *Grand Hotel* in Brighton where the Conservative Government were staying for their conference. Two people were killed and several were severely injured but the primary target, Mrs Thatcher, escaped unhurt. This was the worst terrorist attack ever perpetrated against British politicians. The only reason for it and so many other outrages by the IRA was that we have never had martial law in Ulster and capital punishment for murder.

In December, a fatal gas leak at an American chemical factory in Bhopal in India killed 2,000 people and left some 200,000 injured for life. No one has ever been charged and it was years before any compensation was paid as the company and the Indian Government disputed responsibility. The site has still not been cleared, water supplies are polluted, and defective children still being born.

In 1983 Raul Alfonsin had been elected President of Argentina but the fact that they now had a democratic Government and had put the military *junta* on trial made no difference to our government's refusal to discuss the sovereignty of the Falkland Islands – despite the fact that the islands were, and have remained every year since, a huge expense to garrison.

In April 1985, I bought a Contessa 32 ft yacht, which I intended to sail to Turkey. On my first voyage, when the previous owner sailed with me to show me the ropes, we met a severe gale in the Bay of Biscay and were glad to get into La Rochelle – at 3.00am. We sailed on and up the river Garonne to Bordeaux where, after taking the mast down, he left me to sail the yacht further along the river and into the lock for the Canal du Midi, which was decidedly tricky.

Rosemary came out by train and we spent three weeks motoring across to the Mediterranean. Unfortunately, the yacht drew 5ft 6ins and the canal was only 5ft deep so we frequently got stuck on the bottom. On these occasions Rosemary took a line ashore in the dinghy and after securing it to one of the trees that grow all along the banks, I would winch *Annabel*, as I had named her, off backwards.

The canal was a little deeper in the middle but the trouble arose when we had to get out of the way of a big barge. Some locks were automatic but for the most part, Rosemary had to go ashore and open them.

We spent a couple of nights with John and Deidre Whitfield, now Lord and Lady Kenswood, though I don't think they use the title. They had left their farm at Roch ten years earlier, buying this large farm near Toulouse, on which their three sons worked. They seemed contented but I could never have settled in a foreign country.

We would go ashore for dinner when stopping for the night near a village and spent a day at the beautiful walled city of Carcasonne. We hardly saw another yacht or tourist longboat the whole way. On arriving at Cap d'Agde on the Mediterranean we took a train home spending two nights in Paris on the way.

My mother, who had been living in a bungalow on her own since my father died, had a stroke and fell outside the house. She died in hospital three days later on 31st May without recovering consciousness. When I saw her at the undertakers' she looked younger, with much of her beauty restored.

After her funeral at St Philip's Alderley Edge, we buried her with my father at the cemetery nearby. A tall, good-looking woman and Red Cross nurse during both wars, she had been a devoted wife and mother. It must have been a sadness to her that both her daughters had lived in South Africa the past thirty years but Mark and Sandra lived at Mobberley, only five miles away and visited her most days. And she had always come with my father to stay with us three or four times each year.

In June, Rosemary and I flew out to Montpellier and motored *Annabel* round the coast to Sete, a commercial port. There we found two livestock-carrying ships tied up at the quay. I immediately thought that one would be just right to carry those 20,000 odd sheep, who had their throats cut and were thrown in the sea each year in the Falklands, to a slaughterhouse in Argentina.

On making enquiries I was told by the captain that one, named *Jersey Express*, was going to be sold for scrap, even though she was only 25 years old and in good order, because there was not enough work for two. I talked further with the shipping agents for the Dutch owners, Bruns. I inspected the ship, which was 1,000 tons dead-weight, and it looked fine, although it was due for a 3rd year inspection for certification. I came away convinced that I should buy her. They said she would only fetch about £60,000 for scrap and the idea of owning and sailing my own ship really attracted me.

I put in an offer but it was turned down. We motored on through coastal lakes and waterways across the Camargue to Arles on the Rhone, spending a night at Aigues Mortes from where the last disastrous crusade sailed. There is a magnificent Roman amphitheatre at Arles.

Going fast down the centre of the mighty river Rhone with about a six knot current, we were suddenly thrown off our feet as the keel struck hard against a rock. Only then did we notice that there were marker buoys for the channel close to the right bank and got over to it!

At Port St Louis we got the mast up and sailed through choppy seas with a *mistral* wind blowing to Port de Bouc, where we got the yacht lifted out of the water to inspect the keel that proved to be dented but not seriously damaged. We then took a bus to Montpellier and a plane home.

In July, I flew out again with Mark Shuldham and we sailed along the coast to Marseilles, where the population is half Algerian, spending two days ashore. Next we sailed along the Riviera coast and across to Corsica, staying there for two nights in Ajaccio, before continuing to Sorrento, near Naples. Mark flew home from there but I went on to visit the ancient Etruscan city of Paestum, which was most spectacular and beautifully maintained, and Pompeii, whose ruins I found a bit disappointing.

I also visited the Commonwealth War Graves Cemetery at Salerno, where Anglo-American forces had first landed in 1943 and very nearly got forced back into the sea, before pushing on to Monte Cassino.

Julian and his friend William Adams flew out to join me in Sorrento. Next morning we sailed out of the harbour to find it was blowing a gale and we considered turning back. Pride, however, got the better of us for Contessas are seaworthy boats, so we reefed the sails and proceeded to give ourselves a very uncomfortable 24 hours as the gale increased to near force 10.

Afterwards we heard that there had been an announcement on the a radio warning all yachts to stay in harbour. But then most yachts don't sail if the force of the wind is above force 4 or 5. Many, of course, never leave their moorings, yachting for their owners being more about gin and adultery than sailing!

In the evening I saw the lights of a town and, thinking we'd had enough, turned towards land. When a mile or so away a helicopter appeared and flew low round us, the pilot shaking his fist. I got the message that we should turn around and I think he may well have saved our lives as I later discovered that the sea is very shallow on that coast. I had not got a chart as we would have needed a new one almost every day. I relied on an atlas and a compass which was all that sailors would have had in the days of sail.

Actually, I did also have a Satnav, which should have given me an exact position every six hours but very often the satellite seemed to be sulky and uncooperative. And we had a depth gauge, but in the cabin. So we had to sail on to Reggio di Calabria in the straits of Messina through the night. No one was sick, the boys seemed unconcerned and slept and I sat at the tiller for 24 hours really rather enjoying it.

We went ashore and talked to the natives to hear that, despite strong opposition from the Pope and presumably the local priests, contraception was legalised that year. The rate of birth in Italy, until then the highest birth rate in Europe, dropped like a stone and today is the lowest. Newspapers report that boys now live at home with their parents until they're about thirty years old.

After rounding Calabria and crossing to Cephalonia and then sailing on to Patras, I flew home. James Woosnam and a friend came out and went through the Corinth Canal and around the Greek islands for three weeks. They left the yacht at Piraeus, near Athens.

We then took it over with Fiona and Eddy, who proved not to be very enthusiastic sailors, at least, not when a meltemi was blowing, as it does in September, and left us at Mikonos. Sailing past Ikaria, we were seized by a williwaw, a fierce squall which comes down off island mountains, and nearly capsized the yacht before I could get the sails down. We then sat out a gale tied to a mooring in a harbour for two days before sailing on to Kusadasi in Turkey, where we left *Annabel* at mooring for the winter.

The following spring, Mark Shuldham and his wife, Cherry sailed her for two weeks, leaving her at Bodrum.

In October 1985, I received a call from Bruns that they would, after all, accept my offer of £60,000 for the *Jersey Express* and I flew to Holland to settle the deal. Ronald Thompson offered to drive me down to Sete from his house in Normandy and I arranged with the shipping agents to have the inspection carried out on the ship. I had been in touch with the Falkland Islands development corporation to try to get financial backing, but there had recently been a report by the Labour peer, Lord Shackleton, son of the famous explorer, declaring that the export of sheep meat from the Islands was not practicable, so I was given no encouragement. It was incidentally, Lord Shackleton who had previously advocated the buying of farms for distribution to the workers.

The ship inspector quite unnecessarily ordered that all water tanks along the keel be cut open to check the thickness of the hull, which was found to be perfectly satisfactory, and even ordered the cylinder heads removed from the diesel engines. In doing so they managed to break one.

Then, without consulting me, she was sailed into a shipyard in Marseilles by the crew of her sister ship and when she was returned to Sete the agents sent me an account for nearly £60,000. I was aware that Marseilles was probably the most expensive port in Europe and my intention had been to get a crew and have her sailed to Brazil for the inspection.

I strongly suspected that I was the victim of sabotage, so refused to pay. Fortunately, I had formed a Limited Liability Company to own the ship. Bruns then asked to charter the ship for a voyage carrying cattle to Casablanca, for which they paid the handsome sum of £13,000. The shipping agent, whose boss was in Paris, then demanded that I take them as partners to clear the debt and said they could arrange more voyages to north Africa. I agreed and he formed a new company registered in the Isle of Man and things were looking up. But when the Chernobyl nuclear power station in Russia blew up, spreading radio active dust across Europe, even as far as North Wales the Moroccans refused to take any more of the cattle, which were coming out of Poland.

Meanwhile, I continued to press the Falkland Government with plans to operate the ship as a floating abattoir, with refrigerated storage, which would sail round the islands to each farm in turn. I got support from the Managing Director of the FI Company and several farmers and I found a firm in Smithfield willing to take the meat. But inspectors of the meat and livestock Commission, employed by the FI Government to examine the proposal, produced a report that recommended using a mobile abattoir, which had apparently been tried in the Hebrides, to drive round the islands' farms – a ridiculous idea since there were no roads and hence no means to facilitate exports.

The agents never managed to get any cattle shipments, the *Jersey Express* lay in Sete and I got continuous demands for harbour dues, which was worrying because, under French law, directors are liable for company debts. Eventually the ship was seized and presumably sold for scrap, so ending my dreams to be practically the only private owner of a British merchant ship

I flew out to Turkey in May 1986. With sailing there is always the problem of getting a crew. However I found a man, a yachting junkie, who'd ended up there and wanted to return to Nice.

We sailed to Rhodes and on to Santorini (Thira), believed to be the origin of the Atlantis legend. The harbour is in a vast volcano site and you take donkeys up into the island. Then we sailed to the Pelepponese where, as we rounded Cape Matapan in a half gale and headwind, the engine suddenly stopped. My crewman, who was in such a state of nerves that he had to smoke a cigarette before going forward to lower the sail, then disclosed that the jib sheet had gone overboard and had obviously fouled the propeller. As neither of us was keen to go overboard and free it we sailed for many hours tacking against the wind and getting nowhere until at last I thought that starting the engine and putting it in reverse, while pulling the rope, might free it, which fortunately it did and we reached Kalamati at 10.00pm.

Next day we set sail for Malta, some 400 miles away. It was then, seeing neither smoke nor a sail, I realised just how large the Mediterranean is. In particular, I was conscious of being so rash as to have taken on board only a rubber dinghy and having no life raft. During the second afternoon we were picking up signals on the radio from Malta but then these faded. I feared that we were sailing past and would end up in Libya, so I turned north to hit Sicily, where we arrived late in the evening.

Next morning, we sailed south and hit Gozo, where we entered the harbour and were accosted by police who said that yachts could only land at Valetta, the principal port. So a police launch accompanied us for eight hours and handed us over to a customs official, who remembered the British Navy and, over a bottle of gin, set us free.

Valetta is a pretty town of small streets and many bars. Before the war it was the base of the British fleet in the Mediterranean, where my uncle Jack Gamon served with the charismatic Lord Louis Mountbatten in 1930 before accompanying him and the Prince of Wales on a voyage around the world in the battle-cruiser *Renown*.

During the war Malta was very heavily bombed but fortunately the people remained true to us and our brave fighter pilots just managed to hold off an invasion. Despite losing many ships in supplying the island we just managed to keep it going as a vital base from which our submarines and aircraft inflicted heavy losses on the enemy convoys to north Africa.

For hundreds of years after the crusades the island was ruled by the Knights of Malta, and many of their fine churches remain. Since the war half the Catholic population had emigrated to Australia. I got a very good suit made in 24 hours, flew home for three weeks and on return sailed on to Palma, in Majorca when we were nearly run down by a merchant vessel. It was either sailing on automatic without any lookout or did not know that steam should give way to sail!

I always liked sailing at night as it was interesting to watch the lights of ships and try to calculate their direction. They never answered radio signals. Also, whilst one could cover about 140 miles at night, during the day the limit was probably no more than about 60. There was the bonus, too, that doing watches of four hours, you didn't see much of your mate, and mine was pretty unattractive.

Julian and friends sailed on to Almeria in Spain, where *Annabel* was laid up on land for the winter.

At home, inflation was still rampant and the pound at its lowest level ever against the dollar. Mrs Thatcher had now fallen out with the church, who had produced a pamphlet, *Church and the City*, calling for development of ex-industrial towns, most noticeably Liverpool, where unemployment was at a very high level and the charismatic amateur Test Cricketer, David Sheppard, was now bishop. Eventually, a very large redevelopment of the slum housing and disused docks was put in hand which has transformed the city.

Mikhail Gorbachev became the new leader of Russia, promising reforms and introducing more democratic Government. He also reached agreement in personal meetings with Ronald Reagan to end the Star Wars conflict and to destroy many of the nuclear weapons held by each power.

Having decimated British coal and steel production as well as our engineering industry, Mrs Thatcher was ridiculously suggesting that the unemployed should start individual businesses like her father in his grocer's shop. But 50,000 Indians, driven out of Uganda by the tyrant Idi Amin, had all been allowed to settle in this country and had very successfully taken over most of our grocery shops and newsagents, and some would prosper mightily in other lines of business.

In spring 1987, I flew out with Mark Shuldham to sail *Annabel* from Almeria through the straits of Gibraltar, where in a main shipping line at night it was a bit hairy. In Gib, we explored the extensive tunnels driven through the rock during the war. The frontier with Spain was still closed. It is absurd that we still hang on to this colonial possession which operates mostly as a tax haven for the rich. When we are in the European Union, we would not tolerate Spain owning the Isle of Wight.

Shortly afterwards in Gib the SAS would shoot out of hand three IRA members who were, regrettably, found to be unarmed. However, the usual whitewash enquiry would clear them.

Carrying on around the coast, we struck bottom but Mark leapt forward and pushed the Genoa sail across. We came off and continued to Cadiz where we laid the yacht at a mooring.

When Julian and James Woosnam went out next, they found that *Annabel* had been broken into and that the anchor was fouled. Fortunately, Julian had his diving gear with him and was able to free it. They sailed to La Rochelle.

Mark was unable to come again and sent a man who had been a Hurricane pilot in Malta during the war. The sea was choppy and for two days I was desperately sick – the only time ever. I found my watch quite an ordeal. We left the yacht at Dartmouth and Rosemary collected me.

A day later I was visited by the police as I was reported to have been carrying a gun, which I had deemed wise for protection on the yacht. Why they complained I cannot imagine, but it all blew over.

In 1986, the AIDS plague was announced and the Government, frightened of blaming homosexuals for unnatural practices, disgracefully declared that the whole population was at risk. The truth of the matter was that a relatively small number of people had been unfortunate enough to have had transfusions performed with blood imported from America that, incredibly, had been purchased from homosexual drug addicts, who were thus assisted in financing their vice. AIDS is contracted through sodomy, widely practised in Africa as a form of contraception. In this unjust world, it is passed from mother to child resulting in many millions of orphans throughout Africa and, increasingly, worldwide. Yet, the Catholic church forbids contraception, while Islam and some African leaders strongly discourage it.

Work was started on the channel tunnel which has been the ultimate disaster, now a magnificent engineering achievement which has never been profitable. It has enabled unrestricted immigration ever since and breached our hereditary defence against Europe.

A secret service agent Peter Wright wrote a book which the authorities banned but which was published in Australia and America, disclosing that Roger Hollis, the chief of the service (1956-65), was probably a Soviet agent, as Kim Philby had been during and after the war, and that there had been suspicions about Harold

Wilson, the Prime Minister. He was prosecuted in Australia by the Secretary to the British cabinet, Sir Robert Armstrong, who was famously accused by counsel for the defence of being 'economical with the truth'. The case collapsed and the book has since been published in Britain. Since then, the service has been headed by women, one of whom has also irregularly published her memoirs (as well as a bad novel).

Prince Andrew married Sarah Ferguson only to divorce her ten years later after she had engaged in several affairs. It is fatal for members of the Royal family to marry commoners.

Prince Edward resigned his commission in the Marines, took up film production and organised an unwise royal spectacular *It's a Knockout* show, which did nothing to enhance the dignity of the family. As always, familiarity breeds contempt. Only the admirable Prince Charles did not take part.

Generally speaking, the lives of the Royal family are becoming impossible with the 'gutter' press and photographers recording their every move.

In the autumn, I sailed with Simon Shuldham to the Channel Islands. It was certainly interesting sailing there, with tides of up to 20 feet, running at six or seven knots, when our engine only delivered five if there was little wind.

On the way home, in sight of the Isle of Wight, in half a gale, I carelessly stumbled over the tiller and broke it off. Saying 'Pray for my children', Simon pulled the foresail down and I the mainsail. Wallowing helplessly, I fired distress signal towards the mainland, and then another, but no lifeboat appeared and it was getting dark.

Fortunately, I found that I could get the stub end out of the rudder head and force the broken tiller back into it and we were relieved to round the Needles at midnight and soldier on up the Solent to Gosport.

After that I gave the yacht to Julian, who for several years would take part in races in the Solent and the Round The Island race, in which he had some success. In the course of time, he sold it and skippered a friend's yacht.

Although after an extra year at the polytechnic, Julian had got a degree in economics, there were few jobs looking for graduates, so we bought him a house in Fulham that needed modernisation, hoping that he might take to property development with me. But, after some temporary employments as assistant accountant, notably with the Sock Shop (which went bankrupt), which should have been good experience, he started his own business as an agent between companies and the innumerable training courses that are available.

He has worked hard at this ever since and it may be about to come good, but use of the internet has tended to sideline his firm.

Though professing to be anti-EU, Mrs Thatcher, at a conference in Lisbon in 1986, signed the Single European Act, which tied us closer in. Another of her Jewish ministers, Leon Brittan, Secretary of the Board of Trade and Industry, had to resign over the Westland scandal when he was trying to sell the British helicopter company to the American Sikorsky.

I don't know if there is a Jewish conspiracy to rule the world, as has always been suspected since the French and Russian revolutions, but they have certainly long manipulated American foreign policy and maybe, with the help of the banking financiers, ours also. Their loyalties are firstly to their religion, and the promised land of Israel.

I suppose I may be considered anti-Semitic. In fact, I have never known any Jews personally and much admire them for their remarkable abilities and family solidarity but they do have too many children and it would be remarkable if they did not use their influence to manipulate affairs. They have certainly controlled much British and American press for 100 years as well as film production in Hollywood.

Ever since the rebellious American colonies broke away from Britain as a result of the intransigence of George III, Freemasonry and secret WASP (White Anglo-Saxon Protestant) societies have controlled their policies, culminating in organisations of world government, under the League of Nations, in 1919 and, in 1945, the United Nations, both of which have proved singularly ineffectual, at vast expense. More recently, the machinations of the Masonic Lodge P2 nearly led to the fall of the Italian Government, and the secret

Bilderberg Group, formed in 1954 of selected bankers, industrialists and politicians of the western world, has presumably been trying to influence governments at their annual meetings ever since.

Mrs Thatcher also agreed to let American planes fly from this country to bomb Libya, in retaliation for a terrorist attack on a plane. It was a completely disproportionate act of aggression, leading Colonel Gadafi to arm the IRA, as an act of revenge. Yet in the June 1987 election, the Conservatives again won by a large majority and she was given a third term as PM.

The Church of England offered ordination to women which has proved a great success, but I hope they are not made bishops which would be as disastrous as permitting women to become Prime Minister.

My brother Mark, who had been MP for Runcorn from 1964 – 1983, and Warrington South since 1983, didn't stand and was offered, as I think happened to all ex-cabinet ministers, a life peerage.

As the Earl of Carlisle, whose family name is Howard, is addressed as Lord Carlisle, Mark was obliged to add the suffix, 'of Bucklow', which is the old name of the hundred near his home at Mobberley. It has since been a cause of annoyance to me that a Jewish Estonian immigrant, or son of, had changed his name to Alex Carlyle and become a barrister who was also elected MP for Montgomery. He has since also been made a life peer and calls himself Lord Carlyle of Berriew. I cannot imagine why my brother did not raise any objection.

The next year, Mark was appointed Chairman of the Review Committee of the Parole System and also Chairman of the Prime Minister's Committee on Business Appointments. In 1989, he became Chairman of the Criminal Injuries Compensation Board and in 1990 was made Judge of the Court of Appeal of the Channel Islands. He would hold these last three appointments for ten years, until 1999. Although he never became a top rank barrister, Mark has always been a competent speaker – not suffering from the nervous disposition that has plagued my life – and, I'm sure, a conscientious MP and Committee man.

I think his considerable success in life has been largely due also to his being an easygoing chap, without any strong views, enabling him to get through life without attracting any enemies, unlike my pronounced and sometimes controversial opinions, which I inherited from our Royds forebears. Mark has also been loyally supported by his wife Sandra.

In 1988, we took a holiday in Venice where we enjoyed visiting all the beautiful old buildings and watching intricate glass blowing on an island in the lagoon. But you would have to be much in need of a romantic evening to afford a trip in a gondola. The city is slowly sinking into the sea and they are building an immense barrage to save it.

When we first arrived at Penyrwrlodd, badger digging was an accepted rural 'sport'. I have never taken part but there was a sett on Cae Margaret, a field across the river on a part of the farm known as France – I suppose because it is across the water! All the fields have names, which is common throughout the country.

In c1978 badger digging was made illegal by tough pressure from the pussyfoot brigade. Now the country is overrun with badgers and farmers are loudly demanding their destruction by gassing, as they are believed to infect cattle with tuberculosis. There are reported now to be 300,000 in the country, of which 10,000 are killed annually on the roads, while they have killed all the hedgehogs.

It is reported that in 2002 alone, infection was found in 1,923 new herds, from which 22,377 cattle were slaughtered, and £26m was paid in compensation to farmers. But an NFU report found that the total cost of examination, bureaucracy and investigation of schemes for badger control was a staggering £180m. Incredibly, the government opposes vaccination and refuses to lift badger protection laws, because it would lose them votes among the animal welfare groups.

Fifty years ago children were said to catch TB from infected cow's milk and testing of all cattle was introduced, 'reactors' being slaughtered in the hope of eliminating the disease, which had nearly been achieved by 1980. A cow would have to be very heavily infected to have TB in its udder and I have never read of anyone catching it. Nevertheless, the test is so delicate many thousands of perfectly fit cattle are slaughtered every year, at vast cost to the economy. I am sure that if people were similarly tested for TB, many who had come in contact with the disease would show up as reactors, and don't see why cattle cannot be vaccinated, as children are for polio.

This year a great storm struck the south of England felling many old trees, which should have been felled years before and replaced with new planting. Also by this time, Dutch elm disease had practically wiped out all the elm trees in England.

The Forestry Commission, which had been established after the war and had planted many thousands of acres with conifers, would soon be abolished, putting most of the foresters out of work. Many of their woods have never been thinned and so grow too tall and weak and have been blown down. Besides, the market for pit props for the mines had also gone. And yet, during the whole period, most of the timber used for newsprint, wood pulp and construction has been imported from abroad. Moreover, the demand for firewood, which used to absorb all the rough timber, has collapsed and the west country is getting overrun with useless and dead trees.

In 1989 the Berlin Wall came down, the Russians withdrew from Poland, and Germany, East and West, to their great delight, were reunited. 1,065 people had been killed by communist forces, trying to escape from East to West over the wall. Reunification has, however, proved a disaster. Developing the East has nearly ruined the German economy and many people have moved from East to West. Now, those who have remained look back on the communist regime with fond memories.

Chapter Eleven

In February, Rosemary and I went to New Zealand for a month, stopping three nights in San Francisco on the way. The grim prison of Alcatraz stands in the bay now unused. The town itself is built on a steep hillside with cable cars running up the streets and has a large Chinatown beside the bay. We saw the magnificent redwood forest where trees are as much as 1,000 years old, and we took a trip in a launch under the Golden Gate bridge from which many people commit suicide each year.

Hippiedom began in San Francisco in Haight Astbury in 1960s. Nowadays it is mostly concerned with homosexual and environmental protests.

We flew to New Zealand and landed at Auckland where we hired a motor caravan. We set off round the Coromandel peninsular and on through Rotorua, where we found the geysers rather disappointing. We took a ferry at Wellington, across to South Island and on to Christchurch where we spent three nights with my old friend Peter Hallifax, then sadly starting Altzheimer's disease, and his wife Helen. Since emigrating in 1950, he had started an import business that is now carried on by his son.

We drove inland by Mount Cook. It was their midsummer and to my surprise the country was burnt brown. Visiting sheep stations, we were told how all agricultural subsidies had been removed and though some farmers had gone out of business the majority had managed to survive. We should have followed their example in this country by scrapping subsidies to farmers, which have pushed up the price of land and rents to twice their proper price and encouraged agribusinesses of thousands of acres, some of which get half a million pounds or more in subsidy each year for their chemically grown crops.

Subsidies also cause over-stocking of sheep by hill farmers and cows by dairy farmers, and lend themselves to a certain amount of corruption, while requiring an immense bureaucracy, employing

213

about as many civil servants as there are farmers.

With the best land and climate in the world, there is no excuse in Britain for not being able to compete with imports. If the price of land were halved and mortgages and loans were available at low rates, as in France, keen young men could get into farming as happened before the war; family farms would be secured and the barley barons of the eastern counties would all go bankrupt, as happened after the Great War.

The vast expense of the bureaucracy and inspectors would be removed and a burden removed from the backs of farmers which drives some of them to suicide each year, though half their income is received by way of subsidy.

We flew on to Dunedin, where we stayed three nights with Francis and Joan de Hammel. She had been Rosemary's close childhood friend and he was a doctor. They had emigrated to New Zealand in 1950. From there we crossed to the spectacular mountain country around Milford Sound, where we walked up to a glacier. Kia parrots were a plague, settling on vehicles and devouring anything. On the roads were innumerable carcasses of possums.

The forestry has been most efficiently managed for over 100 years and is much superior to any in Britain. In the later days of sail, ships had to go to New Zealand to get new masts.

We then drove up the west coast and took a ferry to Wellington and explored North Island. That is the Maori homeland. Missionaries first landed near Auckland in 1840. South Island was uninhabited when the first Scottish settlers landed in 1850 at Christchurch and Dunedin.

There were intermittent wars against the Maoris from 1863 to 1870, as settlers moved up into North Island and took their land. Since then there has been considerable intermarriage and New Zealand is the most classless society. In fact, it is the working man's paradise, where he may well play golf, own a yacht and ski in the mountains. A wonderful place to live, if a bit out on a limb from European culture, although cheap air travel is rapidly changing that.

In 1985, the French had been carrying out atom bomb tests on Mururoa Atoll, near Tahiti, an operation that infuriated Polynesians, New Zealanders, and Greenpeace, an independent organisation that campaigns to protect the environment, who deployed their ship,

Rainbow Warrior, to disrupt the tests.

In response, when the *Rainbow Warrior* was lying in Auckland harbour, two French secret service agents planted a bomb on board and sank the ship, killing one of the crew. The two incompetent agents were soon apprehended and put on trial but the French Government denied any responsibility until demonstrations in France at last compelled them to admit the outrage and they discontinued testing after a hydrogen bomb explosion.

The French President de Gaulle in his time had been obsessed with making France a world power, independent of America and Britain, and had refused to sign a nuclear disarmament treaty, which was eventually signed by Reagan and Gorbachev in 1984. British atom bombs had been tested in Australia many years before and some servicemen and aborigines were still claiming to suffer from ill effects.

On the way home from New Zealand, we spent three nights in Hawaii where there are active volcanoes, and streams of lava run down into the sea. We visited the museum at Pearl Harbour, where most of the American Pacific fleet had been sunk by the Japanese in a surprise attack in 1941. Actually, their intelligence services had picked up warning signals but it is suggested, though it seems hardly credible, that President Roosevelt deliberately suppressed the news in order to force America into the war. We also saw the usual tourist show of natives dancing around in grass skirts which was pretty boring.

In 1988, Saddam Hussein, who was still being supplied with arms by America and Britain in his war with Iran, launched a poisonous gas attack on the Kurdish village of Halabja, killing 5,000 people. Now in 2004, a Dutchman is on trial for supplying hundreds of tons of chemicals to make mustard gas at that time.

An American airliner was blown up over Lockerbie killing 259 people but this appalling crime would never have happened if the trigger happy Americans had not shot down an Iranian airliner in the Persian Gulf shortly before. Similarly, an Indian plane had been blown up off Ireland two years before by Sikh terrorists in revenge for the storming of the Sikh temple at Amritsar, which had been ordered by Indira Gandhi and led to the deaths of several hundred people.

Indira Gandhi would herself be murdered by Sikhs shortly afterwards and was succeeded by her son Rajiv, who would also be murdered during an election campaign, in retaliation for sending Indian army troops to massacre several thousand Tamils in Sri Lanka, where they were seeking independence for their homeland in the north.

This civil war in Sri Lanka has gone on unresolved for 15 years. Many thousands have been killed and a few thousand have emigrated to Britain.

General Pinochet, who had murdered the Socialist President Allende of Chile in a coup and had recently been deposed after about ten years of dictatorial rule, in which many political opponents had disappeared, came to London seeking medical treatment. He was sued by a Spanish lawyer and illegally placed under house arrest while his case was heard in the House of Lords.
Mrs Thatcher stupidly gave him support vocally and by visiting him. He claimed diplomatic immunity and after the usual legal farce was released, whereas he should have been deported to Spain to stand trial. He returned to Chile and many years later was eventually tried and convicted but declared too sick to be imprisoned.

Mrs Thatcher then tried to replace the existing tax on house owners, 'rates', with a headage tax on wage earners living in a house. This was in fact the most sensible and just proposal of her reign but the Labour Party were wildly opposed to her so-called 'Poll' tax and, with widespread rioting against it, she weakly dropped the idea.

The perfectly efficient state owned electricity, gas, telephone and water companies were denationalised to make fortunes for their chief executives, who became managing directors of the new companies with no improvement in service and higher charges to consumers, to reward the new shareholders.

In addition to this, the railways, which had been losing money and subject to strikes because of weak management, were sold off to twelve different companies – a disastrous decision whose consequences are felt to this day, even though, incredibly, the railways receive far more tax-payers money than ever before. The merchant banks who organised these privatisations made millions.

Hanbury Park Gate, Needwood, Staffs
Edmund & Rosemary Carlisles' first home 1951 - 1955

Julian Carlisle in the foreground of
Greenway Manor nr Llandrindod Wells 1955 – 1977

Falkland Islands

San Carlos Farmhouse

San Carlos Settlement

San Carlos Water

Peat Bogs, San Carlos

Annabel
Sailed from Southampton to Turkey 1985
Turkey to Portsmouth 1986

Edmund Carlisle 1943
born 1922

Rachel Carlisle, born 1923
Married Barry Crewe Sloane

Mark Carlisle
Lord Carlisle of Bucklow
born 1929

Sylvia Mary Carlisle, born 1920
Q.A.M.N.S
Married Jack Knowles

Penyrwrlodd 1978 – 2002 (before the fire)

Penyrwrlodd 2002 (after the fire)

By this time, the Conservative Party had had enough of the 'Iron Lady's' arrogant ways and she was deposed, being succeeded as leader by her protégé, John Major in 1991. He was not the best candidate! But he turned out to be an uncontroversial PM – except for his signing of the Treaty of Maastricht – and lasted six years.

Mrs Thatcher is still revered by many Conservatives and while undoubtedly she did much good in breaking the strength of the trade unions at the beginning, after her success in the unnecessary Falklands war, power had gone to her head and she finished up destroying much of British industry and the Conservative Party, and letting rip currency speculation and the appalling greed of Company Directors — very different to the days when the City was run by gentlemen whose word was their bond.

For many years I had subscribed to anti-European organisations and now joined The Anti-Federalist League, whose principal policy was to rescind the Treaty of Maastricht, which would tie us further into the EU. I stood in the General Election in Leominster, where the sitting Conservative MP, Peter Temple-Morris had disgracefully transferred his allegiance to Labour.

I was astonished to find that a candidate needed two sponsors whose names were publicly displayed and also that an election address had to be submitted to the post office for their approval before they would distribute it to the electorate. My address stated that immigration should be severely reduced. To this they raised objection though I got it through in the end.

I held no meetings and relied on fly-posting notices over the constituency, and my election address. Of the thirteen candidates standing for the Anti-Federalist League, I polled the most votes, although only 650. Fringe party candidates have little chance in a general election as Britain does not have proportional representation.

Afterwards many people said to me that they would have voted for me had it been a by-election but they were frightened of letting Labour in. It had cost me about £2,000, as I lost my deposit of £600 and had to pay for the printing of addresses and posters – but it was an interesting experience.

After many leadership quarrels the principle anti-Europe party has now become the UK Independence Party, which had considerable success in the EU election but will get nowhere unless it co-operates with the Conservatives. The Referendum Party of the late James Goldsmith similarly failed, after great initial support.

In August 1990 Saddam Hussein invaded Kuwait, which had been part of Iraq until we detached it after the Great War. The American foreign, Secretary Madeleine Albright, another Jew, had met him shortly before and, incredibly, told him that her Government would have no objection.

After he'd committed various brutalities in Kuwait, the Americans demanded that he withdraw and took several months transferring a huge force to Saudi Arabia, joined by British troops, ships and aircraft. It was not concern for Kuwaitis, but for oil supplies that motivated the Americans.

I had a letter to *The Times* published, opposing the war, as did, surprisingly, the journalist Barbara Amiel, a Jew and now the smart Lady Black.

General Peter de la Billiere, whose daughter was a close friend of Julian and whom we got to know when he was commanding South Wales and stationed in Brecon, was about to retire when he wrote to Mrs Thatcher, to whom he had endeared himself by commanding the SAS at the unnecessary attack on the Iranian embassy and during the Falklands war, applying for command of the British forces in the Gulf.

A fluent Arabic speaker, he had served several years in Oman, where he got an MC and DSO, and was given the job over the heads of several senior generals. He would subsequently fall from grace after writing his memoirs, to recover losses in the iniquitous Lloyds debacle. The writing of books about the regiment and its actions had been banned by the SAS, but many more books by former members followed de la Billiere's book.

After several months of bombing with so-called guided missiles, which in fact caused many casualties, the Gulf War was launched and won in a week when retreating Iraqi forces were mercilessly bombed until the pilots refused to fly. The Anglo-American forces never followed up to Baghdad to depose Saddam Hussein but the next year America encouraged the Shia Gulf Arabs and the Kurds in the North to revolt and took no action when they were massacred by Saddam Hussein, whose tyrannical rule would continue until 2003.

In 1990 the leader of the opposition in Burma, Aung San Suu Kyi won an election but was immediately overthrown by the army leaders who had tyrannically ruled Burma ever since the country was given independence by Britain in 1946. This courageous woman has been kept under house arrest ever since. United Nations sanctions were imposed in 1996, but to little effect.

It is reported that some 2,500 villages of the Chin, Kachin and Karen tribes in the north have since been destroyed without UN intervention. These tribes were our loyal allies during the world war.

In Russia, the bellicose Khruschev had been succeeded as President of the Soviet Union in 1964 by Leonid Brezhnev and the cold war had continued under him and his hard line successors. In 1985, however, the liberal Mikhail Gorbachov introduced *glasnost* and *perestroika* – openness – and moved the country towards democracy. On the collapse of the Soviet Union which followed, he was overthrown by the drunken Boris Yeltsin.

As capitalism was introduced, corruption came with it, and a handful of enterprising Russians, aided by western capital, were able to buy up the inefficient state-owned oil industry and would make vast fortunes while the majority of the population got even poorer. Now, while many of the people remain very poor and look back with longing to the stability and certainties of the communist regime, there are reported to be 33 dollar billionaires in Moscow and 80,000 dollar millionaires in Russia overall. Such are the benefits of unbridled capitalism.

After a few years, Yeltsin died to be succeeded by the intelligent ex-KGB officer Vladimir Putin, who has slowly guided the country towards prosperity, if not democracy

In 1991, we took a holiday in South Africa, flying to Johannesburg and taking the Blue Train to the Cape where we stayed with my sister, Rachel and her husband, Barry Sloane in their holiday house on the coast, near their daughter, Jane, who was married to Stuart Walls, a civil engineer. They had two children, Justin and Richard.

We then hired a car and drove 1,500 miles up the Garden Route of the east coast, visiting Grahamstown, where John and Frederick Carlisle had both been sheriffs after leading a party of 10 settlers in 1820 and establishing a 5,000 acre farm nearby, which they called *Belmont*. The farmhouse was now in ruins but *Carlisle House*, built by Frederick is among the finest in Grahamstown.

From there we went inland to the spectacular Drakensburg Mountains, which we climbed, though my hips were getting progressively worse. We stayed two nights at Isaldwana where 1,000 British troops under the incompetent command of Lord Chelmsford had been massacred by the Zulus in 1870 and the next day a company of the Royal Welsh Fusiliers had restored the reputation of the British army by defeating their attack on the mission station at Rorke's Drift, gaining six VCs in the process.

The VC was then the only medal for bravery. It had been instigated by Queen Victoria during the Crimean war, and was mostly awarded to other ranks as it was considered that a British officer acted courageously without the inducement of a medal. There had always been campaign medals but the MC (Military Cross) for officers and MM (Military Medal) for other ranks were introduced at the beginning of the Great War. Now, in these democratic days, the distinction has been removed and all ranks can be awarded the MC.

We also visited the battle sites of the iniquitous Boer War forced on the Boers by the aggressive Colonial Secretary, Lord Milner. They were descendants of Protestant Dutch settlers, who had emigrated to South Africa in the seventeenth century to avoid religious persecution at home and established farms after driving out the native Bushmen.

In about 1800 the British took possession of Cape Town and established government over the whole province, which the Boers found increasingly intolerable. They moved north in about 1850 in the Great Trek, defeating the Zulus at the battle of Blood River and establishing themselves in the Orange Free State and the Transvaal.

Gold had been found at Johannesburg in 1880 and led to a huge influx of prospectors, mostly British, who complained of harassment by the Boer Government.

Cecil Rhodes, who had gone to South Africa for his health, made a huge fortune dealing in gold and led an expedition north across the

Limpopo river to settle the highland country, a largely unpopulated area which he bought from the chief of the Matabele. Later it would be called Rhodesia.

In 1895, a Doctor Jameson led a force back to Johannesburg to support the miners but, known as the Jameson Raid, they were stopped and imprisoned by the Boers.

Milner now demanded the inclusion of the Boer republics in British South Africa and war resulted in 1899. All Europe was outraged and the Germans managed to supply the Boers with modern rifles and even some field artillery. The first major incident was the siege of the British garrison at Mafeking, commanded by Colonel Baden Powell, who would form the Boy Scout and Girl Guides Associations after the war.

The siege lasted several months before being relieved by British troops who were still wearing redcoats at the start of the war. The rifle, the Vickers Machine Gun and the quick firing, recoilless field artillery had now taken over from the bayonet and the cavalry charge.

Meanwhile the Boers, who were excellent marksmen, conducted a guerrilla war with small mounted commandos advancing into the Cape Colony, besieging Kimberley, and into Natal where they laid siege to Ladysmith and inflicted serious defeats on the British at the battles of Spion Kop and Colenso in early 1900.

Huge reinforcements were brought in until 300,000 British and Dominion troops were opposing 75,000 Boers and the British, now dressed in tropical Khaki uniform, advanced to Johannesburg and Pretoria. A truce was negotiated but war restarted in 1901 when Boer commandos raided deep into Cape Colony and only finally surrendered in 1902 after the British operated a scorched earth policy of destroying Boer farmsteads and putting their women and children into concentration camps where many died of disease.

It had been an unnecessary and inglorious war.

We drove to Kimberley, where diamond mining has left an immense hole in the ground of about two acres, and the attractive town of Bloemfontein, carrying on to the Kruger National Park game reserve for two nights, and to Barberton, where Uncle Geoff had been vicar in the 1920s and to Boksburg where Uncle George had been vicar at the same time. He was an army padre during Great War and he was mentioned in despatches.

Returning to Johannesburg via the Drakensburgs, we stayed with Sylvia and Jack and met his daughter Maureen, and her daughter Elizabeth, who was married to a computer expert, Roland Grinker.

We also met Rachel's sons – Christopher, now an independent accountant married to Sheena Connock, who had children Grant, Craig and Mark, and Nigel, a master at a private school. Later he married Monica Bohony, had children Jessica and Michael, and in 2004, became headmaster of a large private school.

In September 1992, we flew to Denver, the highest airport in the world, in Colorado, USA. There we hired a car to visit Mount Hope where Great Uncle Edmund established a farm with his American wife in 1875. It was a 400 mile drive east across flat, treeless Kansas – a country interspersed with huge pivot irrigation towers over corn land and nodding donkeys over small oil wells – to near Wichita on the Arkansas river.

We found Edmund's grave in the churchyard but the farm had been sold by his son around 1950. Nearby was Sand Creek where his brother, Harold had also acquired a farm through an American wife. We then drove back west to Dodge City, where we inspected a beef feedlot, fattening about 4,000 cattle. The roads were straight with little traffic yet the speed limit was only 50mph. We were stopped doing 70 by a police patrol car but fortunately managed to talk our way out of it. Thereafter we used the speed control with which the cars were fitted. There were no hotels but motels which were cheap and adequate.

We carried on over the San Juan Mountains at the bottom end of the Rockies to Durango, a small country town where the Carlisle brothers had established the company office of *The Kansas and New Mexico Land and Cattle Company* that had been formed by my grandfather, Charles, in Manchester in 1880. At that time, some 40 British Cattle companies were formed to graze the great grasslands as all the buffalo had been shot out and the Red Indians driven into reservations after the Civil War of 1862-64.

For over 100 years the Red Indian tribes had resisted the invasion of their territories by European settlers moving ever westwards, with murderous raids and equally brutal retaliation, until the irregular Texas Rangers and the American Army Cavalry embarked on a policy of extermination, shooting women and children out of hand, which amounted to the genocide of these brave, proud and fiercely independent people.

European diseases also did for many of them. By 1875 only a demoralised remnant remained, fed by the government.

Since time immemorial great herds of buffalo, numbered in millions, had roamed the great planes and the Red Indians lived on their meat as they grew no crops, and had no permanent homes, simply following the herds.

As the railways were pushed west and gold was found in the Rocky Mountains, professional buffalo hunters destroyed the herds to provide coats, bed robes and meat for the many thousands of railwaymen and miners.

We drove all over the ranching area, most of it now ruined by over-grazing by sheep, just as so much of the prairie land was turned into dust-bowl by corn growing between 1870 and 1930. In these areas of low rainfall, like in Africa, the soils are easily destroyed and the Europeans who took them were just land exploiters.

There was no tradition of 'Live as if you will die tomorrow; farm as if you will live for ever!' – the maxim of British farmers until the last war, although now replaced here too by farming solely for current profit.

We found Monticello, where my great uncle, Harold Carlisle had built his famous mansion when he had been one of the biggest ranchers in the territory. Now it's a small Mormon town. We then drove south through the spectacular Monument Valley to the great gorge of the Colorado river, 2,000 ft below. We stayed overnight at a motel so were able to see the view and marvel at both the sunset and the dawn.

The descendants of the Red Indians then lived only in reservations where they were not allowed any alcohol and were very poor, but some have now gone into the gambling industry and have built casinos, which has transformed their fortunes.

We drove north through Utah to Salt Lake City, a fine open town and the centre of Mormonism. There we went to the great library where they keep vast numbers of genealogical records, which anyone can consult. This is important to them because, unbelievably, they can baptise their ancestors in the Mormon faith. Their forbears trekked there with great hardship in 1850 to avoid persecution in Pennsylvania. They practised polygamy, have far too many children and have increased ever since by proselytising in Europe and particularly in countries around the Caribbean.

No alcohol is available in the town and unmarried girls who become pregnant are driven out of the family. In many ways they are a very admirable people – God-fearing, honest, hard working and very successful, but you'd have to be pretty credulous to accept the story of John Smith and Brigham Young, their founders.

They followed me up in England afterwards with a visit.

Driving back east over the Rockies, we spent an expensive night at Aspen, the ski resort of the Hollywood stars. The next night we had great difficulty finding a bed, as it was the week when elk hunting was allowed and all accommodation was taken by shooters.

In this part of America, they have a good system for keeping their roads litter free. Stretches of highway are adopted by firms or individuals who have their name displayed and volunteer to pick it up – cheap and effective! Also worth seeing were the autumn colours of the trees, which I can only describe with the ghastly modern word 'fantastic'. Another Americanism I deplored was the habit of everyone in shops or motels telling me to 'Have a nice day!'

On the whole, though, we liked America and the people of the mid-west. Their towns are spacious and law-abiding, quite unlike those of the east coast or California, which must be appalling.

When going abroad for a month, we normally asked a woman to live in at the house, otherwise Julie Williams, who has been a wonderful daily for 25 years, came up to exercise the dogs.

Until about this time, we'd never worried much about locking the house but as ever more immigrants came into the country, crime was spreading to the countryside. I still don't lock the cars at home or in Hay-on-Wye, which, apart from one week in the year, was always a quiet market town. Hay was put on the map twenty years ago by the eccentric Richard Booth who started selling second-hand books and proclaimed himself King of Hay. He has been phenomenally successful and there are now about fifteen book shops in Hay. He has even opened shops, creating book towns in Canada, France and Holland. Now there is a Literary Festival in May, attended this year by the astonishing number of 130,000 visitors.

I have always kept a Welsh Collie sheep dog and a Labrador. Both breeds are really very easily trained as they have the instinct in them to round up sheep and bring them to you, or to go and collect birds when shot. They need only to be taught obedience, to lie down or stop when commanded. Sheep dog puppies will start by rounding up hens. They are not so good at driving a flock forwards and for this the New Zealanders and Australians use a different breed of dogs called Huntaways. Most of our dogs have been killed by cars and burying them has always reduced me to tears.

In 1993 I went on a Saga trip to Egypt. Rosemary had gone two years before with her cousin Penelope while I was electioneering. Cairo is a desperate town, overrun by poor people, as in all Moslem countries where no attempt is made to limit breeding.

We went to see the Pyramids and mausoleums built into the hills and the temples at Luxor and Aswan, which were stupendous. We sailed back to Cairo in a Nile river steamer. We were all very comfortable and well fed. The pyramids built by the Maya in Mexico are equally extraordinary and lead to conjecture that Egyptians might have crossed the Atlantic in ancient times. Or perhaps both cultures were inspired by beings from outer space, as some lunatics suggest!

In 1994 we went on a two week bus tour of Syria and Jordan with a rather downmarket company. Damascus was pretty seamy but we looked at several fine castles built by the Crusaders, who ruled the country and Jerusalem for 100 years of the 12th century, and saw the pillar on which Simon Stylitis sat or stood for several years. People do odd things in the name of religion, like the Sadhus in India.

Then we visited the walled city of Aleppo, situated on a rock, and Homs, where very old, immense water wheels lift water from the river. This was followed by a journey of hundreds of miles across to the Euphrates to see a ruined BC city. Returning across desert, we passed an occasional Bedouin camp, noting their camels, as well as television aerials and often a pick-up truck. We stopped at the Greek city of Palmyra where, like Ephesus in Turkey, there are ruins far finer than any to be seen in Greece itself.

From Palmyra we were taken to Petra, where one walks through a long narrow defile to the temples cut in the rock by the Nabataeans. I had to ride a camel back as my hips were playing up.

In Jordan we visited the capital, Amman, a fine clean colonial-type town, built with broad boulevards, no doubt with British influence. For many years the army officers of the Jordanian Arab Legion had all been British. They were commanded by the romantic Glubb Pasha until King Hussein who, although at school in England and at Sandhurst himself, had to get rid of them in 1956, due to pressure from his Arab neighbours.

Lastly we stopped at Wadi Rum from where Lawrence of Arabia, who led the Arab revolt against the Turks, launched the attack on Aquaba in 1916.

T E Lawrence and Captain Robert Falcon Scott had been the heroes of my youth. Lawrence became a disillusioned man after the war when the Arabs did not get all he had promised them, although Prince Faisal of Saudi Arabia was made king of Iraq. He joined the RAF as an aircraftsman, wrote the Seven Pillars of Wisdom and killed himself on a motorbike in 1930, probably deliberately.

Scott, an officer in the Royal Navy, was given command of the British National Antarctic Expedition and charged with journeying to the South Pole; there was no record of any man having been there before. He set out on 11th November 1911 supported by a team that included sledge dogs, Siberian ponies, and two motorised sledges, but by the time they reached the Polar Plateau, the vehicles had broken down, and the ponies were so weak they had to be destroyed.

The support team returned to base with the dogs and Scott plus his four companions hauled their own sledges and accomplished their mission on January 16th, 1912. But they were not the first to reach the Pole, that honour went to the Norwegian explorer, Roald Amundsen, who had hoisted his flag there 33 days earlier. Tragically, beset by appalling weather, Scott and his companions all perished on the return journey. Scott's son, Peter Falcon Scott, became a naturalist and founded the Slimbridge waterfowl sanctuary after the war, in which he had been the distinguished commander of a motor torpedo boat.

Eddy and Fiona had left London and bought a house at Kingston Langley near Chippenham. William had just gone to Eton and had Prince Harry in his football team but fortunately did not continue the friendship. Since the tragic death of his mother, the prince has been hounded disgracefully by the anti-monarchist press. Eddy and Fiona's daughters all went to Marlborough College, now co-ed. They kept horses and ponies and were very keen on hunting with the Beaufort hounds at nearby Badminton.

Also in 1995, Mark and Sandra's daughter Lucy, a school mistress, married Angus, the younger son of Baron Witold von Schoenberg, who had lost his Prussian estates during the war and lived in Ireland. Angus was a merchant banker. They have produced two children, Alexandra and Emma.

At Treseissyllt and Penyrwrlodd I now started to use big balers, which put hay into round bales of 5 cwt that were picked up by tractor. Silage, wrapped in plastic, was handled in a similar manner. Gone were the days of setting up small square bales in the field and lifting them first on to a trailer and then again into the barns. This saved my back, which had so often slipped a disc.

Ever since the war, an annual price review had guaranteed prices for agricultural produce, well above world prices for corn and sugar, and when the price of lamb and beef fell in the autumn it was made up by deficiency payments. In France excessively generous subsidies had resulted in beef and butter mountains which attracted further export subsidies when sold abroad, further depressing the world price and particularly harming third world countries. So-called wine lakes were converted to industrial alcohol at vast cost.

Under the 1991 McSharry reforms of the CAP, this was changed to a payment of £110 per acre of arable crops and a payment per head of beef cattle and ewes. Quotas were introduced for cows and ewes in milk production, which, incredibly, were allotted to farmers (in this country) not to their farms, and thus could be sold off, or leased.

These quotas soon became very valuable and some

landowners who had taken their farms in hand when tenants retired since a crazy act in 1976 entitled tenants to pass on their tenancy to their sons, sold their dairy herds and milk quota, sacked their men and let the grazing, earning far more profit with none of the worry.

Others formed partnerships with neighbouring farming contractors, gaining an income without any work while retaining possession of the farm. Since that day no farms have been let on long term lease so no young men have a chance of going into farming, except by inheritance or marriage.

'Set Aside' was also introduced, compelling all arable farmers to leave 15% of their land without crop, although horses could be grazed on it. This also collected £110 per acre subsidy. This may have made some sense in France which is twice the size of this country with the same population. In Britain, it was madness as we can produce only 70% of the food we need, so the loss of production had to be replaced by importation from abroad.

The next two years, the world price of wheat was £88 a ton, and many arable farmers were living on their 'Set Aside', but in 1994-96 the world price rose to £120 and arable farmers grew rich beyond belief.

The result of these 'reforms' was that the price of land doubled and the agribusiness farms got bigger and bigger with ever larger machinery and ever fewer workers. A so-called 'Business Tenancy' was also introduced by which land could be let for growing potatoes or such crops at high prices but subject to annual review so possession was not lost.

Penyrwrlodd did not have flower beds, only shrubs, which Rosemary tended as well as growing the vegetables after I had cultivated the patch. Farmers are never gardeners.

Rosemary was a church warden from 1984 to 2001. I only attended high days and holidays and produced and decorated that pagan symbol, a 15' tree, at Christmas.

The heated swimming pool left by our predecessor was a great thing for the grandchildren when visiting and Rosemary would swim regularly. Farmers prefer a hot bath!

While at Penyrwrlodd I was asked to judge the trotting races at the Llanigon sports each year, no doubt because I knew none of the runners. This is a very popular form of racing in Wales. Most of the horses are driven by men or women sitting in light buggies, or 'sulkys', although, curiously, some are ridden in the same races in a sitting trot that never looks too comfortable.

Each year the swallows would arrive within a day or two of the 21st April and reoccupy two nests in the boiler room (despite the disturbance) and several buildings opposite until departure in mid-September. I always think bird migration is a wonder beyond comprehension, particularly the way gannets and penguins find their nests in their teeming colonies. But now we rarely hear a cuckoo, which used to be calling for two months each spring.

All the field birds have been decimated by autumn ploughing for chemical arable farming and early hedge cutting, which destroy their food supply, and early mowing of grassland for silage instead of hay, which destroys the nests of plovers and skylarks.

At Greenways we always heard curlews in the spring, but no more. Now, the only birds to have proliferated are buzzards and magpies, which eat the eggs of other birds and which I occasionally trap.

In November 1995 I went with four other ex-officers of The Rajputana Rifles to a regimental reunion at their depot at Delhi Cantonment. The troops put on an impressive parade with a very fine band, and were much more smartly dressed than in wartime. During the war we had never wasted time on drill parades.

The mess had all the old regimental silver and photos of British Commanding officers around the walls. The officers' wives had been invited to a dance in the garden and I was encouraged to dance but no contact with your partner was allowed. European decadence is now reported to be spreading fast so perhaps unmarried women or even smooching are permitted!

The Honorary Colonel, the Maharaja of Jaipur invited me to stay in Jaipur – I suspect because he had heard that my brother had recently been elevated to the House of Lords. But first I took a bus to Agra to see the beautiful Taj Mahal and the empty Moghul city of Fatipur Sikri.

Jaipur has very fine palaces, castles and an astonishing planetarium. I went on by local bus to Udaipur, again very fine, and then to the Ajanta caves and stayed for two nights at the Taj Mahal

Hotel in Bombay.

Like all Indian towns, Bombay is a seething mass of vehicles, mostly motor rickshaws. Beggars with appalling deformities were still sitting in the street outside the hotel. I then went to Goa by train, on which I had to share the compartment, and was brought an Indian meal on a palm leaf or possibly a plastic one. It was not quite like the old days of the British Raj, although one did still get addressed as Sahib!

A friend had arranged the trip and, stupidly, a flight out to Goa, where we had great difficulty getting a plane on to Delhi. We spent three nights in an hotel there swimming on pleasant beaches and looking at the very fine old Portuguese cathedral and other buildings.

Goa had been the centre of the Catholic church in India for nearly 500 years but they and later Protestant missionaries, have only ever managed to convert the lower Hindu castes. Now there are about two million Christians out of a population of over a billion, which still includes the second largest Moslem population in the world, after Indonesia.

As under the rule of the Moghul emperors, for 100 years the British Raj suppressed religious strife and gave India the best and least corrupt government of any country in the world.

Since the disastrous partition of Pakistan from India the secular Congress party has provided democratic but increasingly corrupt government. The country developed fast, but in 2002 the Hindu Nationalist BJP took over and there were bloody, religious conflicts in Bombay and Gujarat. The Congress Party have stupidly appointed the Italian born Sandra Gandhi, wife of the murdered Rajiv as their leader, who is denounced by the BJP as an agent of Christians and Moslems. The future looks bleak.

Mrs Thatcher created her admirer, William Whitelaw a viscount, the last hereditary peer, although he had no sons. But, incredibly, she was allowed to give the last hereditary baronetcy to her husband, Dennis. As a result, her troublesome son, who was allowed by her to make a fortune in commissions on arms deals with Arab states, and after a chequered career in America was incompetent enough to get lost in the Sahara desert, not to mention being convicted in South Africa for involvement in an attempt to overthrow the ruler of

Equatorial Guinea, can term himself Sir Mark, and his son after him.

My brother Mark agrees with me that the creation of peerages for retiring politicians or party benefactors in these democratic days is quite ridiculous, and that the House of Lords should be renamed the 'Upper House' and its members 'Senators' or whatever.

In 1994, Civil war broke out in Rwanda. The country was inhabited by two tribes. The minority Tutsi were a taller, superior type who had always been recruited into the army and civil service by the French colonial regime but since independence the majority, inferior but more clever Hutus, had managed to get control of the Government and now turned on their erstwhile masters.

Some French troops, still in the country, were disgracefully withdrawn; the United Nations did nothing to stop the massacres and a million Tutsis were killed before a Tutsi force invading from Uganda restored order.

The end of colonial regimes throughout Africa – promoted by Harold Macmillan and the disastrous colonial secretary, Iain Macleod – has been the biggest disaster of our lifetime.

If we had supported the Portuguese in Angola and Mozambique, they could have continued for another 30 years and saved untold misery, massacre and corruption.

In June 1995, I had a letter published in *The Times* protesting that the bigoted 'Kelpers' were still refusing to allow Argentinians to visit the graves of their relatives on the Falkland Islands. If only the Government had accepted my offer of a cemetery at San Carlos, they would have been able to do so without any trouble, ever since the war.

Eventually, a year or two later, a ship was allowed into Stanley but I don't think any has gone since.

In 1998, a new abattoir was built in the islands, paid for by the EEC at vast cost. However, to this day, there is still no export of meat and 20,000 old sheep are wastefully destroyed each year, even though there is a ready market in Africa where people starve. My ship, the *Jersey Express* would have exported them all, as well as the ram lambs for meat, as the wool market has collapsed since 1990.

Britian still maintains a garrison on the Falklands that costs millions of pounds each year to support, in case the Argentinians should strike again, a cost we can ill afford when the army has difficulty in finding troops for policing duties with the United Nations.

Exploration for oil in the seas around the islands has started but not a gallon will be extracted until agreement is reached with Argentina.

About this time, the madness of 'Political Correctness' was introduced into Britain from the USA, and it became illegal to discriminate between gender, race or religion. No longer could an advertisement seek a workman or a female secretary with 'good looks and slim legs'. The Race Relations Board, now, incredibly, presided over by a dark-skinned immigrant, has done nothing but inflame prejudices.

The word 'racist' was invented, and heavy fines awarded to its perpetrators. Employment tribunals have encouraged the idle to claim unfair dismissal – making employers chary of taking on employees – and women to claim substantial sums of money in compensation for sexual harassment, for which they themselves may have been responsible by dressing provocatively.

In short, office flirtation was outlawed and our traditional freedom of speech made a crime.

In 1995 we went on a Caribbean cruise in the *Cunard Countess*, which carried about 600 passengers. It was very comfortable. We sailed by night and went ashore to a different island each day.

On Antigua we found Carlisle Bay, named after a distant ancestor, who'd had a sugar plantation there in 1650. His daughter married the Governor but he left no male heirs. There is now a large hotel above the beach.

I played a little bridge, which I hadn't done since childhood as Rosemary does not play. The attraction of cruising is that you visit many places without any packing, unpacking or travelling in between, but the big objection is that on most cruises, the guests are seated at a table with the same 6 or 8 people each evening for an interminable dinner. Husbands and wives even sit next to each other, although we would break them up, sitting on opposite sides of the table. After a week we usually managed to get moved to a different table.

In 1994 the war-time leader, Marshall Tito died. For a long time he had been President of Yugoslavia, a moderate communist state, independent from Russia.

The Catholic constituent nations, Croatia and Slovenia immediately demanded independence and were supported by Germany, whose allies they had been during the war, when their Ustazi police had been as brutal and run concentration camps as harsh as those of the SS.

The dominant Orthodox state, Serbia which provided most of the army and had been our ally during the war, opposed this. The largely Moslem state of Bosnia Herzegovina rebelled, followed shortly by the large Moslem population of Kosovo in southern Serbia, supported by Albania.

A confused and bloody civil war broke out which continued for two years until American and NATO forces intervened, heavily bombing Serbia and the seat of Government in Belgrade. This was lunatic behaviour, as the Serbs are by far the best nation and should have been supported from the start.

Ten years later NATO forces still occupy the country to maintain peace. About a million lives were lost and a considerable number of Bosnians and Albanians have been allowed to settle in this country. Albania is the most lawless country in Europe and their gangs now bring illegal immigrants, white slave prostitutes and drugs into Britain.

In 1995 a Dutch company of soldiers disgracefully stood by and allowed the massacre of 8,000 Moslem Bosnian men at Srebrenica

The Portuguese had pulled out of their colony of East Timor, which Indonesia now claimed. For two years the Christian Timorese fought for their independence while the Americans continued to supply arms and the British fighter planes to the Indonesians. Eventually the United Nations sent troops there and peace was restored but the country was handed over to Moslem Indonesia which had killed 250,000 Timorese.

About this time also, the Lloyds Insurance scandal blew up. For some years members of Lloyds had suffered from unreasonable awards made by American courts in compensation for illness attributed to asbestos poisoning.

The years 1978 to 86 had seen high inflation, yet the qualification of wealth remained un-changed. Unscrupulous financial advisers encouraged new rich people to become 'names' in Lloyds, using their houses and land as collateral as property prices soared, until membership reached 32,000. Now it appeared that syndicate managers had been hiding their losses by laying them off in offshore companies, which they in fact controlled. Underwriters, who for many years had been enjoying a second untaxed income from their capital, now found to their distress that 'unlimited liability' meant just that, and not a few were ruined.

In 1997 there was a general election, which was won by the Labour Party led by the young Tony Blair. He had recently taken over from the better John Smith, who had died prematurely, and proclaimed New Labour, which in practice meant adopting many Conservative policies. The Conservatives had been in power for 18 years and had been accused of sleaze and sexual irregularities, although John Major's affair with the Jewess, Edwina Currie, who had decimated the poultry industry by creating scares over salmonella in eggs, was not disclosed till several years later when she made a small fortune by writing a book spiced up with politicians' affairs.

The previous year an unbalanced school teacher, who – despite a warning to the police that he was unstable – had been given a gun licence, shocked the country by murdering 16 children in a Dunblane school. The Tory Government had then banned all handguns of more than .22 calibre. Now, seeking popularity, Labour banned all handguns including those used for competition shooting, which was quite disgraceful. They have ever since made it increasingly difficult for sportsmen to get licences for rifles or shot guns.

In fact they have made every effort to disarm the law-abiding population while the police have been frightened to disarm the criminal fraternity, who are reported to own over a million guns. Since then recorded gun crimes have almost doubled to 24,000 last year and murders using guns have risen from 49 to 68 a year in

2004.

We now, in fact, live in a police state where a large number of police are often armed, as they always are in other countries. Only police bodyguards on Royal protection duties used to carry guns and when the local "Bobby" lived in the village or walked the beat in the towns, they were generally liked and certainly respected. Now they only drive around in cars and are alienated from the people. They do little to prevent or investigate robbery and any citizen protecting his property is as likely to be charged as the burglar, or at least as an aggressor, as happened to a farmer, Tony Martin, recently convicted of murder for shooting an intruder, although acquitted on appeal after a national outcry.

Before the abolition of capital punishment, no criminals carried guns. Now the flood of immigrants from the Caribbean, Middle East and Albania has destroyed this once law-abiding country.

Since the days of Karl Marx most revolutions have been fomented in London. Moslem mullahs still inflame terrorists unchecked. Known drug dealers operate with impunity. Gangs of boys and even girls commit violence and vandalism for want of birching and public shaming. The police sit in offices chasing sad paedophiles for exchanging photos on the internet, nowadays a mania in the press

It was in this year that the beautiful and widely loved, though increasingly manipulative Princess Diana was tragically killed in a car accident in Paris with her lover Dodi, son of the controversially successful Egyptian businessman Mohammed Al Fayed, who had snitched Harrods from the equally controversial "Tiny" Rowland, boss of Lonrho.

Fayed has ever since claimed that the crash was arranged by the Duke of Edinburgh. This cannot be believed but there is no doubt that the circumstances were most suspicious and that her death was most convenient, particularly as it is suggested she may have been pregnant Also a car involved in the crash has never been found, which encourages conspiracy theories.

Now, eight years later the police are still investigating the case for the Royal Coroner's court. The poor girl had never been able to accept that she should share the admirable Charles, Prince of

Wales, with his mistress Camilla Parker-Bowles – coincidentally, the great granddaughter of Mrs Keppel, mistress of Edward VII – who had offered herself in adultery.

In revenge, Diana also had many affairs, becoming increasingly neurotic, but she devoted her life to charitable causes and her death provoked national mourning.

Charles was following a royal tradition. George IV ditched his German queen Caroline and lived openly with his mistress Mrs Fitzherbert; William IV had eight bastard children all recognised and ennobled, and Queen Victoria is said to have been intimate with her bodyguard, John Brown after the death of the sanctimonious but brilliant Prince Albert – although this latter liaison seems hardly believable.

George V, a distinguished king and martinet, was succeeded in 1936 by the popular Edward VIII, who had innumerable affairs before becoming obsessed with the American divorcee, Mrs Simpson and abdicating the throne within a year. He was succeeded by his nervous, unwilling brother, Albert as the admirable George VI. His brother, the Duke of Kent, also had many lovers before marrying the beautiful Greek Princess Marina. He died in a mysterious air crash in Scotland in 1942.

Lord Randolph Churchill remarked that, 'The aristocracy and the lower classes are united by a common bond of immorality'. Respectability used to be a feature of the middle classes but they are rapidly becoming equally licentious.

In 1997, in Cornwall, where we hadn't been so much recently, the historic Guidfa tin Mine was closed. This was a sad moment, when one considered that once Cornwall had produced half the world's supply of tin, right back to pre-Roman times.

That same year, we took a holiday in Sri Lanka organised by the Country Landowners Association and led by a retired Major General obsessed with the native birds, which indeed were most colourful. In Colombo we stayed at the celebrated Galle Face Hotel and then drove in a minibus to Kandy, the centre for the tea estates in the mountains, where Ted Thomas had been a planter pre-war, now all taken over by Singalese.

We visited ruined Buddhist cities and temples, including an immense reclining figure of the Buddha. The civil war was still raging in the north where the Tamils were fighting for independence, so we went south to the coast where there was an elephant sanctuary – many still roam wild in the forests – and a turtle farm where they hatched collected eggs and we were given day-olds to race down to the sea.

We also saw the old great fort at Galle built by the Dutch, who had controlled Ceylon for 100 years before being dispossessed by the British.

The following year, I was admitted to the King Edward VII Hospital (Sister Agnes) to have my hips replaced. The surgeon declined to do both together but the first dislocated three times in five days so he had to do a revision operation with an extra long one, which in view of my height he might have used first time.

After a week's recuperation in hospital, Fiona drove me to Osborne, Queen Victoria's house on the Isle of Wight, to convalesce but after three days the hip popped out again so I was taken by ambulance to the NH hospital and later to Brecon NH, both of which were excellent.

Discharged after a week, I had to wear a brace for several months but in the end everything worked out well. Then my doctor, Sandy Cavanagh, who had jumped with the paras during the Suez fiasco, said he could get me into the Abergavenny NH hospital, where there was a good surgeon to do my other hip.

This time I had an epidural injection so was able to hear him say, 'Give me the saw, Jim,' and feel the vibration of his electric saw, but no pain.

After five days I went home and took to driving immediately but ever since have occasionally felt a movement as though the bone was trying to slip out its socket, so have to be very careful picking anything up off the floor or getting off my knees. I have difficulty in doing up my shoe laces and both hips are painful when walking up hill. I don't like walking more than a mile or two, but my sister Rachel never feels hers and is able to go trekking.

In June that year we went on a cruise up the coast of Norway in a smallish ship, which sailed up between the mainland and the islands that skirt the coast, with sorties up several fjords. The spectacular mountains fall straight into the sea and it is all quite beautiful. We visited salmon farms and charming little fishing villages. We also sailed out into the ocean above the North Cape to watch for whales, who did not oblige. I can certainly recommend this cruise.

At home, George Griffiths had retired and I took on John Greenow, who has been a very good worker and excellent stockman ever since. I have only helped a bit at silage or haymaking and kept an eye on the place. John is particularly good with the sheep and has good dogs which he controls with a torrent of abuse. He is also perfectly happy replacing a prolapse, drawing lambs or skinning dead ones to put on the backs of other lambs, so that a ewe will think it's hers and adopt another's twin or triplet.

Ever since one has been able to buy the wonder drug penicillin I have never called a vet except for an occasional prolapse of a cow or one mare, which did it twice in successive years. It looks quite terrible but it is astonishing how rapidly they recover.

Horses always foal at night and won't get on with it if you try to watch; in posh stables they link them up to a CCTV. But they always foal easily unless a leg or the head is twisted back. Cows are another matter. Calves often need pulling, particularly from heifers or if the beast has been fed too well or crossed with a large breed of bull, especially Charollais, which have big shoulders. This used sometimes to entail getting the wife, or possibly a visitor, out in the middle of the night, although for the last twenty years a special jack has been available so one can always manage, providing the animal is tied by the neck in a building.

I once found a cow calving in a field at Treseissyllt and being unable to pull the calf had to use a tractor to save them both; this is not to be recommended. And once at Greenways I had to call the vet in the middle of the night to do a caesarean on a cow; she was up on her feet immediately after.

Three years before, I had finally bought Treseissyllt from my cousin, Lynette Barbour. Now the National Trust, who were buying up all the coastal land under operation Neptune, made me a good offer for half the farm, which I accepted. I also sold most of the rest to a neighbour. Rafael Colella, who had worked for me loyally for thirty years had acquired 100 acres in St Nicholas, where I bought the materials for him to build a house.

I then passed on the house at Tresiessyllt, the buildings and remaining forty acres to Fiona and Eddy, who have since converted some of the buildings to another house. Tessa and Julian also regularly take holidays there.

In some ways, farming in Pembrokeshire, through Rosemary's obsession with the county, has blighted my life, as I always felt a foreigner in Wales and wanted to get my feet back in England. Having farms 100 miles apart for forty years has limited my involvement in local affairs.

Election Communication
Leominster Parliamentary
Constituency

THE
ALL PARTY
ANTI-FEDERALIST LEAGUE

Candidate: CAPTAIN E. P. CARLISLE

SAY **NO**

TO BRUSSELS RULE

Vote
CARLISLE

FEDERATION WILL FAIL

DON'T LET BRUSSELS
RULE BRITANNIA!

A WORD ABOUT THE CANDIDATE

Educated at Radley College, Edmund Carlisle is descended from a family with strong church, military and political connections. He joined the Life Guards as a volunteer in 1941, was commissioned in the Indian Army in 1942 and retired in 1946.

Since then he has spent his life as a farmer in Radnorshire, Pembrokeshire and Breconshire.

During that time he served 10 years in the Territorial Army, Shropshire Yeomanry and 10 years as County Commissioner Radnorshire Scouts. He has been a member of Council of the Royal Welsh Show and Chairman of Brecon & Radnor Country Landowners Association. He has a wife, three children and three grandchildren.

His message is:-

"I am not a professional politician but one who believes fervently in preserving our national independence and freedom under our Queen, for which so many friends gave their lives.

This may be your last chance to stand up and be counted."

TEMPLE-MORRIS
ACTIVELY SUPPORTS THE EURO-STATE

STOP HIM!!

MAKE YOUR VOICE HEARD

VOTE CARLISLE

Printed by Piggott Press, 15 Bridge Road, Hay-on-Wye, Hereford and published by the Candidate, Penywrlodd, Hay-on-Wye Hereford

WHAT FEDERATION MEANS FOR US

1. A puppet government in Westminster.

2. German control of economic and foreign policies.

3. A huge British financial gift to the 'poorer states' - Eire, Portugal, Spain and Greece.

4. A vast influx through Southern Europe of immigrants from North Africa.

5. No chance to change our Brussels masters, or even to have real influence on them.

6. Loss of our own currency. No control over interest or exchange rates.

7. The Queen loses her authority, and instead of being British subjects we all become 'European citizens'.

8. No border controls on drug smuggling and rabies.

9. Rising resentment on the part of the French, German and others, who also have national pride.

10. In the end, the inevitable collapse in ruin and chaos of the whole unworkable centralised European State (as in U.S.S.R.).

FEDERATION WILL FAIL

DON'T LET BRUSSELS
RULE BRITANNIA!

WHAT DOES "FEDERAL" MEAN?

It means a political system in which a number of states are allowed very limited powers, but are ruled by a central government, with its central armed forces, foreign policy, economic policy and legal systems.

CAN A FEDERAL STATE WORK?

Yes, if its people share a common language, a common culture and a common loyalty. The United States is successful, so is Germany, because each developed as one nation with one language.

CAN A FEDERAL EUROPE WORK?

No. There are already twelve different nations, with different traditions and loyalties and nine different languages. A "Federal Europe" would end, like the U.S.S.R., in confusion, misery and possible bloodshed.

WHO WANTS A FEDERAL EUROPE?

1. Fainthearts who have been persuaded that Britain cannot survive as an independent nation (*The Labour Party*).

2. Woolly-headed idealists who do not like nation-states, and believe that they can achieve the brotherhood of men through politics (as in the U.S.S.R.) (*The Liberal Democrats*).

3. Leaders of multinational companies, who jet around the world, have no national loyalties, and see greater profits for themselves if European frontiers are abolished (*The Tory Financial backers*).

MAKE YOUR CHOICE

BRUSSELS	NO	WESTMINSTER ✓ YES
DELORS	NO	THE QUEEN ✓ YES
FREE ENTRY	NO	IMMIGRATION CONTROL ✓ YES
THE ECU	NO	THE POUND ✓ YES
RABIES	NO	QUARANTINE ✓ YES
POLITICIANS KNOW BEST	NO	REFERENDUM ✓ YES
TEMPLE-MORRIS	NO	CARLISLE ✓ YES

THE ALL-PARTY ANTI-FEDERALIST LEAGUE (AFL)

The AFL was founded in November 1991 by Dr. Alan Sked to mobilise public opinion in defence of British sovereignty, and to prevent the UK becoming a province of a united European super-state. It calls upon people to put their country before their traditional political party.

IS THE AFL ANTI-EUROPEAN?

Certainly not. The AFL welcomes the breaking down of trade barriers, and the increased co-operation between European countries. We wish to work with Europe, but not to be merged with it. Our surrender of sovereignty should go no further.

IS THE AFL SATISFIED WITH THE PRESENT SITUATION IN THE COMMUNITY?

No. The agricultural and fishing policies are disastrous, and cost the average British family over £16 per week. The Brussels system is much too bureaucratic, and issues 4,700 regulations and directives per year, many of them trivial or ridiculous.

Billions of pounds go in export subsidies and in massive fraud by Mafia and other criminal organisations, particularly, but not only, in Southern Europe.

The first priority of Brussels must be to put its house in order. The AFL will work for the thorough reform of the Community, the protection of Britain's interests and the prevention of further loss of sovereignty.

Chapter Twelve

My next project was to buy a derelict Queen Anne mansion, Caynham Court (listed Grade II), near Ludlow, for £80,000, hoping that Julian would help me restore it, sell it, and buy a tenanted estate for the family, which has always been my aim. But Rosemary was dead against the idea, and Julian was seduced by life in London.

However, at the sale, I'd met a retired builder, who asked to go into partnership with me. It seemed an attractive idea at the time. He would pay half and then work at it while I financed the restoration. It soon turned out, however, that he had no money and although he owned two houses in Knighton, they were heavily mortgaged. Besides that, he had a tiresome wife who was trying to leave him.

Nevertheless, work proceeded well with him and a carpenter for a year when the poor man developed a brain tumour and was not able to work again. My niece Elizabeth and Roland Grinker had got in trouble with a farming venture in South Africa, so I sponsored their immigration and he worked for me for two years at Caynham doing the plumbing and rewiring.

The house, which had been the centre of an estate owned for three hundred years by the Curtis family, had been bought by a property developer, who had built a dozen 'executive' type houses behind it and then gone bankrupt. This, coupled with the fact there was a turkey hatchery to one side was the reason for its low price.

I had instructed Ludlow architects John Needham Associates to apply for routine planning permission and paid them £2,000, but later, without reference to me, they submitted plans to the building inspector that were quite different from my intentions and demanded a further £3,000, which I refused to pay. They duly took me to court and to my amazement I lost. Professional men support each other, particularly if they are Freemasons, although I have always found country auctioneers and land agents honest and admirable to deal with.

Some time before this I had acquired by lease from my bank a second hand Range Rover, which from a date on the window I

242

discovered to be three years older than advertised. It was, I realised, a 'ringer', which had been reregistered, had its number plate changed and milometer clocked. When I suggested to the dealer, Bromyard 4 Wheel Drive that he take it back, he laughed at me, so I considered it my duty to take him to court.

The bank, who in fact owned the vehicle, disclaimed any responsibility for it, even though they owned it under the Consumer Credit Act. When I applied to a judge to include them as third party to my claim, he refused, predicting that if I were to sue the bank I would lose, yet ordering me to do so. The bank, one of the big high street banks, were notorious for this illegality and of course, it doubled my difficulties.

I have recently read in the newspapers that no London solicitor will sue the banks! It took two years for me to get the case set down for a hearing, during which time both parties changed their evidence at interlocutory hearings. I considered I needed a professional advocate and the local secretary of the National Farmers Union recommended one of the leading firms in Hereford.

I met a partner who assured me he was experienced in court advocacy and would represent me at the hearing, which was due in ten days. I left the papers with him and two days later received a letter from a junior solicitor saying that the case had been passed to her and she had instructed a barrister. I protested to no avail.

The day before the hearing I received a letter from my new solicitors saying that they had dropped the case and handed it to another firm because the banks' lawyers had objected that my solicitors had represented them at one of the interlocutory hearings. Although the firm I was using must have been aware of the position, they denied that they were, and in any case only I could reasonably object. One is required to submit one's pleadings to the court a week in advance of the hearing but my lawyers hadn't even sent them.

At the hearing a young barrister arrived late, irregularly went to talk to the judge and came back to say I would lose, and tried to persuade me to drop the case. Neither my barrister nor the judge made any attempt to question the car dealer or the bank's solicitor, who remained silent throughout. The judge, however, was hostile to me from the start. After my examination and evidence, the barrister asked for an adjournment and told me that the judge had indicated to him, in 'Bar Speak', that he intended to find against me so that he could get finished that day. The car dealer, of bad local reputation, made no attempt to justify the re-registration. Against the evidence of the only expert witness, an experienced insurance assessor, who said that I had been overcharged £3,000, the judge stated that the evidence of the assessor was mere speculation and that he preferred to believe the evidence of the 'honest' car dealer, who declared that he had told me the vehicle was three years older than represented and I had just forgotten about it! The judge accordingly dismissed the case and awarded costs of some £9,000 against me, in a 16 page judgement, presumably written in advance.

But in our archaic court system, although the proceedings are recorded, the defendant is not given a copy of the judgement, but has to apply to licensed translators, who supply it at considerable expense after about three weeks and after the judge has approved and possibly changed it. Although a copy of the full trial proceedings is extremely expensive, you are not allowed to tape-record it yourself in court.

I had discovered that the senior partner of my Hereford solicitors was a very prominent Freemason, as also were the bank's local managers, and I asked the judge if he were a Mason. But, in defiance of a recent order of the Home Secretary requiring membership of the Freemasons should be disclosed, he refused to answer, as have all judges before whom I have appeared since.

I appealed to the High Court and went before Judge Millet, a very senior Freemason and Judge Saville, who has been engaged for the past three years on the farcical 'Bloody Sunday' enquiry into the paras' shooting of rioters in Londonderry 10 years before – an enquiry ordered by Blair which has cost £150 million. Before I had finished my evidence I was cut short and permission to appeal was refused on the basis of a judgement of seven pages, which, as before, had obviously been written in advance!

There was no other case pending. I had had to pay the second firm of lawyers £700 for taking the pleadings to court too late and attending uselessly, but I refused to pay the original firm I'd engaged for their disgraceful behaviour and they sued me in Brecon County Court for £690, although their statement showed only £165 owing, and I had already been required to pay £250 in advance, which no other solicitor had ever demanded of me.

It was ordered for arbitration but these crafty lawyers applied for the case to be transferred to Hereford where they knew all the judges, one of whom considered their illegal behaviour perfectly acceptable and found against me, with costs, needless to say. When I protested he shouted me down and threatened me with arrest. At this and other hearings these solicitors, the plaintiffs, were presenting themselves as witnesses and charging £150 per hour; I could have claimed a mere £6.50 per hour.

In the meantime, the car dealer who had been charged by the police for selling 20 stolen Land Rovers and taken to court, was perversely acquitted by the jury, no doubt fed up, perhaps bought or intimidated, by a trial that had lasted five weeks. He went out of business shortly afterwards. The police told me that the case had cost them £500,000. A few months later Judge Geddes wrote an article in the *Spectator* criticising jury trials and quoting this case as having been a miscarriage of justice. Yet he had presided over it!

Five months later the Hereford lawyers submitted a bill for costs of £7,823, without any detailed account. This claim was ten weeks out of time and illegal, at eleven times the sum of the judgement but was awarded at a taxation hearing by a district judge, well known to the firm's partners. I had paid the £691 as ordered but refused to pay these outrageous costs claim.

For over a year the solicitors made no attempt to get the money by distraint through court bailiffs but when they discovered that I owned Caynham Court they registered a charge against it in Brecon County Court, now claiming some £10,000. A few months later, having failed to get a result, they again applied in Brecon for an order for the house to be seized and sold. It was refused as being completely disproportionate to their claim, which they had done nothing to recover.

So back they go to Hereford where the same Judge Geddes, who had acquitted the car dealer, grants them permission and costs.

I appealed to the High Court and again was dismissed by a Lord Justice, who had obviously reached his verdict beforehand as he soon shut me up (although he had no other case that day) and awarded them costs.

The house was seized by the Hereford solicitors and soon after a leak developed in the roof which they did nothing to repair.

Nearly a year later this firm applied to another Hereford judge for an order to prevent my attending the sale. The judge spent the first hour reading the case, which he should have done beforehand, and refused the order, yet illegally awarded them costs of another £4,126.

The solicitors instructed one of the leading Hereford estate agents to sell. These agents disgracefully advertised it as in need of extensive restoration, especially to the plasterwork, and treatment of timber infestation. In fact, the house had been completely restored, except for decoration, and all timber treated, although there'd been little evidence that it needed to be done. The only fault was the roof leak, which Matthews had refused to attend to. A guide price was advertised at £150,000 - £200,000, which was near half its real value. The estate agent had himself valued the property at £300,000, when discussing a possible sale a year earlier.

Before the sale my solicitor, David Jones-Powell, who unfortunately never did court work, advised me to pay the original solicitors' demands, now £22,000, so that I could regain possession and put a proper reserve price on it. Apart from the first claim, these cost claims had never been taxed and no detailed account had ever been submitted to me. But, reluctantly, I paid, only to find that the estate agent refused to accept a higher reserve than he had put as guide price on the advertisement. This I later discovered to be illegal. The house sold for £250,000, which was £50,000 less than I had previously been advised by him.

The dishonesty of the bank, once renowned as an honest Quaker firm, of which my cousin, had been a director, and whose customer we had been for 30 years, in failing to support my claim against a corrupt car dealer and colluding with the Hereford solicitors against me, had cost me £35,000, as well as an immense amount of time and a considerable loss on Caynham Court, as prices were just beginning to rise very substantially. The chairman of the bank was kept fully informed by my letters, but would not intervene, saying, 'Leave it to the courts.'

It is reported that one of the directors of the bank, has been paid the obscene sum of £100million over the past 10 years, while many employees have been sacked, while their profits exceeded £4billion last year.

I had arranged for a reporter from the local paper, *The Hereford Times* to attend the court but found they will do nothing to report abuse by the banks or solicitors. Gone are the days when the newspapers stood up for our civil liberties. Now they are terrified of the protective libel laws of this country and are interested only in advertising revenue.

The moral of this sad saga is never ever trust the courts. The much-vaunted British justice is just a bonanza for lawyers who have every interest in prolonging a case. Only the seriously rich or those on legal aid can afford to use the courts and yet it is fatal to act as a private litigant without an advocate. But you cannot instruct a barrister except through a solicitor, which doubles or trebles the cost. There is an old Spanish proverb: 'Better to be a mouse in a cat's mouth than a man in a lawyer's hands.' Charles Dickens memorably wrote, 'The law is an ass,' and George Bernard Shaw declared, 'All professions are conspiracies against the laity.' How right they were.

Furthermore, never, ever get involved with Freemasons, who are sworn to support each other even when in trouble. Many of the top detectives and Police Commissioners in this country are Masons and no solicitors will sue them, or the banks.

Ever since Chief Constables have been appointed from the Force, the Police have been corrupt. Before 1960, the Chief Constable of a county force was always a retired army officer, who was honest and respected. Since then any policemen under investigation simply retire early on 'health' grounds and vast sums, £300 million in 2003, are paid to policemen suffering from phony stress. It is much the same in the prison service.

I read recently in the obituary of an honest and courageous Judge Gerald Sparrow, who had stood for parliament against Harold Wilson for Desmond Donelly's Democratic Party in 1970, which I had supported, that he warned: 'Never go to law. Avoid lawyers like the plague. They will not champion your cause but try to compromise and you can do that better and more economically yourself.' This is the best free advice I've ever been given by a lawyer.

It's a pity I was not aware of it ten years earlier, when I still believed justice could be obtained in a British court. It would have saved me a great deal of time and expense. Now, we even have lawyers defeating the Home Secretary and laws of parliament to deport unlawful immigrants, acting on legal aid and every day on television encouraging people to sue for trivial or imagined grievances. It has become as bad as American litigious society. Someone has to be blamed for every trivial accident or misfortune!

It is also a waste of time to complain to the Law Society which is meant to examine complaints but, in fact, is just a protection agency for lawyers.

In 1999, devolution brought another tier of government to Scotland and Wales in a quite useless move that is wildly expensive, furnishing a lot more soft jobs for politicians and civil servants to define and deal with more regulations.

In November of that year, we had two weeks holiday at Kyrenia in Northern Cyprus where my friend from Indian army days, Ben Brocklehurst, and his wife Belinda, who ran Cricketers' Holidays, had a house. It was still warm enough to bathe in the sea.

Unlike the south, there are few tourists in northern Cyprus since the Turks drove out the Greeks in the nineteen-seventies. The country is mountainous and green and there are several Crusader Castles of the Knights Hospitalers, who occupied the island for 300 years after being driven out of the holy land by Saladin in 1200. They then moved to Malta, where they ruled as Knights of St John until c.1700.

Britain still maintains a large army base in southern Cyprus and whilst there has been a United Nations force there ever since partition to prevent another war, there is at last hope of a settlement of the dispute between the two factions.

For some years, a disease, Brucellosis Spongiform Encephalitis (BSE), or 'Mad Cow Disease', had started to appear in cattle in this country. Government scientists claimed they had caught it through eating imported feed. However, there are many to whom this seemed improbable, particularly as no other countries were suffering from the disease. They considered it more likely to be caused by organophosphates, which, by government order, were used to treat the backs of cattle as a means of eradicating Warble Fly. However, the Ministry has refused to investigate this possibility, despite being pressed by independent veterinary surgeons.

It was alleged that the disease could cause the rare Creutzfeldt-Jakob disease in humans but this has never been proved and the number of cases each year has been a mere handful – 16 deaths in 2004. Yet mad scientists caused scares by predicting many thousands of deaths and it was ordered that no cattle over 2½ years old could be used for human consumption. All the waste from abattoirs which had previously been processed into meat and bone meal and included in animal feeds has since been wastefully incinerated.

The substantial export trade in cattle was stopped and ever since, all cattle over 2½ years have also been incinerated at a cost of about £8 billion, even though perfectly healthy and by that age, in many cases, not even mature. In the past, sick or dead cattle were collected by knackers' yards, who paid up to £50 for a carcass. The meat went for pet food, the hides and tallow were profitably sold.

Now farmers have to pay about £50 to have them collected and all are wastefully destroyed. Hunt kennels feed the meat but have to pay £100 per week for the offal to be collected and get nothing for the hides. Sheep may no longer be buried on farms and collection has to be paid for, although I usually feed ours to the dogs. The skins which used to be sold to fellmongers for up to £5, are now worthless. Hides and sheep skins are now all imported from the Middle East or South America.

Farmers had also been ordered to use sheep dip containing organophosphate for several years, which was highly effective against lice and fly strike, until some found they suffered from serious neurological symptoms, which the authorities have again refused to examine or admit, although they have now banned its use and it is now mandatory to attend a training course and acquire a licence to dip sheep – bureaucracy gone mad again!

I bought a secondhand Czech Zetor tractor. I have never bought a new one since I started farming when I bought Fergusons, £330 for paraffin and £420 for diesel, made in Coventry. Practically all tractors were then British made and many were exported.

Ever since, I've used Massey Fergusons which never caused trouble. Now, new tractors are more powerful and more sophisticated and cost around £20,000, but are much more likely to break down. In fact, if tractors are kept topped up with oil and water they never wear out except for the clutches which we replace on the farm. Rafael still runs two that are thirty-years old, which I passed on to him.

Today, no tractors are manufactured in Britain.

The same goes for all farm machinery. Once produced in this country, the vast majority are now imported. A great British industry has been destroyed by striking workers and incompetent management.

In 2000, we went to Cuba where Fidel Castro had presided over a communist regime for 30 years, despite every American attempt to remove him. The tourist hotels were perfectly good but the people were very poor. Havana, which had been a beautiful Spanish city, was much dilapidated. The countryside was attractive enough but the roads were full of potholes. The few cars there are old American models, held together with string.

We visited the house of the reprobate author Ernest Hemingway and the pub where he drank himself to oblivion, and went around a cigar factory, the products of which were surprisingly expensive. I was disappointed to find that the girls do not roll them on their thighs as rumour always had it!

Although their schools and hospitals are of a very high order, few people appreciate living in this socialist paradise and many risk their lives every year on unseaworthy boats or rafts to escape to Florida, where a large ex-patriate community is already well established.

The tyrannical President Mobutu of the Congo died, followed by the eruption of a civil war which is said to have resulted in the deaths of some five million people as a struggle for the country's mineral wealth has been unleashed. At long last a United Nations force was sent to the country but has proved to be unable to stop the massacres and themselves have been involved in corruption.

Meanwhile, in Afghanistan, a United Nations report has stated that the country has 220,000 acres growing poppies, which provide 80% of illegal opium consumption worldwide. This is the only profitable crop on their poor soils, keeping several war lords in power. The total crop is 4,000 tonnes, earning $650m a year but more is being spent on its destruction. 80% of legal opium, which produces Codeine and Morphine is consumed by six rich countries, and 10,000 tonnes is needed to provide cancer relief and other treatments in developing countries. Why doesn't the UN buy this crop for legitimate and constructive use, providing legal income to farmers, instead of destroying it?

In 2001 we flew to Thailand for two weeks, spending three nights in Bangkok where the traffic is quite appalling. We had a trip on a Dragon boat along the canals of the city and visited spectacular Buddhist temples and a ruined city of an ancient civilisation. We also visited the celebrated Bridge over the River Kwai, which is a steel structure quite unlike the wooden bridge shown in the famous film.

There is a War Graves Commission cemetery nearby, with the graves of 12,000 of the 50,000 British and Australian prisoners of war who died during the construction of the infamous Burma railway by the Japanese. A museum, which contained photographs and artifacts, seemed to me to gloss over the appalling brutalities of the Japanese. Far larger numbers of Asian coolies who were forced to work on the railway died but they lie in unmarked graves.

We then flew to Chiang Mai in the north, an attractive town on the Mekong river close to the borders of Burma and Laos. This is the area of the Golden Triangle – after Afghanistan, the principal source of heroin in the world and controlled by local warlords. Here we saw elephants dancing around and doing all the remarkable things that elephants are able to do. We then flew down to Patong, near Phuket and spent several very comfortable nights in an hotel on the beach, since then, all destroyed by the Tsunami of Christmas 2004. The Thai Government had 24 hours warning of it but failed to broadcast it to the coastal areas.

Also in 2001, a general election was held, and won again by the Labour party led by the charismatic but deceitful Tony Blair, described by the distinguished Tom Dalyell, father of the house, as the worst Prime Minister he had ever known.

Cabinet Ministers became of little importance, as Blair, with a very large majority has operated in Parliament more in the style of a dictator than a Prime Minister, commanding far more power than the President of the US.

In September, Moslem terrorist, mostly Saudi Arabian, hijacked four American airliners and crashed two into the twin towers of the World Trade Centre in New York and one into the Pentagon Military Headquarters in Washington. The fourth, in which the crew or passengers managed resistance, crashed in open country.

Some 2,800 people died, provoking President George Bush to declare war on terrorism and to name countries harbouring it as an 'Axis of Evil'. Shortly afterwards, America bombed and then invaded Afghanistan where the terrorist leader Osama Bin Laden was believed to be hiding under the protection of the fundamentalist Mujahadeen. Aided by a few troops from Britain and other countries the Americans are still bogged down there today, trying to impose democracy on an unwilling population who now grow even more heroin than before whereas cultivation of poppies had been almost eliminated by the Mujahadeen. Osama Bin Laden's Al Quaeda terrorists are till active.

The brave General Musharraf of Pakistan, who has survived several attempts at assassination, has sent his army, which used to support the Mujahadeen, into the Pathan province of Waziristan, where we kept the peace during the war. They have suffered 250 dead but have not found bin Laden. Meanwhile his fundamentalist Mullahs continue to indoctrinate terrorists in their religious *madrasas*, some to return to this and other countries.

There is an immoral idea propagated today by the Americans that it doesn't matter how many of the enemy or civilians are killed, so long as our boys don't come back in body bags. Yet it has always been understood that if you live by the sword you cannot complain if you die by the sword. Suicide bombers are dismissed as terrorists but in fact they are very brave and indoctrinated by religious beliefs of eternity in paradise. They can only be defeated when the causes of their grievances are removed.

In September 2001, Julian married the charming Anna, daughter of Mary and Tim Taylor, a retired stockbroker and old Radleian, who gave them a large wedding at Goudhurst in Kent. His best man was Tom Cripwell, whose young wife has tragically suffered a serious cancer. Julian's close friend, James Woosnam is crippled with ME, and another, William Thrupp, by a brain tumour. Why does it happen? Is pollution to blame?

I always reckon there are two sorts marriage. Most people marry their similarities in looks and characteristics, as have Julian and Fiona, and live happily ever after. A few marry their opposites, tall marrying short and highly strung marrying phlegmatic, as we did, resulting in a battle of the sexes.

Nowadays, however, with the decline of religious belief, an increasing number, particularly among the lower classes, don't get married at all, with the appalling result that 20% of children are born to single mothers. Ever since the stigma of illegitimacy was removed by law some 40 years ago, governments have done everything possible to encourage this by financial support. The inevitable result is that society has sorely deteriorated with many fatherless children, brought up without discipline, often taking to crime and drugs.

Until the swinging sixties women were moral and respected, divorce was difficult and expensive. Divorcees were generally shunned and not allowed into the Royal Enclosure at Ascot. The feminist revolution and the birth control pill changed all that and now women are more immoral than men ever were. In state schools Sex Education instructs the young from puberty to adultery.

For many, marriage vows are a farce, to be kept only until a more attractive model comes along. This has been encouraged by the appalling cult of 'Celebrity', which promotes vastly overpaid film stars, pop-musicians and footballers as a new aristocracy, to be admired and imitated.

In 2001 the Zimbabwean dictator Mugabe started to evict white farmers, who had made the country the breadbasket of Africa. Violent gangs invaded the farms and by now practically all Europeans, including several thousand British subjects, have been forced to leave the country, which is facing starvation as a result. Yet this country and the United Nations have done nothing to stop it. In

1870 Lord Palmerston sent our army into Abyssinia to rescue one Englishman.

Mugabe has remained in power by fraudulent elections, against the wishes of the vast majority of his terrified subjects. The South African President Mbeki has given him every encouragement and may well also go the same way – very different from the charismatic Mandela.

In February 2001, Burnside Farm in Northumberland was found to be in a disgraceful condition where pigs, being fed on unprocessed swill, were dying and although the farm had been inspected by officials no action had been taken. It was then scandalously announced that Foot and Mouth disease was the cause, although this has never been proved and, in fact, has recently been admitted to be untrue.

European countries immediately banned the import of any British meat. Two large dealers who had bought a great number of ram lambs to export to France, as Moslems eat them at the end of the Ramadan fast, were stuck with them. It should have come as no surprise that they both suddenly announced they were also suffering from foot and mouth, and collected massive compensation for their slaughter.

The Government veterinary department then went mad, demanding that the livestock on any adjoining farms or those from which livestock had come, should also be slaughtered. In fact, no vets in this country could recognise the symptoms of the disease as the last outbreak had been in 1967 and very many sheep show lesions around the mouth through grazing heather or hedgerows. Also, although they get seriously debilitated by the disease, very few sheep or cattle actually die from it. The slaughter policy dates from the days far away when this country was a great exporter of pedigree livestock all over the world. There is also a vaccination available but this was never used.

Philip Hughes, who lived in a bungalow at Penyrwrlodd, had acquired land on the other side of the Black Mountains, and kept, with his brother, an excessive number of ewes on the bare mountain. He ran into trouble after a heavy fall of snow, which prevented him from feeding them. Some sheep died, so he called in the vet, who found that the sheep were in a disgraceful condition and diagnosed foot and mouth — and an order was given for them to be slaughtered.

As Hughes' bungalow was on my farm, another vet arrived and demanded to inspect my sheep. A Swiss – one of the vets taken on by the Government to cope with the emergency – it transpired he too had never seen foot and mouth but claimed, nevertheless, that 6 or 7 of my sheep had mouth lesions and proposed slaughter.

I told him to take blood samples and send them for a laboratory check. This he did but said he must ring London for instructions and was told the entire flock must be slaughtered. Men arrived next day to perform the wicked deed.

I was reduced to tears at the sight of 500 ewes in prime condition and 40 healthy cattle lying dead in the buildings. Later they were incinerated in a field on a great funeral pyre, using many tons of prime coal.

Afterwards, a team of six men arrived to cleanse the buildings that the sheep had never been in. They were on the farm for 12 weeks, stripping out and burning any timber, washing and disinfecting yards, even under the roofs, and generally idling about. No one seemed to care that the germ can only live for a short time in buildings and is destroyed by sunlight, and the results of the blood tests had already proved that my livestock were not infected.

Meanwhile another farm in the valley was wiped out as well as three on the other side of the mountain.

At a meeting three weeks later, the veterinary department admitted that foot and mouth had not been proved on the Hughes farm or any of the others.

The blow was softened when compensation was paid at about twice the value of the animals and also for restoration of the buildings. Not surprisingly some farmers jumped on the bandwagon. Over that summer of madness, some seven million sheep, cattle and pigs were slaughtered and contractors made vast sums on cleansing buildings, while some farmers made greatly inflated claims for pedigree livestock valued by local auctioneers.

This wicked waste cost the country some £7 billion and it now appears certain that the disease never existed. I was recently told by an official in DEFRA (Dept of Agriculture) that an elderly vet who had experienced the 1968 outbreak had told him that he had inspected farms all over the country and had been unable to confirm a single case of Foot & Mouth. In any event, all the stock could have gone for human consumptions as the disease doesn't affect humans.

Passports were then introduced to register the movement of cattle, as well as the ear-tagging of sheep, which has caused a huge amount of work for farmers and auctioneers, controlled by another bureaucracy to no apparent advantage, as auctioneers already have records.

Now, five yeas later, forms still have to be submitted for movement of any animals. Officials are uselessly employed in supervising all this paperwork, and farmers are required to keep records of all medicines bought, what livestock are treated and by whom. This is all quite unnecessary but carries threats of prosecution for non-compliance.

Feeding of waste food as swill to pigs was banned and still is. Some 60 swill processors were rendered bankrupt without compensation, for which they are still demanding £40 million, yet unbelievably the pig farmer whose disgraceful conditions started the holocaust did receive compensation.

As movement in the countryside was restricted, many hotels and B&Bs suffered heavy losses, as did farmers who were not allowed to move their stock to market when needed. Incredibly, it has recently been officially reported that 40% of the food produced in this country goes to waste to be dumped in landfill sites as it can no longer be fed to pigs. Whereas in wartime nothing was wasted, now we live in a society of waste, encouraged by multifarious regulations of hygiene and sell-by dates and general affluence. The supermarkets demand such exacting standards, whereby carrots must be straight and cauliflowers uniformly shaped and unblemished, that 30% of the vegetables and fruit produced by farmers has to be discarded and fed to livestock.

Before 1994, exports of lamb, mutton and beef far exceeded imports, now, since BSE and FMD, imports exceed exports by £100 million a year. Most abattoirs have closed, as have many creameries, now that dairy products are also flooding in from abroad. Half the chicken and pork we consume is now imported, where once it was all home produced.

In 2002, I joined the organic farming scheme, as £25,000 over three years was being offered by a generous government for joining. So-called 'organic' farming is just what was considered good farming practice forty years ago; that is to say, not using nitrogen fertilisers, which promote excessive growth, and chemical sprays, which kill weeds and wild flowers, insects and bacteria and pollutes all fruit. This has caused the disappearance of almost all our farmland birds.

Previously, all farms kept livestock and practiced rotation of crops to maintain fertility and control pests and diseases. Tenancy agreements stipulated that half the farm be kept in grass. Since the disgraceful abolition of controls by the 1946 Landlord and Tenant Act, arable farmers have been able to dispense with livestock and practice monoculture of root, corn and rape crops grown with inorganic fertilisers. This has resulted in much heavier crops but renders the soil a sterile medium. It will now grow nothing without fertilisers.

The obvious way to correct this situation would be to tax nitrogen fertilizers and chemical sprays but the oil and chemical companies and barley barons who control the Farmers Union have managed to prevent this.

In my case, as the farm was all in grass, rearing cattle and sheep, 'going organic' has resulted in little change, except for having to put up with a lot of bureaucratic paperwork and inspections.

Some farmers convert to organic, collect the grant, and then revert to their wicked chemical ways without penalty. A tax on fertilisers and chemical sprays would compel traditional good husbandry and healthier food without the great expense that has arisen through overloading the system with bureaucracy and civil servants.

In spring 2002 we flew to Mombasa where we joined a small cruise ship for a week for a trip, taking in Zanzibar, with its old Moorish buildings and a slave market, Madagascar and Reunion, which was very French and attractive, returning to Mombasa. We managed to leave our appointed dining table and join Ann and Ivan Stewart, who have a cottage at Abergwesyn and with whom we have remained close friends ever since.

Ivan had served in Probyns Horse, Indian Army before and

during the war, gaining an MC in Burma. We flew up for a couple of nights in the Masai Mara game park, where we were driven round and saw many buck and a few lions and, of course, a Masai village. Hippos were said to come into the camp but I did not encounter any. The hotel at the coast was good but the climate very enervating, and the beach disappointing.

Kenya is now a sink of corruption, although supported by British aid funds. Gone are the hedonistic days of the Happy Valley when, in 1940, Jock Delves Broughton was tried for the murder of Lord Errol who was having an affair with his wife Diana. He was acquitted but committed suicide a year later. Diana went on to marry Lord Delamere, leader of the settlers. Jock's uncle, Frank Delves Broughton, was a cousin of Rosemary's father.

In November 2002, our daughter-in-law, Anna produced a son, Hugo, who, after early worries, is now progressing well. Julian's business is picking up and there are hopes that it can be sold at a useful profit.

In the same month, our house caught fire. At about 4.00pm, I went out to the boiler room adjoining the house to find timber blazing. I dialed 999 to call the fire brigade and expended several fire extinguishers to little effect. When Rosemary appeared, I said we had better remove the good pictures. We had no sooner started in the dining room when two police, a PC and a burly WPC appeared and demanded we leave the house.

I said, 'Don't be ridiculous! Help us take these pictures out.' Whereupon I was seized and forcibly removed from the house and with the help of an ambulance driver, Ken Francis who arrived a few minutes later, thrown on my head into a small space at the back of their police van. There had not even been any smoke in the house, as a strong south westerly wind was carrying it away over the road.

The sergeant from Hay-on-Wye, Brian Jones arrived and Rosemary was locked in a police car, while Brian Dennis and two other men, who had come up from his garage below to help, were prevented from going to rescue our possessions and threatened with arrest.

The Brecon Fire Brigade were on strike and the police

headquarters delayed 33 minutes in passing on the alarm to the volunteer Hay-on-Wye firemen, who arrived nine minutes later from their station 1½ miles away, but now too late.

The fire had now been raging for 42 minutes and flames were coming through the roof at the back of the house against the road on the east side. A little later, another volunteer fire engine arrived from Talgarth, but they carry little water and I had been prevented from speaking to the chief on arrival to tell him of the water supply in the swimming pool in the garden and other information, as he would have expected.

The fire took 1½ hours to reach the west half of the house and then break through the roof. All the principal rooms of the house were on that side and contained all our possessions of value that could easily have been saved. If the fire had been fought from that side it would never have got past the immense central chimney as there were only doorways on each side and the west half could have been saved.

By then, nine police, another ambulance, even a television crew had arrived, and all stood by uselessly while the whole house was consumed – the straightforward result of police malice!

The local newspapers reported that Constables Skyrme and Swales had reported to Brecon hospital complaining of smoke inhalation, which strongly indicates conspiracy by Police Headquarters, as there had been no smoke whatever in the house when we were seized in unlawful arrest and a police report, obtained later, states that they were immediately discharged as fit. The ambulance service refused to disclose the name of their driver, who had aided the police in assaulting me.

Since then I have been trying to sue the police for illegal arrest and our loss and have approached 20 firms of solicitors in Hereford, Bristol, London and Birmingham all of whom have refused to act. When lawyers feel they cannot protect our civil liberties, we are living in a police state.

The Police Complaints Authority also refused to take any action; they were, in fact, just a Police protection association. Now at keas in 2005 they have been made independent and thus may offer some protection from police abuse.

Magistrates, who used to be gentry, are nowadays just shopkeepers who always find for the police. Incredibly, they are now advertising in Brecon for people aged between 25 and 60 to apply to become JPs and judge their contemporaries! To my mind, they should only be successful, retired people of age and experience and with time for the job. When MPs can remain active into old age, why not magistrates?

Dyfed Powys police have an appalling record and are universally distrusted in this area. Eight people have told me they have suffered from police harassment.

When robberies are reported to them they take no action to investigate. For many years they have plagued law-abiding motorists, stopping them at night when no offence was being committed and unlawfully demanding breath tests. I had written to the local papers complaining of this abuse of our civil liberties and complained both to the Chief Constable and the Police Complaints Committee, with no result except to attract harassment.

A few months before, fire broke out in the middle of the night in a large house in Herefordshire. Although the entire house was destroyed, the greater part of the furniture and possessions were saved with the help of neighbours and firemen.

The Chief Constable, Terence Grange, had been a corporal in the parachute Regiment and notoriously stated in the press that all drug dealers should be shot. The Chairman of the Watch Committee had an Italian name and ran a fish and chips shop in Carmarthen. This was all very different to the old days, when the Chief Constable was a retired army officer and the Watch Committee comprised local gentry. Then the police were honest and respected, like television's Dixon of Dock Green, living in the villages, patrolling the beat in the towns and calling in at the pubs at night. Now they just drive around in cars and are frightened to walk the streets of towns to prevent vandalism and crime. Hundreds turn out to confront a crowd or demonstration, probably just to get overtime pay.

At Notting Hill Carnival this year, 2005, the monstrous number of 4,000 police were on duty to maintain law and order. Not surprisingly, there was very little criminal behaviour. It is even reported that some police in London get their wages up to £100,000 a year through overtime pay.

In 1993, I had been invited to a Lions Club dinner and on returning home through Hay in a red Jaguar, which I then owned, was followed by a vehicle flashing its headlights. I drove slowly keeping to the middle of the road, stopped beside the back door of my house and went inside, foolishly omitting to lock the door behind me.

A few moments later a constable burst in, saying I had a faulty tail light and demanding to breathalyse me. I told him to get out but he refused and even followed me into Rosemary's bedroom when I went upstairs to call her as witness to the situation.

I then rang my solicitor who said he believed they could claim entry when 'in hot pursuit'. By this time two other police had arrived so I agreed to take the test, whereupon they said it was 'too late', and they were arresting me to take me to Brecon for a breath test. I checked the tail lights and proved that the man was lying.

In Brecon, after the test had proved completely negative, I was charged with failing to stop for an officer on duty.

The case was heard in Brecon Magistrates court where I had the AA's solicitor, John Llewellyn to represent me and, unbelievably, was convicted and fined the maximum of £600 by a shopkeeper magistrate, doing the police's bidding.

I appealed in the Crown Court, without an advocate this time, and the case was thrown out because the police car had had no 'Stop' sign and flashing headlights did not constitute an order to stop. The hearing in the Magistrates' Court had achieved banner headlines on the front of the local paper. Typically, the result of my appeal was not reported. Foolishly, I forgot to demand costs.

There was some background to the vindictive behaviour of the police towards me. In 1997 some people 'from off' had bought a farm higher up the valley and the wife regularly drove through the farm at excessive speed, without regard to people, horses or dogs.

Having written to her several times over two years to no effect, during which time, she had nearly crashed into five neighbours, I asked the police to have a word with her. Apparently these neighbours had close relations with the local police and complained that I was harassing the wife. Constable Lyndon Heard came to visit me and insolently accused me of this.

Two months later my firearms certificate for a .22 rifle, occasionally used as a humane killer, was due for renewal in February. My cheque was cashed but the new certificate not supplied, which was illegal.

On 20th April a police constable arrived, saying that he wished to question me about it. I replied that he had all the information on the application form. He then officiously tried to shake my hand. I refused this unwanted familiarity, known in the army as 'dumb insolence'. Whereupon he left, threatening to cause trouble.

Four days later, Rosemary and I were driving to a dinner in Brecon when we were overtaken by a police car in the main street and another, unmarked car stopped behind.

Another constable and the same WPC who had attended at our house demanded that I take a breath test. I gave them a piece of my mind at this unlawful hold-up but had to submit to the indignity, which proved me to be completely sober.

They then said I had been driving without due care and attention, as I had crossed a white line, which is, as it happens, in no way an offence. However, they charged me but could not proceed with a prosecution. In fact, I've had a clean driving licence for 60 years.

Police drivers are reported to have killed 35 people and injured 2,015 during the year 2004, when in pursuit or answering emergencies, yet practically none have been convicted of manslaughter or dangerous driving. They are even required to attend driving courses of two to five weeks, yet this year, a policeman was caught driving on a motorway at 150mph for no operational reason, and was never charged.

In August, a notorious police sergeant, of whom I had heard several complaints of harassment, and the PC who'd been previously, arrived one night bringing a letter, dated June, from the Assistant Chief Constable saying he was not renewing my firearms certificate and was cancelling my shotgun licence as I was unfit to own firearms. Disgracefully he quoted the failed hold-up in Brecon. The letter stated that I had 30 days to appeal, which I did immediately.

In their panic after the September 2005 bomb attacks on the London Underground, plain clothes police followed a young Brazilian man onto a train, held him down and cold-bloodedly shot him with eight bullets. The Chief Commissioner of the Metropolitan Police lied and covered up and no charge has been brought against the perpetrators.

A member of the SAS unit which trains the police in firearms use has recently written to *The Times* to say that he found many of them 'gung-ho' and unsafe with firearms. It is also reported that Scotland is now the most violent country in the developed world with three times the murder rate of America. Yet our police devote more of their time to removing sporting guns from law-abiding citizens than tackling the huge number of criminals holding handguns.

I heard nothing more about my appeal, and in September I set off to India for a bus tour of the North West Frontier, Swat and Chitral. It was rather low grade and we sometimes went 'native', eating at local restaurants.

The romantic Hunza, Nagir and Gilgit proved rather disappointing with camel trains and mules now replaced by lorries and 4-wheel drive vehicles, and of course the same old, brilliantly painted buses. We returned along the new highway built by the Chinese and Indians through deep gorges between the spectacular mountains, which had cost a life for every mile in construction.

Rosemary, who had driven me to Heathrow and then spent the night with Fiona at Chippenham, returned home to find that six police had arrived that morning to search the house with a warrant, illegally issued by another patsy magistrate, 'Wally' Elliott, as the appeal hearing was still pending.

They turned out our 'daily', Julie and rifled the house, including all drawers and our personal papers, finding a gun, bolt removed, belonging to Julian, on top of a cupboard in Rosemary's bedroom as she was alone in the house during my absence. My guns were in a locked a cabinet.

When I returned I found no acknowledgement of my appeal and on enquiry, the Crown Court denied receiving it until I proved it had been sent by recorded delivery, when they admitted it and set a date in December. I instructed the Brecon solicitor, Llewellyn, who said he would represent me but two days before the hearing, refused and never sent my pleadings to the court.

When solicitors will not tackle the police and the local papers and judges refuse to defend our civil liberties, it really is hard not to come to the conclusion that we are living in a virtual police state, which is getting progressively worse as common informers are encouraged by the appalling increase of bureaucratic regulations, and the traditional freedom of an Englishman is eroded.

I went to the appeal, taking three friends to attest to my good character, confident that I could not lose against this conspiracy by five lying police, who had all produced colourful, coordinated statements three days after the Brecon hold-up, claiming that I had become uncontrollably angry and they were frightened that I was going to assault them! In fact it is not in my character to lose my temper or even to express anger except on paper.

The police concerned did not even appear in court to support their lying witness statements, nor did my neighbours from up the valley, whom I had demanded should appear. However, the patsy judge, Gareth Davies, illegally quoted from their evidence statements. He also illegally refused to answer my question as to whether or not he was a Freemason. In fact I was prosecuted only for the gun not being shut in a cabinet, an offence with which I had never been charged and which the police later admitted is not a requirement by law, merely a recommendation.

This disgraceful judge then dismissed my appeal with £200 costs though it's difficult to imagine anyone more suitable to possess firearms than me. Statistically the most unsafe users of weapons are the police, who have often shot dead unarmed men, sometimes mental defectives, and are never charged with manslaughter. My guns were later released to my son who lives in Battersea, a high crime area, where they are far more likely be stolen.

It has recently been reported in the press that James Hewitt, who had an affair with Princess Diana, has had his licences cancelled, out of spite, no doubt. Many other people in the county have also had trouble over cancelled gun licences. The police just plague the law-abiding while they themselves are frightened to tackle the criminal fraternity, reported to own a million unlicensed firearms, although one never reads of their houses being searched.

After the unlawful search of our house, I had written to the Home Secretary, Jack Straw asking him to sack the Chief Constable, to whom I sent a copy of my letter, which no doubt made him determined to have my appeal refused.

I had also written to the Lord Chancellor complaining of the magistrate, Wally Elliott who had issued the illegal warrant, in both cases getting only an evasive reply from a junior member of staff.

I then sued the Chief Constable and Deputy for defamation in Brecon County Court. The police solicitors first sent me witness statements and then applied for an interlocutory hearing to get the case struck out and, in a letter to me, dishonestly said that this would not be the final hearing.

At court, their barrister from London, presumably sympathetic, gave me the report of a case which stated that a defamation charge should be heard before a jury. But this judge, Lloyd Davies, in another kangaroo court refused this demand and reserved judgement, which incredibly he delivered two months later illegally striking out the case and awarding costs of £3,200 against me.

I appealed to the High Court in Swansea and instructed a Swansea solicitor, who professed to stand up for our liberties and said he was happy to represent me. A few days before the hearing he dropped the case, again, presumably, under police pressure. The judge hardly listened to me, refused my application for trial by jury and confirmed the striking out of the case. The police, however, made no attempt to collect the £3,200 costs awarded.

There is a leaflet instructing those dissatisfied with the court to write to the Lord Chancellor. This I did and got only the usual evasive reply from a junior member of his staff as had happened when I complained previously. Letters through an MP get no better attention. In fact, writing to MPs or Ministers is a waste of time.

In May 2002, I wrote to John Denham, Minister of State at the Home Office in charge of the police, demanding that the Chief Constable be sacked after several local residents had complained to me of police harassment.

A thousand gallons of petrol had disappeared from the police pump in Brecon and after lengthy enquiries it was declared to have just leaked from the pipe, which was impossible as it is regularly pressure tested and anyhow would have been smelt.

A drunken policeman wrote off a car and another covered up for him. At Brecon Magistrates' Court, they were both charged with driving under the influence of alcohol and perverting the course of justice. The case was transferred to Carmarthen Crown Court after a year and they were acquitted as, incredibly, it was deemed there was 'no case to answer'.

A friend of ours, spotted by speed cameras driving over 70mph at night on an empty motorway in Scotland and being involved in a very minor accident, collected 12 points on her licence, which was suspended for two years. Moreover, she was ordered to report weekly for instruction in Brecon, 15 miles away without transport, which she needed to carry her elderly mother and for her extensive charitable work. She was also ordered to retake the driving test, which required three attempts.

A similar, ludicrous instruction course was imposed on the wife of my solicitor and a friend, who died before he could pass the test after a very minor accident.

Two men had been forcibly searched for cannabis and even convicted when 'magic mushrooms' (not an illegal drug) were found in a search of their house.

Some common informer reported to the National Park authority that a neighbour had put a mobile field shelter close to her listed cottage while she built a stable for her horses. She was ordered to remove it and refused as it was in no way illegal. She was convicted in the Magistrates Court of refusing to obey the order and later, on appeal to the Crown Court, the judge illogically imposed no fine but ordered her to pay costs of £2,000, which was half what the Park solicitor was demanding and her daughter unfortunately paid. She is a strong believer in our liberties and gave all officials a piece of her mind. This malevolent prosecution must have cost the Park several thousand pounds and wasted much time at four court hearings over two years.

Many years ago she had suffered a mental breakdown and after a minor traffic accident and an incident in Hay when she had lost her cool, four police had broken into her house on two occasions and forcibly removed her to Bronllys hospital where she was injected with tranquillizers. This brutal behaviour puts one in mind of communist Russia, where dissidents were regularly locked in mental homes. I had written on her behalf to the chairman and vice chairman of the Park protesting at their disgraceful harassment, but it did no good and they refused to name the informer who had laid the complaint, leaving suspicion in the neighbourhood.

In the past, when they lived in the community and walked the beat, police were respected as the servants of law-abiding people, their job to prevent crime. Now they only drive around in cars, alienated from the public, of whom they consider themselves the masters, and may occasionally investigate crimes after they've failed to prevent them.

As I've already said, more then once, it is no exaggeration to say that we live here in a police state, encouraging informers as in Nazi Germany. All this has, of course, cost me a great deal of time and it is outrageous that the police should devote so much time and expense to malicious witch-hunts when they should be tackling crime.

No doubt my efforts to have the Chief Constable sacked were the reason that, when I rang his headquarters to raise the alarm on our house fire the following November, his police arrived six minutes later and dragged me out of the house and he failed to pass the alarm to Hay-on-Wye fire brigade for 33 minutes, thereby causing the loss of our house and all our possessions.

The house, which I am rebuilding by direct labour, and hope to do so within the sum insured, will not include an attic floor but will be more convenient, warmer and less draughty than the old one. The loss of her furniture was a great blow to Rosemary as she had some good pieces and pictures passed down over generations. But the greatest loss of all is our heritage of photograph albums, portraits of the family painted by Elizabeth Pulford, letters, records and so on, which can never be replaced.

At times like these, it is said; you discover who your friends are. Three offered me accommodation while Rosemary went to stay with Fiona. I was given suits and other clothes and many friends subscribed to photograph albums and other gifts of china and linen. One offered us their coach house for the winter and another, their holiday home near Llanigon, in June.

In July we bought a bungalow in Cusop, just outside Hay. It is a delight to Rosemary as it is very convenient and warm but I do not like living in such small rooms. She had long complained that Penyrwrlodd was too large and the wind blew through it. However, the bungalow is not overlooked, being surrounded by a 2-acre paddock and bounded by a small river. It is only two miles from Penyrwrlodd farm, which I visit every day.

Chapter Thirteen

In February 2003, we spent two weeks in a very comfortable hotel in Tenerife with Cricketer Holidays.   The island is completely dependent on tourism with practically no cultivation of crops except bananas.   Puerto de la Cruz was a most attractive town and the centre of the island was dominated by a huge extinct volcano, around which we were driven in a coach on narrow roads with terrifying precipices and gradients.

In March, America invaded Iraq without United Nations approval, claiming that Saddam Hussein supported terrorists groups, such as Al Quaida, and that he was still producing weapons of mass destruction, even though inspectors had been scouring the country for several years without finding any. For six months American planes had been bombing Iraqui sites on the so-called 'No Fly' zones, to provoke reaction, but without success.

The duplicitous Tony Blair, acting without the consent of Parliament, although stupidly approved by the Conservatives, sent British troops to support them. Why didn't the Queen forbid it? Constitutional Monarchy has gone too far.

Disgracefully the Americans started with a week of bombing by aircraft and missiles, killing many thousands and, after considerable fighting, occupied Baghdad and arrested Saddam Hussein, with the British occupying Basra in the south.

Then, unbelievably they disbanded both the Iraqi army and police, instead of just changing the commanders, so turning them all into unemployed potential adversaries. The British army has, of course, long experience of dealing with urban guerrillas and getting the goodwill of the population, as in Northern Ireland for the past 15 years. The Americans, on the other hand, haven't a clue and shoot anything or anybody on sight. The result has been two years of strife with the death of some 100,000 Iraqis, the loss of 90 British and over 1,000 American soldiers, and wholesale destruction of cities.

A so-called democratic government has at last been

established which, it is hoped, may spread to the other Moslem countries in the region, but democracy does not fit well with Islam. It is equally possible that fundamentalist theocratic regimes will take power in all Moslem countries, resulting in an expanded Christian-Moslem war, which would be extremely dangerous in view of the huge numbers of Moslems now living in the Western world.

That year, too, the Moslem Sudanese government unleashed a reign of terror on the largely Christian population of the southern province of Darfur, massacring 180,000 people and driving some 2 million into refugee camps.

Despite threats of sanctions the United Nations has done nothing to check these barbarities, except to provide food and shelter for the refugees.

In Zimbabwe, AIDS is decimating the population, as in all African countries and it is reported that 100,000 immigrants have been admitted to this country without any health checks whatever, to be a burden on the country and the NHS.

The devastation and appalling corruption of all African countries is the direct result of the end of the colonial regime 40 years ago – 50 years too soon, and all due to American anti-colonialism and American/Russian antagonisms of the cold war. Since then there have been 186 coups, 26 wars and 7 million have died

All African heads of state own fleets of Mercedes, many stretched or armoured models costing over £100,000 each. The jovial King of Swaziland last year spent £7 ½ million on Mercedes cars and parties for his 13 wives, out of the £14 million we gave him in foreign aid, while 70% of his people live in poverty and 4 out of 10 suffer from AIDS.

In Kenya, MPs are paid £65,000 tax-free to discourage them from corruption while the average income of their people is £210 per year. The British ambassador recently stated that corruption is as bad as ever and was nearly sacked for his candour.

In April 2004 Rosemary and I went on a cruise round the Baltic. After sailing through the Kiel Canal with immense locks each end, I took a day trip on a coach to Berlin, which I was surprised to find a very fine city with wide avenues.

Tallin, the capital of Estonia, is also a beautiful town, built on a small hill. We spent two nights in St Petersburg again. I think what impressed me most in the Hermitage this time were the beautiful parquetry floors in woods of different colours and patterns. Although the town was under siege for 2½ years during the war and a million people died, it is now completely rebuilt, as is Berlin. It all looked much more prosperous than when I was there ten years earlier, with far more cars around, but many Russians are said to find the abuses of capitalism less attractive than the old certainties of the communist regime, when they at least had a job for life and a pension.

We went on coach tours around Helsinki, Stockholm, Copenhagen and Oslo, all beautiful cities with none of the poor industrial housing that exists in all British ports. Everywhere looked clean and was surrounded by beautiful mountainous country.

Back in England, this year saw the final collapse of the once mighty steel industry with the closure of its mill at Port Talbot, caused by militant unions and incompetent management, yet an Indian tycoon called Mittel has managed to make an immense fortune out of steel in this country and abroad. But the demise of the industry here has caused a collapse in the demand for scrap metal and the littering of the country with old cars and other machinery.

Now there was an announcement of intention to reform the Common Agricultural Policy, which ever since we joined the EEC had paid subsidies to farmers based on the number of cattle or sheep they kept, the amount of milk produced or the crops grown, and even land left uncultivated in "Set Aside". Yet pig and poultry farmers have always managed to operate without subsidies.

Now, unbelievably, we were being told that production is not of interest, only the environmental beauty of the landscape, so all previous schemes were to be scrapped and much the same level of subsidy would be paid, even if no livestock is kept or crops grown. You can get £113 per acre per year for growing wild flowers and £150 for a picnic site.

I am told, however, that even more civil servants are being employed to administer and police this madness, and that farmers will even be able to sell their 'Single Farm Payment' to others, which, in the end, can only lead to a great increase in the price of land and a vastly greater bill for food imported from abroad.

As the world's population inexorably rises, surplus stocks of food stocks will disappear and the price of it will escalate. More farms are now being sold to the city new rich than to farmers, who will be able to collect the innumerable environmental development grants.

The lunatic townies who govern us will be able to enjoy more wild flowers and birds in derelict fields, until starvation faces when, as practically all manufacturing industry has been destroyed and services industries are fast going abroad, the country will slide into bankruptcy.

It has now been announced that grants will be paid for felling conifer plantations, established with grants over the past 60 years to replace them with hard woods, which will take 200 years to mature. It takes about £1,000 per acre to put good agricultural land under forestry. There is no demand for hardwoods except the very best, as there are no mines needing pit props. Soft woods, most now imported anyway, build houses and the demand for board, pallets and pulp newsprint increases inexorably as junk mail proliferates.

Despite this looming crisis, Blair fiddles, Nero-like, and more parliamentary time has been devoted to the iniquitous ban on hunting than to any other business of governing the country – a recipe for civil unrest if ever there were one. The trouble is that, whereas in the past Members of Parliament were gentlemen with country interests, nowadays they are all lawyers, social climbers and professional politicians - just lobby fodder with no country interests. The aristocracy have deserted it, killed off by two world wars and the remnant at home, managing their estates or merchant banking, and not producing enough children!

No one under 40 years old should be an MP. Only people with experience of life and a successful career are fit to govern the rest of us and can afford to be independent of the party whip, as was the case in the past, except for some Labour MPs supported by the trade unions.

Then the lunatic EU produced their new draft Constitution, amounting to 557 A4 pages, compared with some 10 pages that comprise the American Constitution. It is even proposed to bring in

Turkey and Bosnia Herzegovina, which would introduce a Moslem population of some 100 million, all of whom would have free movement within Europe – and our Prime Minister traitorously supports the proposal. There is already a fifth column of near to 10 million Moslems within the EU, ready to cause turmoil if Moslem countries are able to unite in a theocratic Caliphate, which could lead to the Christian-Moslem conflict at which some Mullahs aim.

Fortunately, the tide is turning, several countries are likely to prevent both measures. The six Eastern European countries recently admitted will soon absorb the agricultural subsidies we have so long enjoyed and as opposition to the mad bureaucracy increases in many countries there is every hope that the EU will fall apart.

Set up as the 'Common Market' after the war to heal the ancestral hatred between Germany and France, it has been developed by politicians wanting to make their name in history into an uncomfortable union of the stable, honest, freedom loving Protestant peoples of northern Europe with the feckless, corrupt, bureaucratic, regimented Catholic nations of the south.

On the night after Christmas 2004, a major earthquake in the sea off Indonesia caused the catastrophic tsunami that led to the death of some 300,000 people round the Indian Ocean. In Indonesia they had no hope but the many thousands in Thailand, Malaya, Sri Lanka, India and Somalia could all have been saved if their governments had issued warnings in the 24 hours available. Hundreds of millions of pounds/dollars were offered in international aid but re-building of shattered communities has been very slow and as usual subject to much corruption. It is even reported that 7 months later, 2,000 containers are still sitting on the docks in Sri Lanka, held up by bureaucracy, and that Oxfam has had to pay £1m to Customs in demurrage charges, while nearly 5 million people had lost their homes.

Prince Charles unwisely decided to marry his discreet and admirable paramour, Camilla Parker Bowles in a registry office in Windsor, to be followed by a spectacular blessing in the royal chapel of the castle – a union likely to cause all manner of trouble in the future. Why he could not have continued with an unofficial liaison as before, and as his forebears would have, I cannot imagine.

The ceremony was actually postponed for a day, out of respect for Pope John Paul II, who had died and whose funeral was due to take place on the day previously set for the wedding. This Polish prelate, who had shown great courage in opposing communism and spreading the gospel worldwide, had developed into the most reactionary incumbent, banning birth control and abortion, encouraging his Catholic subjects to put another bambino on the streets of Bogota and the appalling spread of AIDS throughout the world. Yet, unbelievably, prime ministers and even royalty from around the world attended his funeral. It would have been more appropriate if the Catholic Cherie Blair and perhaps the Archbishop of Canterbury had represented this country.

In April 2005 there was another general election, again won by Labour although with a much reduced majority, in fact polling only 35% of the votes cast. Democracy is madness unless there are only two parties, as in America, or proportional representation as in all other European countries.

The Conservatives lost, through being led by Michael Howard, the son of a Rumanian Jewish immigrant, who, though a competent speaker was too abrasive and had supported the invasion of Iraq. The intervention of the anti-European and anti-immigrant party UKIP, which the Conservatives should have long ago embraced, further impeded them.

Now the Labour party is determined to remove the 92 remaining hereditary members of the House of Lords, who represented our only protection against a parliamentary dictatorship. They have appointed another twenty life peers of socialist leanings to gain a majority and, incredibly, their leader in the Lords is a black baroness.

The last British-owned car maker Rover/MG went out of business after being robbed by its management of £40 million. We have used Rover cars for the past ten years and found them excellent and have never bought a foreign car. The company has now been sold to the Chinese, while the once proud British marques of Rolls Royce, Bentley and Land Rover have long been German owned.

Government statistics reported that the incredible sum of £400 billion, the proceeds of drugs, crime and fraud, has been laundered during the past 10 years and only £40 million has been recovered at a cost of £400 million in investigation and court costs. Secretive Swiss banks have long held the ill-gotten funds of African tyrants and international crime syndicates, although they do claim to have disclosed some lately. While money laundering in this country is a serious crime, no attempt is made to control the secret banks in the Caribbean islands.

It is obvious that British and American banks have also been participating in this racket. The Financial Services Authority is practically useless and whenever they do bring charges, highly paid lawyers frustrate their efforts in fraud trials extending over many months, much to the bemusement of reluctant juries.

The Americans are much tougher. There the top-ranking world accounting firm, Arthur Andersen was brought down after being convicted of helping Enron, the US energy company to disguise a multi-billion dollar fraud in its accounts, and the second-ranking firm, KPMG has been fined $500m for assisting its clients in avoiding taxes.

The Caribbean island of Anguilla has 8,000 inhabitants and 300 banks and many British businessmen keep their money in these banks or in the Channel Islands, Isle of Man or Gibraltar, all little supervised by the Bank of England. Though the government repeatedly talks of prohibiting the use of offshore banks it has done little to control it.

Between these practices and the obscene salaries paid to company directors, the city of London is a sink of corruption. The phrase, 'Greed is Good' was introduced during the 1980s under Mrs Thatcher's Conservative Government, but since this so-called socialist government gained power seven years ago, the number of millionaires has multiplied seven times.

Ever since the abolition of fixed exchange rates in the 1970s, huge fortunes have been made by currency speculation, commodity trading and now the disreputable hedge funds, all of which just increase the price of everything. As Harold Wilson once said we need people to make things, not money.

The price of houses is now so high, at an average of £180,000 throughout the country, that none of the young can afford to buy them, even though innumerable mortgage companies offer

3/4 or more of the price. Until the 1980s all councils had large numbers of houses to rent at modest prices but Mrs Thatcher, in order to encourage them to vote Conservative, disgracefully allowed the tenants to buy their houses at appreciably discounted prices, which, naturally, all of them did.

Further inflating the price nowadays, about quarter of the price of a house – anything from £20,000 to £100,000 – is in the building plot with planning permission. In the 1970s, development tax charged at the rate of 95% on the change of use of land was abandoned by the Conservative Government because the supply for building houses had dried up. Since then any farmer selling a field for housing for a vast price has always been able to roll over the proceeds into buying farmland, without paying any tax. It is incredible that Labour Governments have allowed this to continue.

Since they first made their ungainly appearance on British horizons, I have campaigned against wind farms, which desecrate the hills and produce very little electricity. To reduce pollution from power stations burning fossil fuels, the obvious answer is nuclear power, which the French use to produce 75% of their electricity and the present government is at last considering the possibility of replacing our ageing stations, which led the world 50 years ago. The protesters have at last gone quiet.

Poisonous emissions from cars are much reduced but nothing is done to discourage air travel by taxing the fuel. It has recently been reported that the pollution emitted by aircraft per person flying the Atlantic is equal to that produced by a Range Rover in a year. Cheap air travel and tourism have become a menace and have allowed the people of the third world to flood into developing countries.

All this has caused global warming, which, over the past twenty years, has given us milder winters with warmer autumns and later springs.

Many people complain of our climate but in fact it is the best in the world. You have only to live in a hot country to realise how blessed rain is. We never suffer serious drought; seed times and harvests never fail. But chaos lies ahead unless steps are taken to curb the excesses of our wasteful, throwaway society with water, power, packaging and junk mail all encouraged by the menace of advertising, and the unrestrained breeding of Moslem, Catholic and African nations. Only the protesting ecologists of the Green Parties speak out about it while governments irresponsibly indulge their people.

I am glad to say that I have never had to sack an employee. Except on leaving a farm all have stayed until retirement. But I have lived through a revolution as complete as any in Russia, albeit a peaceful one. It began with the country governed by a landowning aristocracy, rich but responsible, a god-fearing professional and fiercely patriotic middle class and a working class that was industrious but seriously poor, at the same time, mostly moral and patriotic. All classes were pro-monarchy and proud of our empire. It was a class-ridden and deferential society in which everyone knew their place, and for that reason extremely stable. All people were good mannered and formal and Christian names were used only in the family. A small number rose to be termed 'nouveau riche' for a generation and a very small number sank and 'went to the dogs'. Talk of money, and ostentatious display were considered vulgar.

There was very little crime except for the poaching of game. Vandalism was unknown. The small number of professional burglars never carried weapons as murderers were hung. Rape and assault were very rare. There was very little shop-lifting as all goods were handed out by shop assistants. There were no supermarkets enabling people to help themselves.

All children were spanked at home, caned in state schools and more severely beaten in the public (actually private) schools. Juvenile criminals, though very few, were birched. Children left state schools at 14 to be labourers, miners or apprentices to tradesmen or factory workers. The cleverer ones got scholarships to grammar schools, academically higher than many public schools, and went on to universities.

The vicar or rector was universally respected in country villages where he visited his parishioners when they were sick, and some social workers had appeared in the towns.

Few people locked their houses and fraud was practically unknown. The police lived in the community and patrolled the streets on foot or bicycle. They may not have been loved but were certainly respected and could give tiresome juveniles a cuff on the ear without repercussions. They were not afraid to call in the pubs to discourage drunkenness. Now young drunks, both girls as well as boys, are out of control. The police are also bogged down with bureaucracy and accused of racism, perhaps with good reason when confronting blacks or Asians.

The doctors were all in private practice and visited the sick in their homes. They gave treatment free to the poor at their surgeries under a panel insurance scheme. District nurses and mid-wives visited the poor. The better off employed a resident mid-wife/baby nurse.

On the British Empire, the greatest ever in world history, the sun never set and the British navy policed the world. Sterling was the world currency and rock steady. From 1870-1940 the pound devalued by 7d, or 3p today. Currencies were fixed and there were $5 to the £. The disastrous end to fixed currencies in the '50s has caused speculation ever since, earning fortunes for banks and financiers.

During the world depression of 1929 there was a national strike which was broken by the middle classes driving the trains and buses. There were hunger marches, notably Jarrow shipbuilders to London, but no violence in the demonstrations.

Domestic service and nursing were the only employment for women apart from a very few secretaries. All the middle classes had a cook and a housemaid. Since the First World War there had been a low level of unemployment pay and old age pension.

Homosexual acts in public lavatories or parks earned a prison sentence but it was tolerated in private and there was no victimisation of people known as 'queers' or 'dykes'.

Cars were owned only by the upper classes so there was little traffic on the roads apart from lorries, some of them steam-powered. There was no driving test and the breathalyser had not been invented.

Some of the aristocracy went to the Riviera after the hunting season, whilst the middle classes took holidays at the seaside where the beaches were empty. The working classes took day trips to seaside resorts and the Lancashire workers spent 'Wakes Week' at Blackpool. A very small number of the rich went skiing or climbing in Switzerland which had just become fashionable.

Women were on something of a pedestal, fully clothed and practised modesty, except Lancashire mill girls. Virginity on marriage was important and illegitimacy shameful so any such children were given for adoption or brought up by their grandparents. Cohabitation before marriage was unknown and there were no single mothers. Contraception was practiced only by the upper classes who bred few children, whereas the working classes had large families.

Respectability was important to all classes and adultery practiced only among the *louche* aristocracy who accepted the results as their own.

Elderly Ladies carried laudanum smelling salts (opium) for their nerves. Drunkenness was fairly common but drugs were not available to the general population.

There was also a considerable Jewish community in parts of London and some northern towns but they kept their heads down and there were no coloureds except a few in Cardiff and Bristol.

Debt was shunned, women worked only until marriage when they reared their families while their husbands were the breadwinners.

The only advertising was for cigarettes, Oxo, Bovril, soap products and seaside holidays at the railway stations. Britain was a proud, free, law-abiding country.

The war and the Labour party which was elected after it changed the country, introducing socialism, which is communism without the secret police, which the Conservative party has never reversed, along with the concept that the state should look after everyone from the cradle to the grave.

The National Health Service was set up in 1946, which gave better medical treatment but is now failing as medical science has developed to keep alive the terminally ill and people are now living far too long. Unemployment pay became so generous that many people were discouraged from working. Socialist school teachers, who encouraged self expression not discipline, have destroyed the state schools.

The removal of the slur of illegitimacy and the contraceptive pill has destroyed morality and the state now encourages and supports single motherhood. Separated couples are reported to be

£8,000 a year better off than those who remain married.

Fifty years ago this country had a stable, homogenous population of 50 million. Since then life expectancy has risen but reproduction of the native population has declined. Now, with the surge of immigrants and their excessive breeding rate, the population is approaching 60 million and unstable – more than France with half her land.

Communist shop stewards took over the trade unions and have destroyed British industry. Immigrants from the Caribbean arrived in 1951 to be followed by a flood from India, Pakistan and Bangladesh, although there were still a million unemployed who could not be directed to work.

Now there are six million Moslems and Hindus living in this country and they are breeding twice as many children as the native British population. Soon they will number one quarter of the population. Encouraged by disreputable lawyers, rights became more important than duties and the sex discrimination act was promulgated.

High pressure advertising has created wants and encouraged people into debt. Homosexuality was legalised; now the so-called 'gay' community claims the right to be married in church.

Joining the European Union transferred most of the powers of Parliament to Brussels and has resulted in a torrent of regulations that have imposed a huge burden on business and an immense bureaucracy to enforce them, and allowed people from all member countries to settle in ours.

Laws against sex, race and religious discrimination have been a bonanza for lawyers. Now a 'Racial and Religious Hatred Bill' is proposed, to outlaw free speech and even the jokes of comedians. The Human Rights Act, promulgated by the EU, is the ultimate lunacy, encouraging phoney claims.

The mad bureaucrats of the EU are spending E150m a year on advertising against smoking, while they give E600m a year in subsidies to European tobacco growers (mostly Greek). In moderation, their warnings may provide solace to many but it doesn't take a nanny state to tell you that if you chain smoke you are heading for an early grave.

Immigrants from the Caribbean and Africa have brought drugs, dealers in drugs and gun crime, previously unknown. Chinese 'Triad' gangs have brought violence and intimidation.

Since the collapse of Yugoslavia and the enlargement of the Union, Eastern Europeans, and particularly Albanians, have engaged in smuggling people and white slavery of prostitutes. This Labour Government has done little to stop the flood of immigrants, now running at some 200,000 a year and its feeble efforts are frequently defeated by Liberal do-gooders and corrupt lawyers, usually with foreign names. It is now proposed that immigrants should take an oath of allegiance to the EU, not to HM the Queen.

Women are taking over the country, as girls out-perform boys in school, and they are becoming a majority in all professions including, the boardrooms of business companies. Unfortunately adopting the appellation of 'sexy', which used to be called 'tarty', they are also promoting decadence. These women routinely discriminate against men, whereas discrimination against women by men has long been outlawed.

Not only sleazy magazines but now most national newspapers and all television channels actively promote immorality. Lord Reith, who maintained such high standards for the BBC, must be turning in his grave. Sky Television produces so-called 'Adult' programmes which are straight pornography on eight channels every night.

The present policy of this class-ridden Labour Government to gain popularity is to push half of all pupils from the state schools into universities, which are disgracefully urged to discriminate against children from public schools whose parents have paid vast sums for their education. In practice, many drop out and there are not enough jobs requiring graduates anyway. The result is a shortage of craftsmen and skilled workers, all being filled by immigrants.

Napoleon called the British a nation of shopkeepers. Now it appears we are a nation of accountants, consultants and financial services, which account for 31.7% of national GDP, whereas retailing and wholesaling accounts for only 15.7%. A more serious concern, though, is that manufacturing output is now only 14.9% whereas in 1960 it was 35% and, of this sum, only 3% is attributable to farming and mining.

In 2004 exports amounted to £167 billion but manufactured imports cost £209 billion, leaving a trade gap of £42 billion. The financial wizards of the City of London, however, achieved a trade surplus of £19 billion, but that still left us with a national payments deficiency of £23 billion – second only to the United States of America.

With North Sea oil running out, the population increasing through immigration, food production falling as the country is put under concrete and farmers are encouraged to grow wildflowers instead or crops and livestock, it's obvious that we are headed for bankruptcy.

When so-called New Labour, led by Tony Blair took power in 1997, the laws of this country were recorded on 4,500 pages. Now, eight years later, they amount to over 9,000 pages, mostly having originated from Brussels. Before we joined the European Union it was communist trade union leaders who tried to destroy the country. Now it is laws, regulations and lawyers.

The Health and Safety Act is the ultimate madness. Anyone erecting scaffolding for building repairs, dipping sheep or using a chain-saw must have a licence, obtained only after attending a training course. When I take wool to a depot in a trailer, the employees are forbidden to help me unload it. Village fetes are cancelled because of the cost of insurance.

Until 1950 the British shipbuilding industry was the greatest in the world. Then the Japanese and Koreans took over and now we build no merchant vessels and we cannot even build an aircraft carrier without French participation. Yet Norway, Germany, Italy and France have managed to continue construction.

In the days when the bankers and brokers of the City of London were Gentlemen of honour, whose word was their bond, near all was honest. Now, following the major takeovers by the great American banks, it is as corrupt as Wall Street. Since the so-called 'Big Bang' reforms of 1986, financial institutions have been able to float companies, sell the shares and also deal in them themselves, previously done by separate firms with clearly delineated roles. The major brokers will only act in an advisory capacity for a portfolio of over £100,000 and the dividends obtainable from blue chip companies are no more than annual inflation. As a result, many have been tempted to buy shares on the AIM market, or Penny shares, hoping for capital gains. In fact 50% of new companies fail in a year or so and you soon discover that they are operated only for the enrichment of the directors at the expense of the shareholders.

During the Dot-Com boom of 2001, these 'boiler room' share pushers made fortunes but a friend of my son, who worked for one, told him that none of their clients made any money. One such company with a London telephone number and address was in fact operating from Barcelona to where calls and correspondence were transferred.

In a full page article, *The Sunday Times* reported that very many people had been taken for a ride but the Financial Services Authority, sixty of whose executives are reported to earn over £100,000 a year, would take no action against the miscreants as they were companies registered in an island in the Caribbean; yet they had previously been closed down in New Zealand.

Nor have the FSA made any attempt to stop Nigerian fraudsters who for many years have persuaded gullible people to assist them in moving large sums of money abroad, at an initial cost, of course, which disappears. This year the self-aggrandising Tony Blair hosted a meeting of the G8 countries at the Gleneagles Hotel near Edinburgh, promoting himself as the saviour of Africa, taking over from the Live Aid campaign of the charismatic rebel Bob Geldof.

Fifteen miles of 8' high wire fencing were erected, and 10,000 Scottish and English police brought in to protect the delegates from some 300 so-called anarchist demonstrators. The cost is reported as £100 million, while 300 million Africans live on 50 pence a day. The meeting could have been held on a ship at sea at little cost, or on the Royal Yacht if it had not been decommissioned. In any case, the cancellation of African debt and pledges of more financial aid will only encourage tyrannical rulers in their wicked ways. The president of Tanzania, Benjamin Mkapa, for example, has a private jet which cost £15m, while his people starve.

What is needed is the removal of European trade protection and export subsidies and the encouragement of African enterprise, but this is contrary to the Socialist policies of many of the aid agencies.

Greed rules in the City where, the TUC report, the average pension fund of the directors of the FTSE100 companies is £2.5 million, or £167,000 a year. The average for the leading companies is £4.6 million, which is 45 times the average pension of their staff. *The Lawyer* magazine reports that 30 barristers earn over £1m a year and 10 QCs over £2m. There are too many criminal barristers, who struggle along on £40,000-£50,000 but the average at the commercial Bar is £332,000 pa.

      The big London solicitors are equally avaricious, while good country ones are modestly rewarded. Until a few years ago solicitors were not allowed to advertise, now unscrupulous firms are daily on TV, encouraging people to make claims for trivial accidents or medical negligence, on the basis of no win no fee, but double fees for solicitors if they win. As a result, doctors' insurance escalates and the NHS is deprived of millions for the treatment of the sick. Until about 20 years ago no one could sue the state. Now it's a goldmine!

To placate the murderous IRA, some four years ago Tony Blair ordered a third enquiry into the 'Bloody Sunday Massacre' in Londonderry 24 years ago. It has cost us £150m already, without result. It's been a bonanza for the lawyers. There will be no charges, but no doubt compensation will have to be paid.

The morale of the British army in Iraq is being undermined by soldiers being put on trial for mistakes made under great stress. Recruiting will suffer. The most dangerous occupation has long been that of the war photographers, of whom many have been killed.

      The ex-President of Serbia, Slobodan Milosevic is, absurdly, still on trial for war crimes at the International Court at The Hague, after five years, at a cost of £57 million a year.

The Internet menace invades most homes. 60% of its content is devoted to sex and paedophilia. The search engine, Google alone can access 7 million photographs of children and sex.

      Last year, the incompetent or corrupt Customs and Excise lost millions when they allowed the import of lorry loads of alcohol without duty or VAT. The importers were charged but acquitted when they claimed they had been framed. This year, several have been imprisoned for encouraging the import of drugs to catch the Mr Bigs. Some men who had been convicted got off on appeal, claiming they'd been set up.

Now some 200 hundred drug dealers in prison are expected to challenge their convictions, aided by shady lawyers defeating the state, on the grounds that they had been set-up by informants. Why don't they remove the duties on alcohol and free drugs. This would remove the cause of a huge number of crimes of violence. Of course, a few more people will kill themselves through taking drugs but this cannot be stopped; in fact cannabis is probably less addictive than alcohol or smoking.

The National Lottery encourages gambling and mostly attracts it from the poor, hoping for a windfall. Having refused the admirable Richard Branson, who offered to run it free, it was given to a company who make vast profits and the proceeds are given to very dubious causes. It would be better if many smaller prizes were distributed to many more people. But for the state to encourage gambling is anyhow immoral.

The Inland Revenue have sold their property portfolio for £600 million to Mapeley Bermuda, a company based in the Caribbean. Yet they are expected to outlaw offshore funds. The Child Protection Agency has written off £1 billion which it should have collected from separated fathers.

The Child Tax Credit Scheme introduced with a flourish by this Government costs 45p for every £1 distributed.

This government has lost billions of pounds on the computerisation of the NHS, the Police, the Ministry of Defence, Labour Exchanges and Air Traffic Control. None has worked.

Packaging of every thing has created great problems of waste disposal and the transport of food worldwide causes immense pollution. Since the attack on the Twin Towers, rabid Moslem Imams have openly preached terrorism against America, Israel and this country. Bigamy, forced marriages and honour killings have been tolerated. Although Islamic modesty of dress is admirable, the overall covering of women should not be allowed.

2.7 million people claim incapacity benefit to be idle. 750,000 are unemployed, including 61% of Bangladeshis and 45% of blacks. 200,000 people who have been refused asylum are kept for two or three years at public expense, yet are not allowed to work, while half a million students and workers from Eastern Europe have flooded in.

If everyone were paid a basic £80 a week by the state and all allowances scrapped, the vast bureaucracy of benefit offices and inspectors could be scrapped too, saving £30billion and providing an incentive to work.

Despite our admiration for our beloved Queen, our national anthem is outdated in these democratic days and should be replaced by *Land of Hope and Glory* – not *Jerusalem*, as some advocate.

I have been fortunate to have enjoyed good health and to be approaching old age. So many people never get there. Of people I have known, or known of, twenty have committed suicide, twenty have been killed on the roads, ten have died in other accidents, thirty have died prematurely from cancer, heart attack, stroke or diabetes, and ten relations or close friends were killed in war.

It used to be said that 'Whom the Gods love die young'. It seems to me a matter of luck, or carelessness, depression or, lately, obesity. Since childhood I have hardly had a day in bed except for surgical operations, but farming is stressful and for many years I carried bicarbonate pills for gastric pains but never got an ulcer. Mostly I have been optimistic, believing anyone can do anything but at times have suffered from worry and depression.

For thirty years, home brewed beer has been a great aid to sleeping although I always wake in the middle of the night to read a book for an hour and reinforce it with aspirins which gives me another couple of hours' sleep.

For those who survived the war or were born after it this has been a golden age in the western world. Poverty, except for some elderly, has been abolished and medical science has removed most suffering and extended life. All people work much less and have long holidays. Electricity has taken the drudgery out of house work. All have cars and telephones, which have greatly expended their horizons. Television provides entertainment in every home. Cheap air travel enables most people to visit places in the world their forebears could not have dreamt of. Class distinctions have been largely removed and opportunity exists for everyone.

But liberty has brought licence, drugs, crime, and the fear of crime to many people.

Competition has brought stress; excessive population and motor transport the same.

Globalisation and the development of the Eastern nations threaten to put many of our people out of work. Climate change, pollution and the exhaustion of fossil fuels threaten the future. Religion, the great solace of our forebears gets ever more aggressive as guns and every form of arms proliferate in the world. It looks as if the golden age is over and that our descendents will not have it so good. The Four Horsemen of the Apocalypse loom ever close on the horizon.

That great statesman Enoch Powell reckoned that all lives end in failure. Confucius said that a man should, in his lifetime, have a child, plant a tree, build a house and write a book. I have now achieved that but failed to hand on to my children the landed estate I had hoped to. Perhaps there is time yet.

Our country is no longer the land of the free where an Englishman's word was recognised as his bond worldwide.

Political spin doctors, corrupt financiers, trendy clerics, academics and teachers have undermined our traditional social and sexual morality. But in America the tide is turning, perhaps it can happen here.

In the words of that patriot, G K Chesterton, 'Smile at us, pay us, pass us, but do not quite forget. For we are the people of England that never have spoken yet.'

Postscript

Sadly, my brother died in June 2005, aged 75. As well as having considerable success in life as a Member of Parliament, Minister and Life Peer, he was also a QC, Judge of Appeal in Guernsey and for many years Chairman of the Criminal Injuries Compensation Authority.

He was evidently widely liked and respected, as an astonishing 450 people attended his funeral in Mobberley while 350 peers, their wives and lawyers also came to his memorial service at St Margaret's, Westminster in November.

Fortunately Rosemary and I and our children have always enjoyed good health and they and our grandchildren visit us frequently. I do not suffer the boredom of retirement as I am able to visit the farm, only 2 miles away, daily where John Greenow does all the work admirably. I only have to supervise him and the re-building of the house by the skilled John Barber and his apprentices and deal with the ever increasing bureaucratic regulations.

I have now reached the fourth stage of my life where one is supposed to contemplate death. Regrettably I have long ceased to believe in a personal relationship with a loving or retributive Almighty God which sustained my forebears, but, when one considers the wonders of television which brings dozens of perfect pictures and voices into our home at the press of a button and the miracles of radio telephony, computers and the internet, it is not difficult to believe in a spirit world and I have occasionally believed I have received guidance. So perhaps there is some existence after death as well as characteristic inheritance through one's descendants.

War Service Record of the Carlisle Family
Great War 1914 – 1918 & World War 1939 – 1945

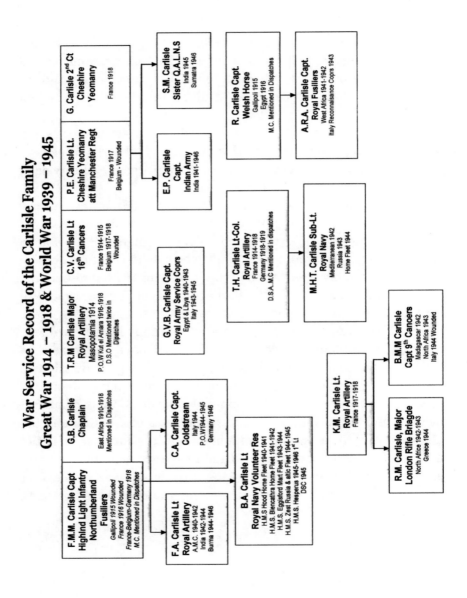

F.M.M. Carlisle Capt
Highlnd Light Infantry
Northumberland
Fusiliers
Gallipoli 1915 Wounded
France 1916 Wounded
France-Belgium-Germany 1918
M.C. Mentioned in Dispatches

G.B. Carlisle
Chaplain
East Africa 1910-1918
Mentioned in Dispatches

T.R.M Carlisle Major
Royal Artillery
Masopotamia 1914
P.O.W Kut el Amara 1916-1918
D.S.O Mentioned twice in
Dipatches

C.V. Carlisle Lt
16th Cancers
France 1914-1915
Belgium 1917-1918
Wounded

P.E. Carlisle Lt.
Cheshire Yeomanry
att Manchester Regt
France 1917
Belgium - Wounded

G. Carlisle 2nd Ct
Cheshire
Yeomanry
France 1918

F.A. Carlisle Lt
Royal Artillery
A.M.C. 1940-1942
India 1942-1944
Burma 1944-1946

C.A. Carlisle Capt.
Coldstream
Italy 1944
P.O.W1944-1945
Germany 1946

G.V.B. Carlisle Capt.
Royal Army Service Coprs
Egypt & Libya 1940-1943
Italy 1943-1945

E.P. Carlisle
Capt.
Indian Army
India 1941-1946

S.M. Carlisle
Sister Q.A.I.N.S
India 1945
Sumatra 1946

T.H. Carlisle Lt-Col.
Royal Artillery
France 1914-1918
Germany 1918-1919
D.S.A.M.C Mentioned in dispatches

R. Carlisle Capt.
Welsh Horse
Gallipoli 1915
Egypt 1916
M.C. Mentioned in Dispatches

B.A. Carlisle Lt
Royal Navy Volunteer Res
H.M.S Hood Home Fleet 1940-1941
H.M.S. Blencathra Home Fleet 1941-1942
H.M.S. Eggisford Mart Fleet 1943-1944
H.M.S. Zest Russia & altic Fleet 1944-1945
H.M.S. Hesperus 1945-1946 1st Lt
DSC 1945

M.H.T. Carlisle Sub-Lt.
Royal Navy
Mediterranean 1942
Russia 1943
Home Fleet 1944

A.R.A. Carlisle Capt.
Royal Fusiliers
West Africa 1941-1942
Italy Reconnaisance Coprs 1943

K.M. Carlisle Lt.
Royal Artillery
France 1917-1918

R.M. Carlisle, Major
London Rifle Briagde
North Africa 1942-1943
Greece 1944

B.M.M Carlisle
Capt 9th Canoers
Madagascar 1942
North Africa 1943
Italy 1944 Wounded